THE AMERICAN NUMISMATIC SOCIETY

MUSEUM NOTES

28

THE AMERICAN NUMISMATIC SOCIETY
NEW YORK
1983

ISSN 0145-1413
ISBN 0-89722-199-0

COMPOSED IN BELGIUM AT CULTURA, WETTEREN

PRINTED IN THE U.S.A. AT BRAUN-BRUMFIELD, INC., ANN ARBOR, MI

CONTENTS

Greek

Byzantine

Sasanian

Islamic

Methodology

CONTENTS

Greek

Byzantine

Sasanian

Islamic

Methodology

ANSMN 28 (1983)

THE CHRONOLOGY OF THE FOURTH-CENTURY B.C. FACING-HEAD SILVER COINAGE OF LARISSA

(Plate 1)

Thomas R. Martin

The mint of Larissa was the most important and the most prolific civic mint in classical Thessaly. To judge from modern collections and the contents of hoards, a great deal of the mint's production came in the fourth century B.C. when the standard obverse type became a female facing head portrayed in a three-quarter view. More than fifty years ago, Fritz Herrmann published what remains the only attempt to establish a chronological arrangement for this important coinage in his article on the silver coinage of Larissa in Thessaly.[1] Since these numerous issues are distinguished only by often subtle variations in their obverse and reverse types and not by any overt indications of chronology, Herrmann's chronological scheme depended almost exclusively on his own criteria of style. He settled on ca. 395 B.C. as the date of the introduction of the new facing-head issues and 344/3 B.C. as the date when these coins ceased to be produced. Since these are the final issues of the city's mint, 344/3 B.C. also became the date when the minting of silver coinage at Larissa came to an end permanently.

[1] "Die Silbermünzen von Larissa in Thessalien," *ZfN* 35 (1924–25), pp. 1–69, hereafter cited as "Herrmann." Additional abbreviations are: *ACGC* = Colin Kraay, *Archaic and Classical Greek Coins* (Berkeley, 1976); and *CH* = *Coin Hoards* vols. 1–6 (London, 1975–81).

As we shall see, Herrmann established these chronological termini with historical rather than numismatic arguments.[2] His procedure was in itself reasonable, but in this case the arguments are too weak to stand. The lower terminus in particular, which carries with it important implications for numismatic and political history, is disturbing because Herrmann based it purely on the assumption that Philip II of Macedon suppressed the coinage of Larissa in 344/3 B.C. This notion was apparently too self-evident to require any documentation, and Herrmann offered none.

In fact, the question of the date of the end of civic coinage at Larissa is extremely difficult to answer with precision and assurance on current evidence. Nevertheless, the hoard evidence published since the appearance of Herrmann's article, although far less copious than one would like, indicates that the end of silver coinage at Larissa cannot be as early as 344/3 B.C. and, furthermore, that Herrmann's chronological arrangement of the fourth-century facing-head issues is suspect. The evidence calls for a re-examination of his scheme and the outlining in at least preliminary fashion of a new arrangement for these issues.[3]

A full-scale treatment of the chronology of these issues could only be attempted if a comprehensive die study were made of the enormous amount of material from the Larissa mint that survives in modern collections. Since that sort of study is not in immediate prospect for practical reasons, it seems desirable for the present to begin work on this coinage based on the currently available evidence. That evidence comes from Herrmann's own work and from hoards that have been well enough published to identify the coins of Larissa which they contain.[4] Many hoards that might contribute to this work do not fall into this category. I hope in time to be able to assemble by correspondence and autopsy the precise information on types and conditions of wear that will help to test and to refine the hypotheses that are formulated in this study.

[2] Herrmann, pp. 41, 50–51 (upper terminus); pp. 49, 58–59 (lower terminus).

[3] This study will focus almost exclusively on silver coinage. The bronze coinage of Larissa appears too infrequently in hoards to be studied in detail by the method adopted in this paper.

[4] The information on hoards comes in the first instance from *IGCH* and *CH*, vols. 1–6. Original publications have been consulted when they exist.

HOARDS AND THE END OF SILVER COINAGE AT LARISSA

The broadest indication of chronology for these Larissan issues comes from the statistics on their occurrence in hoards. That is, one can hypothesize that the appearance of very small numbers of these coins in hoards of a certain period from an area where the coins are more numerous in hoards of earlier periods indicates that minting had severely declined or ceased. For this study, the obvious area to investigate is Thessaly. Coins of Larissa are very common in Thessalian hoards of the fourth century and become less common in hoards of the third century, but their almost complete absence from hoards of the second century points immediately to a terminus ante quem of ca. 200 B.C. for the end of civic coinage at Larissa. Of the 19 Thessalian hoards on record for the period ca. 200–100 B.C., only one has any coins of Larissa.[5] This numismatic evidence correlates with the historical evidence because the coinage of the reorganized Thessalian confederacy of the early second century served in place of civic coinages such as that of Larissa.[6]

Further evidence from hoards shows that the date for the end of coinage at Larissa comes much earlier than ca. 200 B.C. From published sources, I can identify 18 hoards of silver coins which were discovered in Thessaly (including the southern perioikic area) and have been assigned dates later than ca. 300 B.C. but earlier than the mid-second-century date of the first Thessalian hoards to contain coins of the Thessalian confederacy. Only seven of these hoards have coins of Larissa, and two of these include only a single specimen. Three of the five

[5] *CH* 6, no. 35 (5, no. 42): 3+ Larissa drachms in a total of 450+. The other eighteen hoards are *IGCH* 214, 220, 228, 234, 237, 239, 247, 289, 304, 305, 306, 313, 314, 315; *CH* 1, no. 83, 3, no. 57, 4, no. 56, 5, no. 45.

[6] On the establishment of this new federal organization, see J. A. O. Larsen, *Greek Federal States* (Oxford, 1968), pp. 281–94, especially p. 291 on its coinage. The silver coins of the Thessalian League are very common in Thessalian hoards of the second century: *IGCH* 239 with 1 of 52; 247 with only League coins, a total of 75+; 313 with 1192+ of 1199+; 314 with only League coins, a total of 36 (possibly part of no. 313); 315 (see *CH* 5, no. 45) with only League coins, a total of 203+; *CH* 1, no. 83, with only League coins, a total of 50+; 3, no. 57, with only League coins, a total of 38.

remaining hoards have small numbers of coins of Larissa, with only *IGCH* 168, a mid-third-century hoard, containing a large number of these coins, 156 of a total of 591.[7] As shall be shown, the coins of Larissa in this hoard are all the same type and generally quite worn. This evidence from the third century clearly contrasts with that based on Thessalian silver hoards from the fourth century. There are 22 such hoards, 11 of which contain coins of Larissa.[8] Furthermore, the coins of Larissa represent 10% or more of the contents of 10 of these 22 hoards. The comparable statistic for hoards post 300 B.C. is three of 31. In sum, the pattern of the statistics on the frequency of the appearance of coins of Larissa in Thessalian hoards suggests that the mint of Larissa was no longer producing silver coins at least by the last half of the third century B.C.

It is difficult to estimate how early the terminus of this coinage can safely be put, as figures concerning the frequency of appearance in hoards are far too imprecise an indicator of chronology to provide any further help in this investigation. Rather, conclusions must be drawn from another indicator, an analysis of the comparative state of wear of the coins of Larissa and the coins of the Macedonian kings that appear together in hoards. Since the Macedonian coins can be more accurately dated on external criteria than can the coins of Larissa, this comparison can be exploited in the search for a plausible chronology of the facing-head issues.

Seventeen hoards are recorded as containing silver coins of Larissa and Macedonian regnal coinage, but regrettably, information on the state of wear of the relevant coins is available for only five of these

[7] In the following list, the identification number of each hoard is followed by the number of Larissan coins and the total number of coins in the hoard. *IGCH* 117, 1 of 38; 133, 0 of 11+; 141, 0 of 16; 144, 0 of 115; 146, 1 of 26; 150, 0 of 5000–7000; 159, 0 of 61; 162, 5 of 30; 168, 156 of 591+; 220, 0 of 10+; 228, 0 of 130; 234, 0 of 100–150; 237, 0 of 2500–3000. *CH* 1, no. 52, 0 of 75+; 3, no. 43 (2, no. 72), 4 of 38+; 4, no. 56, 0 of 162+; 6, no. 24, 26 of 569; 6, no. 35 (5, no. 42), 3+ of 450+.

[8] *IGCH* 45, 0 of 92+; 49, 0 of a small number; 52, a large number of ca. 2000; 55, 2 of 4+; 56, 7 of 16–18+; 57, 2 of 6; 58 (including *CH* 4, nos. 20–21, 5, no. 20), 541+ of 626+; 61, 13+ of 20+; 62, 0 of 1647+; 71, uncertain; 80, 0 of 12; 82, 0 of 37+; 93, 0 of 112; 96, 2 of 13; 97, 0 of 16; 111, 10 of ca. 69. *CH* 1, no. 25, 0 of 149; 1, no. 27, 0 of 6; 1, no. 33, 0 of 4+; 1, no. 40, 10 of 90+; 2, no. 51, 1 of 9+; 6, no. 20 (2, no. 52), 1 of 7.

hoards as a result of the generally brief publications of the hoards in question.[9] Nevertheless, it is possible to make some progress on this scanty evidence toward the construction of a cumulative case for a lower terminus for the facing-head issues of Larissa. Throughout this discussion I will refer to the facing-head issues, Herrmann's group 7, by means of Herrmann's alphabetically designated series, which will be discussed in detail later in this paper.

IGCH 385 from Macedonia, now dated by Georges Le Rider to ca. 337/6 B.C., has 62 drachms of Larissa from a total of at least 240 silver coins, of which 136 lifetime tetradrachms of Philip II are the most recent coins. Fifty-four tetradrachms and two drachms are illustrated in the published reports. Sixty of the drachms are the facing-head type, Herrmann's group 7, of which it seems 58 are series A or M.[10] The other drachms represent one specimen of series B, one of series C, E or F, and two of group 6 (not facing-head types).[11] The very limited size of the illustrated Larissa sample of course makes any conclusions tentative at best, but it is noteworthy for the sake of the cumulative force of the evidence that the two illustrated drachms are as little worn, if not less, than the majority of the tetradrachms, even those which Le Rider has identified as the most recent series of Philip's coins in the hoard, Pella group 2 A 2 (see, e.g., nos. 221 and 232 in Le Rider, pl. 10). For example, one can compare the condition of the hair and of the nose

[9] These 17 hoards are *IGCH* 70, 74, 76, 111, 117, 146, 162, 168, 385, 386; *CH* 1, no. 37, 1, no. 40, 2, no. 51, 3, no. 43 (2, no. 72), 6, no. 20 (2, no. 52), 6, no. 24, 6, no. 35 (5, no. 42).

[10] I will argue below that Herrmann's series A and M in fact represent only one series, which I will call A-M, with a subgroup to be called A-M 168.

[11] The original notice of this hoard is by Irene Varoucha-Christodoulopoulou, "Athenai-Antike," *ADelt* 19 (1964), pt. 2, 1 *chronika*, p. 8, pl. 1, nos. 2–7 (Philip), 8–9 (Larissa). The coins are fully described (except for the state of wear) and the date for the hoard is given by Georges Le Rider, *Le monnayage d'argent et d'or de Philippe II frappé en Macédoine de 359 à 294* (Paris, 1977; hereafter cited as "Le Rider"), pp. 286–89, 341–42, hoard no. 4. He illustrates 48 tetradrachms.

According to Le Rider, 58 drachms "appartiennent à la série courante (tête de la nymphe Larissa presque de face/cheval paissant)," which I take as a description of the type I will refer to as A-M. His catalogue does not allow a decision on whether the one specimen belongs to series C, E or F. Varoucha illustrates an A-M 168 and an A-M drachm respectively.

on the Larissa obverses, raised areas which are very susceptible to wear on this type of coin, with the condition of the hair and beard of the tetradrachm obverses. Similarly, the details of the representation of the horse on the reverse of the drachms appear to be, if not better, at least as well preserved, as comparable features on the horse on the tetradrachm reverses. Since smaller denominations like drachms tend to show wear more quickly than do larger denominations like tetradrachms due to their smaller surface area and faster circulation, it is worth pointing out that the drachms are as well preserved as the tetradrachms of Le Rider's thunderbolt-N series and are in fact better preserved than most of the tetradrachms which he places before this series. (See, for example, 187a and 193 in his pl. 8.) The evidence of *IGCH* 385 is certainly no barrier to believing that some of the facing-head issues of Larissa in the hoard are at least contemporary with the issues of Philip, the most recent of which Le Rider dates to the period ca. 342/1–ca. 337/6 B.C. Since under Herrmann's system the two drachms illustrated from *IGCH* 385 belong to his group 7, series A or M (as do 56 other coins in the hoard) and are therefore to be dated to ca. 395–363 B.C., it is easy to see how Herrmann's chronology of the facing-head issues is at variance with the hoard evidence.

Unfortunately it is impossible at this time to make a complete analysis of the comparative state of wear of the relevant coins of *IGCH* 386 from Macedonia ca. 340 B.C. Four of its 18 silver coins are drachms of Larissa, and the most recent coins are two lifetime tetradrachms of Philip. Both the tetradrachms and two of the drachms are illustrated in the publications of the hoard.[12] Of these four coins the most severely worn is Larissa drachm b, an example of Herrmann's series Q whose condition is not noted in the original publication (Plate 1, 1).[13] The other drachm which is illustrated, a, belongs to series C and is rated "bien." The two tetradrachms from Le Rider's group Pella 2 A 1 receive "très bien"

[12] The original publication is by Irene Varoucha-Christodoulopoulou, "Acquisitions du Musée Numismatique d'Athènes," *BCH* 86 (1962), pp. 417–18, pl. 9, nos. 4 (Philip), 5–6 (Larissa a and b). See Le Rider, p. 285, hoard 3, pl. 7, no. 169a, for the other tetradrachm.

[13] The reverse type, the rare dolphins on the obverse, and the treatment of the neckline clearly place this coin in series Q, which I will discuss below. The head on the obverse is gazing left, a variation not listed by Herrmann.

ratings, as do the two remaining drachms of Larissa. Although they are not illustrated, the published references show that these drachms belong to one of Herrmann's series K to M 1.[14] Difficulties in Herrmann's chronology immediately arise because the less worn Larissa drachms should according to Herrmann be dated to ca. 370–363 B.C., even though they are of a smaller denomination and apparently comparable in condition to the tetradrachms of ca. 348/7–ca. 343/2 B.C. Moreover, the drachm b, apparently significantly more worn than the drachms of series K to M 1, should by the same scheme be dated ca. 361–353 B.C. as part of series Q. It is of course impossible to draw firm conclusions from the condition of so few coins, but again this evidence is worth recording as part of the cumulative case in favor of a revised chronology of the facing-head issues.

The photographs provided with *Coin Hoards* 2, no. 52 (6, no. 20), permit a judgment on the state of wear of another relevant but tiny selection of coins. Discovered in Thessaly, of its seven coins the hoard includes one facing-head drachm of series A or M and, as its most recent coins, two tetradrachms of Alexander III from Babylon and one drachm from Miletus of Alexander III which belongs to the period ca. 325–323 B.C.[15] A comparison of the wear on this coin with that on the comparable denomination from Larissa indicates that the latter coin is in similar, perhaps even better condition. Both coins show signs of wear on the raised surfaces of the obverse, but the Larissa drachm seems to have a less worn reverse with a clear, sharp legend even below the ground line, a spot where wear is common on this type. The one illustrated Alexander tetradrachm is better preserved than either of the drachms with almost no visible signs of wear, while the tetradrachm of Philip, a posthumous issue from ca. 336/5–ca. 329/8 B.C., is comparably worn, especially on the obverse.[16] Since the Larissa drachm belongs to series A or M, dated ca. 395–363 B.C., the evidence of this hoard, too, undermines faith in Herrmann's chronology.

14 Varoucha (above, n. 12), p. 418.

15 This coin is part of the ΑΙ series, on which see Margaret Thompson, *Alexander's Drachm Mints I: Sardes and Miletus*, ANSNS 16 (1983), pp. 43-50.

16 The coin belongs to Le Rider's group Pella 2 B, nos. 376–82.

No further information is currently available on other fourth-century hoards with coins of Larissa and Macedonia, but there are two third-century hoards to consider, one of which fortunately contains a large sample of relevant coins. The smaller hoard, *Coin Hoards* 3, no. 43 (2, no. 72), is from Thessaly ca. 229–228 B.C. The evidence of this hoard is problematical because the pattern of wear of the various issues included in it is very inconsistent and misleading.[17] The four drachms of Larissa which the hoard contains are severely worn, as one would expect of fourth-century issues by the date of this hoard. Likewise, the three Alexander drachms also show signs of much wear, although perhaps less than the coins of Larissa. However, all the drachms are so worn that it is probably futile to argue that one group is significantly more worn than the other, especially in the light of the peculiar pattern of wear exhibited in the hoard as a whole. The Larissa drachms are from series A or M. The Alexander drachms unfortunately cannot be identified precisely from the published photographs, but they are probably posthumous issues from the period ca. 320–300 B.C.[18] One perhaps would be justified in assuming that the Larissa drachms are roughly contemporary with or slightly older than the Alexander drachms, but such a judgment cannot be made with confidence. Criteria of comparative wear necessarily become more unreliable after coins have circulated for as long as these drachms seem to have done and therefore have become so very worn.

The one large hoard which I have examined personally is *IGCH* 168 from near Larissa, dated ca. 250 B.C. or perhaps later.[19] The relevant coins are 156 facing-head drachms of Larissa, series A or M, and 288 drachms of the standard Alexander type with the legends of Alexander, Philip III and Lysimachus. Almost all these Alexander-type drachms belong to the period ca. 325–300 B.C., but some of them are as recent as ca. 290 B.C. As a group the Larissa drachms are quite worn, as are the Alexander-type drachms except for the most recent examples. On the whole, the Larissa drachms are comparable in condition to the

[17] J. Morineau Humphris, *CH* 3, pp. 10–13, points this out.

[18] I am indebted to Margaret Thompson for this information.

[19] T. R. Martin, "A Third-Century B.C. Hoard from Thessaly at the ANS (*IGCH* 168)," *ANSMN* 26 (1981), pp. 51–77.

lifetime Alexander drachms and perhaps the early posthumous issues. For example in Plate 1, compare three typically worn Larissa drachms from this hoard, 2–4, with a lifetime Alexander drachm of Salamis, 5, and two of Miletus dated ca. 325–323 B.C., 6–7.[20] Since the size of the sample is larger in this case than in the others previously discussed, greater confidence can be placed in an analysis of comparative wear. In fairness to the evidence, however, an additional reservation must be admitted. Since *IGCH* 168 cannot have been hidden before the middle of the third century,[21] the fourth-century coins in the hoard could have circulated for over fifty years before their extraction from circulation for hoarding. In that span of time, a small denomination such as the drachm could be subjected to so much use that even coins of significantly different dates of issue could be worn down to a similar state of poor preservation. Alternatively, coins of the same date could exhibit different degrees of wear if some of them had been withdrawn from circulation for a period of time, as could have happened if some of the coins had been previously hoarded and then restored to circulation before being hoarded for the final time. In short, it would be foolhardy to claim undue precision or reliability for any conclusions based on an analysis of comparative states of wear. Nevertheless, the evidence of *IGCH* 168 is certainly striking because it agrees with the evidence of the other hoards already surveyed: coins dated by Herrmann early in the fourth century, in this case ca. 395–363 B.C., exhibit a pattern of wear comparable to that of coins of demonstrably more recent date, in this case of the 320s B.C., and perhaps a little beyond. To sum up, the evidence from published hoards militates against the assumption that the silver issues of Larissa ended as early as 344/3 B.C. and reveals serious problems in the chronology established by Herrmann for his group 7, the facing-head issues. As a result, there is a need to establish a more plausible date for the closing of the civic mint at Larissa and to examine the standard chronological arrangement of these coins.

[20] The Salamis drachm is no. 495 in Martin (above, n. 19); the Milesian drachms are nos. 107a and 118b in Margaret Thompson's study (above, n. 15).

[21] Martin (above, n. 19), pp. 66–70.

The 156 drachms of Larissa in *IGCH* 168 constitute the second largest group of coins of Larissa yet found in a single hoard.[22] In view of the large number of these drachms in the hoard, it is extremely remarkable that all these coins are one main type with a female facing head, three-quarters left on the obverse and a horse with three or four legs bent, grazing right on the reverse (Plate 1, 2–4). In no other recorded hoard with a sizable group of drachms of Larissa do we find this consistency of type. For example, *IGCH* 58 has at least ten different types.[23] Also noteworthy is the variety found in the types which closely resemble the one type found in *IGCH* 168. For example, in *IGCH* 58 the facing head can be left or right, as can the horse.[24] Significantly, *IGCH* 58 includes no Macedonian regnal coinage and therefore probably belongs to the second or third quarter of the fourth century before the coins of Philip and Alexander had made their way into Thessaly.[25]

As A. R. Bellinger was the first to point out, the startling uniformity of type of the drachms of Larissa in a third-century hoard should indicate that these coins are the most recent issues of the mint of Larissa;[26] otherwise, we would expect to find other contemporary or later types mixed in. But Bellinger's acute observation on the uniformity of types in *IGCH* 168 cannot be reconciled with Herrmann's chronological scheme. According to Herrmann all the coins of Larissa belong to series A or M and should therefore not have been issued after ca. 363 B.C.;[27] if this dating were correct, *IGCH* 168 with its large number of coins of Larissa should then definitely contain at least some of Herr-

[22] *IGCH* 58 (ca. 350 B.C.?) has 266 drachms of Larissa, a total which can be raised to 541+ with the addition of *CH* 4, nos. 20–21; 5, no. 20.

[23] See n. 77. Notice of *CH* 6, no. 24 (270 B.C. with 25 Larissa drachms), reached me just as this article was going to press.

[24] See, e.g., coins 7 and 18 in fig. 1, *ArchAnAth* 2 (1969), p. 106.

[25] Since none of Philip II's coins turns up in Thessalian hoards earlier than late in the reign of Alexander (*IGCH* 80), the absence of Philip's coins from a Thessalian hoard does not mean that the hoard could not have been hidden as late as 340–330 B.C. Tony Hackens, in a general meeting (*RBN* 1967, p. 250), dated the hoard "d'avant Philippe II."

[26] "The Thessaly Hoard of 1938," *Congresso internazionale di numismatica Roma 1961*, vol. 2 *Atti* (Rome, 1965), pp. 57–60. Cf. *ACGC*, p. 117.

[27] That is, Herrmann's lower terminus for series M. The end of A he put in 370 B.C. See Herrmann, pp. 41, 44.

mann's later issues. In addition, the presence of a large number of the coins of Alexander in the hoard in contrast to the complete absence of the coins of Philip II represents a circumstantial argument in favor of placing the lower terminus of this type of Larissa drachms substantially later in the fourth century than Herrmann did.

Taken by itself, *IGCH* 168 presents a readily comprehensible picture of the fate of the silver coinage of Larissa. The earlier preference for a multiplicity of types and marked variation in similar types was abandoned in favor of an almost uniform type. This change probably took place some years or even decades before the closure of the mint, and in the ensuing period the older, more diverse types gradually disappeared from circulation as they were replaced by the new uniform issues. These final issues of Larissa continued to circulate for quite some time and became generally well worn because the mint was no longer open to receive and restrike worn silver. Since the new drachms of Alexander began to appear in Thessaly in large numbers in the last decades of the fourth century, they eliminated the necessity to renew local production of the customary drachm coinage even if conditions permitted the reopening of the city mint in, say, the early third century. But, the retention of Herrmann's chronology for the facing-head issues of Larissa would make *IGCH* 168 evidence for dating the end of this coinage no later than 363 B.C., an impossibly early date. It is time to examine his system in detail.

HERRMANN'S CHRONOLOGY

Herrmann arranged the facing-head issues of Larissa in chronological order from older to more recent primarily on the assumption of a gradual deterioration of the style of the female head on the obverse. The less the Larissa obverse resembled its model, the Kimonian Arethusa of Syracuse (Plate 1, 8), the more distant in time it had to be from its inspiration, or so the argument goes by implication.[28] Herrmann divided

[28] On the Arethusa type of Kimon and its imitation at Larissa, see Katherine P. Erhart, *The Development of the Facing Head Motif on Greek Coins and Its Relation to Classical Art* (New York, 1979), pp. 181–87, 241-43.

the facing-head issues of his group 7 into 19 series (*Reihen*) designated by letters of the alphabet from A (the oldest) to R (the most recent) with the letter J omitted and the letters M and N supplemented by M 1 and N 1.[29] The grouping in series depends on an analysis of style for the most part, and in the course of his discussion Herrmann forthrightly declared the difficulties and the limitations of his method of classification.[30] The assumption that die cutters at Larissa became worse rather than better at imitating the complex representation of Arethusa as they acquired more experience with the passage of time apparently bothered Herrmann, and he admitted that "auch braucht die Stilverschlechterung nicht immer spätere Zeit anzudeuten, sondern mag hie und da auch als Arbeit geringer Hände zu erklären sein, die gleichzeitig mit dem Meister arbeiteten. Meine Endziffern sind also oft vollkommen hypothetisch."[31] He also expressed reservations about the relative chronology of all the facing-head issues outside the so-called "schöner Stil" series, that is, all the issues outside series A through I. In fact, Herrmann stated that his theory of a deterioration in style as a guide to chronology could not be easily applied to series K through R and that the alphabetic order of these groups did not necessarily represent a well-established relative chronology.[32] On the basis of work by K. Regling, Herrmann dated series A through I to ca. 395–370 B.C., series K through M 1 to ca. 370–363 B.C., series N through Q to ca. 361–353 B.C., and series R to 353–344/3 B.C.[33]

[29] Herrmann, pp. 41–49.

[30] Herrmann, pp. 49–59.

[31] Herrmann, p. 50.

[32] Herrmann, pp. 53–54. I have tried to provide a sufficient number of illustrations, but for the discussion which follows some readers may prefer to use the plates in Herrmann's article. Since his series are not indicated on the plates, I append for the readers' convenience a list of the examples of Herrmann's series as they are arranged on plates 5–8 in *ZfN* 35 (1924–25). Series A is represented by pl. 5, nos. 1–14; B by 5, nos. 15–19 and by 6, nos. 1–3; C by 6, nos. 4–6; D by 6, nos. 7–9; E by 6, no. 10; F by 6, nos. 11–13; G by 6, no. 14; H by 6, no. 15; I by 6, nos. 16–19; K by 7, nos. 1–3; L by 7, nos. 4–5; M by 7, nos. 6–8; M 1 by 7, nos. 9–10; N by 7, no. 12; N 1 by 7, no. 13; O by 7, nos. 14–17, and by 8, nos. 1–2; P by 8, no. 3; Q by 8, nos. 4–8; R by 8, nos. 9–16.

[33] Regling's arguments are quoted by Herrmann, pp. 59–63.

Herrmann's own words sufficiently demonstrate that his arrangement of the facing-head issues is too insecurely based to stand against the evidence from hoards that has already been surveyed. In the tradition of Barclay Head's canon developed for the coinage of Syracuse that a worse style meant a more recent date, Herrmann evidently found it natural to organize his chronological scheme on the basis of a gradually developing "Stilverschlechterung."[34] There is, however, no need to assume any necessarily progressive evolution of style, for the worse or for the better, in the issues of a large and productive mint like that of Larissa. One might compare the style of the female head found on Roman Republican denarii, whose dates are approximately known. The style of this head is not a reliable guide to the relative chronology of the denarii.

Nevertheless, of necessity Herrmann based his chronology on considerations of style. It was obviously difficult to establish absolute dates for his series, but the dates about which Herrmann felt the most confidence were those of his series R, the final fourth-century issues of the mint of Larissa in his opinion. Since these coins bore the name of a man whom Herrmann took to be tyrant of Larissa from 353 to 344/3 B.C. as a minion of Philip II of Macedon, he could peg series R to that period and then align all the other alphabetical series to run backwards in time toward the fifth century.[35] Since Herrmann's chronology depends on his dates for series R, it is important to make clear the nature of the evidence on which those dates are based.

Herrmann derived his absolute dates for series R from G. F. Hill's interpretation of the tiny inscription ΣΙΜΟ which appears on these coins.[36] In brief, Hill's argument is that Simos, while serving as Philip's tyrant in Larissa, placed his own name on the city's coins during the period between Philip's intervention in Thessaly on the side of Larissa against Pherae in 353 B.C. and Philip's reorganization of the Thessalian tetrarchies in 344/3 B.C.[37] The historical evidence used to link the coins

[34] On Head's canon, see C. H. V. Sutherland, *ANSMN* 4 (1950), p. 1.

[35] Herrmann, pp. 58–59.

[36] *Historical Greek Coins* (London, 1906), pp. 93–97. Kraay, *ACGC*, p. 119, refers to the Simos issues as a "fixed point" based on Hill's arguments.

[37] Diod. Sic. 16.35, 38 (intervention); Dem. 9.26 (tetrarchies). For detailed discussion of the intervention, see N. G. L. Hammond and G. T. Griffith, *A History*

of series R with this period, however, is tenuous. Above all, it is clear that Philip exploited the situation in Thessaly to his own advantage by maintaining a façade of constitutional normalcy as far as possible. For example, he led the Thessalians not in his capacity as the Macedonian king but as the chosen leader of the Thessalian confederacy, a post he secured in the late 350s B.C.[38] Since this leader customarily issued no coins under his own name nor did he interfere in civic coinage, it is very unlikely that Philip himself made any changes in the traditional coinages of Thessaly or that he encouraged others to do so.[39] Furthermore, Philip seems to have avoided overt interference in the traditional forms of civic government in Thessaly for the most part in order to make propagandistic use of an official policy of preserving or restoring the "ancestral constitution" of Thessaly.[40] Tyrants in the cities were not part of that policy, and Philip consistently intervened in Thessaly to expel tyrants, not to install them.[41] The position adopted by Herrmann which dates the coins of series R on the assumption that the inscription "Simo" refers to Philip's tyrant in Larissa is untenable.

of Macedonia. Vol. II. 550–336 B.C. (Oxford, 1979), pp. 267–81 (Griffith); T. R. Martin, "Diodorus on Philip II and Thessaly in the 350s B.C.," *ClassPhil* 76 (1981), pp. 188–201. On the tetrarchies, see Griffith, pp. 528–34.

[38] For Philip's leadership of this confederacy, see Griffith (above, n. 37), pp. 220–23; Marta Sordi, *La lega tessala fino ad Alessandro Magno* (Rome, 1958), pp. 249–60.

[39] The only leader of the confederacy to issue coins with his name inscribed on them was the tyrannical Alexander of Pherae, whose leadership was contested by the members of the confederacy because of its revolutionary character. See Sordi (above, n. 38), pp. 193–234 on Alexander and pp. 334–39 on the normal functions and privileges of the leader of the confederacy (the *tagos* or *archon*).

[40] Philip's reorganization of Thessalian federal government meant that he could forge effective control of the cities without subverting their traditional civic governments. On Philip's ostensible respect for Thessalian tradition, cf. Griffith (above, n. 37), p. 534; J. R. Ellis, *Philip II and Macedonian Imperialism* (London, 1976), p. 140. If, as Ellis, pp. 141–42, 238, and M. Sordi, "La dracma di Aleuas e l'origine di un tipo monetario di Alessandro Magno," *AIIN* 3 (1956), p. 20, suggest, the Thessalian confederacy under Philip issued a federal bronze coinage, there was a federal silver coinage of the fifth century as a precedent. For this latter coinage, see Peter Franke, "ΦΕΘΑΛΟΙ—ΦΕΤΑΛΟΙ—ΠΕΤΘΑΛΟΙ—ΘΕΣΣΑΛΟΙ. Zur Geschichte Thessaliens im 5. Jahrhundert v. Chr.," *AA* 85 (1970), pp. 85–93.

[41] Diod. Sic. 16.14.1–2, 35, 38, 69.8.

The matter does not end here, however, because subsequent attempts to maintain the chronological connection between series R and a career for Simos in the 350s and 340s B.C. have taken another direction. The consensus is that at some point after the entry of Philip into Thessalian affairs in the 350s, Simos became tyrant of Larissa without the help of Philip and indeed contrary to his wishes. Philip therefore intervened in 344 B.C. to expel Simos and his fellow Aleuads from Larissa, thus putting an end to series R.[42] The evidence used to support this reconstruction is, as in the previous case, insufficient. The clearest piece of evidence is Demosthenes' brief reference to a Eudikos and Simos of Larissa who were called friends of Philip until they had put Thessaly into Philip's hands.[43] The implication seems to be that Simos along with the other collaborators mentioned in the same passage suffered exile as the penalty for Philip's lost favor, but the chronology is not specified.[44] The rest of the evidence is either too vague to be of help or completely worthless.[45]

[42] See Griffith (above, n. 37), pp. 525–26; Ellis (above, n. 40), pp. 137–38; Helmut Berve, *Die Tyrannis bei den Griechen* (Darmstadt, 1967), pp. 295, 672; Sordi (above, n. 38), pp. 286, 364–68; H. D. Westlake, *Thessaly in the Fourth Century B.C.* (London, 1935), pp. 190–91.

[43] *De Cor.* 48.

[44] In any case, Demosthenes cannot be trusted implicitly in such assertions about the fate of collaborators. For example, Aristratos of Sicyon and Perilaos of Megara, who are named as exiles after the list in which Simos appears, reappear later in the same oration in a list which names traitors who gave away the freedom of their cities first to Philip and *now* to Alexander (*De Cor.* 295–96). One might also notice Euthykrates of Olynthos, another friend of Philip, who Demosthenes says "came to the worst ruin of all" after betraying his city to the king (Dem. 8.40). Hypereides reports that the same man was alive and apparently influential even after 338 B.C. (frag. 76 OCT = frag. B 19.1, LCL *Minor Attic Orators*, vol. 2).

[45] Harpokration, s. v. "*Σῖμος*," says only that Simos was an Aleuad who seemed to have cooperated with Philip. Aristotle at *Pol.* 1306a25–30 refers to a Simos in describing an incident at Larissa in which an oligarchic government was made into a tyranny, but his description is so compressed that it is very uncertain what role this Simos played. The date of the incident is in any case unknown. Diod. Sic. 16.69.8 succinctly reports that in 344/3 B.C. Philip "expelled the tyrants from the cities" in Thessaly, but the cities are not named. Pherae was certainly one, but Pagasae is more likely than Larissa to have been another. Polyaen. 4.2.11 does not indicate that Philip expelled the Aleuads from Larissa because, according to this story, the Aleuads forestalled any action to undermine their position. This passage

It is possible to summarize as follows the historical evidence which bears on Simos and the coins of series R. A certain Simos, a noble of Larissa, was involved in the summoning of Philip to Thessaly in the 350s B.C. for help against the tyrants of Pherae. At some point after he and a confederate, in the words of Demosthenes, "had put Thessaly into Philip's hands," Simos lost the special favor of the Macedonian king. We do not know when the loss occurred or with what specific consequences for Simos. For example, if in this context Demosthenes meant by "putting Thessaly into Philip's hands" the reorganization of the Thessalian tetrarchies in (it seems) 344 B.C.,[46] a plan which Simos could have helped Philip to devise, the loss of favor could have meant only that Philip betrayed Simos' hopes by failing to make him one of the tetrarchs and not that Simos was driven from Larissa.[47] In sum, it is certain that Simos cannot have been Philip's tyrant at Larissa from 353 to 344/3 B.C., as Herrmann believed, and if he ever exercised tyrannical power in this period, it would have been in 345–344 B.C. for only as long a time as it took Philip to return to Thessaly and unseat him.[48]

By now it should be clear that the historical evidence used to date the coins of series R to the period 353–344/3 B.C. is largely a mirage, changing its appearance or even completely fading away in substance depending on the point of view of the interpreter. The consequences of the unsatisfactory nature of the historical evidence are obvious. There is no choice but to look above all at the evidence of the coins themselves in any attempt to give a date to series R and to the other series of the facing-head coinage of Larissa.

is evidence only for tension between the king and his collaborators, nothing more. Finally, the scholia to Dem. 1.22 and 2.14 are worthless because they confuse the Aleuads of Larissa with the tyrants of Pherae.

[46] Griffith (above, n. 37), pp. 528–35.

[47] The names of only two tetrarchs are attested, but neither is Simos: Theopomp. *FGrH* 115 frag. 209; *SIG*^{3} 274, no. 8; Ellis (above, n. 40), pp. 141, 276, n. 64.

[48] This is essentially the view of Westlake (above, n. 42) and Ellis (above, n. 40), and the date is established as follows. The stasis described by Aristotle occurred in peacetime (*Pol.* 1306a26), therefore after the peace of 346 B.C. The best time for Simos to have become tyrant against Philip's wishes was while the king was away fighting the Illyrians in 345 B.C. (Isoc. *epist.* 2.3; G. L. Cawkwell, *Classical Quarterly* 13 [Oxford, 1963], pp. 126–27). Philip intervened in 344 B.C. (Diod. Sic. 16.69.8).

NUMISMATIC EVIDENCE FOR A NEW CHRONOLOGY

RELATIVE CHRONOLOGY

According to Herrmann, series R and its neighbor, series Q, are the most recent issues of the mint at Larissa, dated ca. 361–344/3 B.C. A glance at their obverses and reverses shows why Herrmann put these coins together (Plate 1, 9 = R, 10 = Q). On the obverse, one sees a rather elongated version of the female facing head ultimately derived from Kimon's head of Arethusa on the coins of Syracuse. On the reverse, the horse in series Q and most of R grazes with all four legs extended instead of crouching in the position which G. F. Hill described as "about to lie down" which is so common on the other series at Larissa.[49] This grazing horse is replaced by a prancing horse on some specimens of R.[50] As for the legend on the reverse, R regularly has ΛΑΡΙ, which also occurs in Q along with ΛΑΡΙΣΑΙ. Particularly noteworthy in these series are several details in the treatment of the obverse type. First, all the examples assigned by Herrmann to Q exhibit a scalloped or indented neckline on the female head.[51] This particular refinement otherwise appears on a facing-head coinage, oddly enough, only on the Arethusa-type imitations from Carthaginian Motya around the very early years of the fourth century B.C.[52] Second, in Q certainly, and perhaps in R as well, the nymph is wearing a chlamys fastened by a

[49] *NC* 1923, p. 220.

[50] Herrmann, p. 48, lists two examples. He says he cannot decide whether specimen alpha is genuine, not having seen it in person, because its reverse resembles a forgery by Christodoulos. The reverse of specimen beta is described as "wohl derselbe Stempel," but he expresses no doubt about its authenticity. This coin he had seen personally in the Berlin collection on which he worked for this article on the coinage of Larissa (p. 2). See below, n. 87.

[51] Herrmann, p. 47.

[52] On the facing-head issues of Motya, see G. K. Jenkins, "Coins of Punic Sicily," *SNR* 1971, p. 31, and Erhart (above, n. 28), pp. 233–34. Erhart suggests in n. 481 that this indented neckline may be Punic in origin. It also appears on the profile heads of some fifth-century Syracusan issues, e.g. Kurt Regling, *Die griechischen Münzen der Sammlung Warren* (Berlin, 1906), nos. 331–33.

button or similar clasp at the base of her neck.[53] Like the scalloped neckline, the chlamys is not characteristic of Kimon's Arethusa but rather appears on fourth-century facing-head issues from western Asia Minor which carry a representation of Apollo.[54] Third, all the issues of Q and all but one of R lack the necklace characteristic of other facing-head series at Larissa (except P), and the earrings common in other series are generally absent as well.[55] Finally, series Q exhibits one additional oddity. Some specimens from this series have dolphins alongside the facing head on the obverse, which otherwise appear nowhere else in the facing-head coinage of Larissa.[56] The dolphins presumably reflect the influence of the dolphins to be seen sporting in the hair of Arethusa as depicted by Kimon, but on these coins of Larissa, as on the facing-head issues of Motya, the dolphins are placed around the nymph's hair rather than in it.[57]

In sum, the issues of R share a number of the characteristics which serve to distinguish series Q from the other series in Herrmann's classification. Therefore, his decision to place these series together seems reasonable based on their overall similarities, although, as I see it, the two series are probably not exactly contiguous.[58] But we can no longer accept Herrmann's chronology which makes these series the last silver coins of Larissa because that position belongs to the type found in *IGCH* 168. Furthermore, the grounds on which Herrmann based his

[53] The chlamys is clearly visible in Herrmann's illustrations of Q. On nos. 11 and 12 of Herrmann's pl. 8 from series R, there is a bulge along the neckline that might be the fold of a chlamys, but the spot where the button or clasp should appear is off the flan on both these coins. Herrmann recognized this bulge but wrongly called it a necklace. See n. 55. If it should be proven from other examples of R that a chlamys does occur in this series, one should then consider moving R close to the start of the facing-head issues.

[54] See the issues of Klazomenai, Miletus and the satraps of Karia described by Erhart (above, n. 28), pp. 213–19.

[55] Herrmann, pp. 47–48, who failed to recognize the chlamys, erroneously described the fold of this garment fastened at the neck as a necklace on the coins of these series. Herrmann's series R, coin beta, is his only example with earrings in the series.

[56] Herrmann, pl. 8, 8, and Varoucha (above, n. 12), pl. 9, 6. See Plate 1, 1, for a reproduction of the latter specimen.

[57] Cf. Erhart (above, n. 28), p. 233.

[58] See the discussion which follows on the order of the series.

absolute dates for Series R are unreliable. The same observation applies to the chronology of series Q. Herrmann dated these coins to the period ca. 361–353 B.C. on the grounds that they were the series just before R, whose start he put in 353 B.C., but were later than the issue inscribed ΑΛΕΥ (Herrmann's group 8), which he dated to the period ca. 363–361 B.C.[59] But just as 353 B.C. has no claim to authoritative status as a chronological fixed point, neither does 361 B.C. because no compelling stylistic or hoard evidence can be marshalled to date these coins. First, the obverse and reverse types of this "Aleuas issue" are so markedly different from those of the other facing-head issues that it makes little sense to attempt to date the issue closely on the basis of style (Plate 1, 11).[60] Second, the hoards are of no help because no examples of this issue are on record from any hoard. In the absence of any relatively objective criteria for dating, scholars are forced to rely on interpretations of the types and legend of the issue as the basis for their chronological suggestions. In this way Herrmann arrived at his date of ca. 363–361 B.C.[61] In the same manner, Marta Sordi has subsequently argued that the Aleuas issue belongs considerably later in the century at the start of the reign of Alexander the Great, probably in 336 B.C.[62] Sordi's arguments are intricate and exhaustive, but when two such different chronological conclusions can be drawn from the same evidence, it is necessary to admit that we cannot in truth date these coins with any confidence. Since the Aleuas issue is not precisely dated, it cannot safely be used as a chronological peg from which to hang other facing-head issues. In other words, Herrmann's date of ca. 361 B.C.

[59] Herrmann, pp. 60, 63–66.

[60] Obv. ΑΛΕΥ, male helmeted head facing l., double ax; rev. ΛΑΡΙΣΑΙΑ ΕΛΛΑ eagle on lightning bolt l.

[61] Herrmann, pp. 64–66. His most substantive argument rests on his interpretation of the legend ΛΑΡΙΣΑΙΑ as contemporary with the similar adjectival legends on the coins of Alexander of Pherae, but this legend appears on several other issues of Larissa, some of which Herrmann dates as early as the fifth century, e.g. groups 3 D, E, F and G (Herrmann, pp. 21–22). It is obvious that this criterion is ambiguous at best in this case. For the view that the coin was issued by Jason of Pherae, see H. T. Wade-Gery, "Jason of Pherae and Aleuas the Red," *JHS* 44 (1924), pp. 63–64, with references to earlier attributions by various scholars.

[62] "La dracma di Aleuas e l'origine di un tipo monetario di Alessandro Magno," *AIIN* 3 (1956), pp. 9–22.

as the upper terminus of series Q is just as unsubstantiated as is his lower terminus of 353 B.C. We are free to place Herrmann's final series, Q and R, wherever they appear to belong based on the numismatic evidence.

The record of the various types of the facing-head issues as they occur in hoards helps to provide a rough guide to the relative chronology of these coins. In the latest hoards to contain coins of Larissa, instead of specimens from Herrmann's final series Q or R, there are only examples which he would put earlier than these series.[63] In fact, with the exception of four well-worn didrachms in *IGCH* 162, all the coins of Larissa in the hoards of the third and second centuries B.C. whose contents have been adequately described are the same type.[64] These drachms carry on the obverse the familiar female facing head turned slightly to the left and on the reverse a horse to the right in an odd crouching position with bent legs.[65] The reverse legend is uniformly the genitive plural ethnic, ΛΑΡΙΣΑΙΩΝ, with part of the word inscribed above the horse and part below in the exergue (Plate 1, 2–4). This is of course exactly the type found in *IGCH* 168 which Bellinger identified as the final issue of the mint of Larissa. Under Herrmann's classification, the didrachms of *IGCH* 162 belong to series A and *IGCH* 168 type drachms belong to A or M. One must say A or M because the drachms of these two series are, in my opinion, too similar to represent different series. Herrmann's explanation as to why the coins of A and M should constitute two series appears to rest above all on the assumption that the coins of M do not achieve the "beautiful style" of the coins of A, although he does claim that the facing head of A always has earrings but that of M does not and that the nymph's lips are more closely pressed together in M.[66] Herrmann's judgment on the style and lips of M seems to me subjective, and, to judge from Herrmann's own plates, earrings

[63] I should reiterate that my discussion of the hoard evidence depends on currently published information.

[64] *IGCH* 168 (Thessaly, ca. 250–240); *CH* 3, no. 43 (2, no. 72, Thessaly, ca. 229–228); *IGCH* 232 (Euboea, ca. 171–169).

[65] The one drachm of Larissa in *IGCH* 162 (Thessaly, ca. 250) is described only as "of the fourth century," but it seems very unlikely that this coin is not the same type as the other drachms in late hoards.

[66] Herrmann, pp. 41, 45, 55.

are not always visible on the coins of A. (See, for example, Herrmann's pl. 5, 12, from series A, and his pl. 7, 8, from series M.) I will therefore treat the coins of A and M as one series, to be called A-M. The subgroup of A-M found in *IGCH* 168 which has the nymph three-quarters left and the horse right will be called A-M 168.

If one proceeds backwards in time in terms of the dates of the hoards in which coins of Larissa appear whose types can be determined, the next relevant hoards are six which belong to the 330s and 320s B.C. The types in these hoards support the claim of A-M 168 to the status of the final issue of the mint of Larissa. In two of these hoards there is only a single drachm of Larissa, in both cases an A-M 168 type.[67] The only hoard in this group with a large number of Larissa drachms is *IGCH* 385 with A-M and A-M 168 types as 58 of its 62 specimens from this city. As mentioned earlier, the other drachms belong to series C, E or F (one specimen), B (one) and group 6 (two).[68] Herrmann placed group 6 at the beginning of the fourth century.[69] Two other hoards in this period have two drachms of Larissa in each, an A-M and a "K or Q" type in one hoard and one D and one E type in the other.[70] We are now beginning to encounter types other than A-M 168, but unfortunately it is not possible at this time to report on the condition of the great majority of these coins. The situation improves somewhat in the sixth hoard of this group, *IGCH* 386.[71] This is the hoard that has two drachms from one of Herrmann's series K to M 1 which are described as "très bien" in condition, an E type in "bien," and a Q type whose condition is not rated but which appears to be more worn than the E coin in the published photographs.[72]

[67] *IGCH* 76 (Messenia, ca. 327); *CH* 2, no. 52 (6, no. 20, Thessaly, ca. 323–320).

[68] See n. 11.

[69] Herrmann, p. 40.

[70] *CH* 1, no. 37, in Le Rider, pp. 290–92, hd. 5, Macedonia, ca. 337/6, and pp. 292–93, hd. 6, in commerce, ca. 337/6. The date of these hoards is derived from the coins of Philip of Le Rider's group Pella 2 A 2 of ca. 342/1–ca. 337/6 B.C. The identifications of the Larissa drachms are Le Rider's.

[71] See n. 12.

[72] Varoucha (above, n. 12), p. 418, pl. 9, 5 (E) and 6 (Q). Since the two drachms of K to M 1 are not illustrated, it is impossible to determine their precise series. I suspect it is M, i.e. A-M.

The next hoards in this survey provide limited but useful information. One worn didrachm, the denomination Herrmann places with series A, appears in at least one hoard of ca. 348 B.C., and several more are perhaps included in a contemporary hoard.[73] Another small hoard of approximately the same date contains at least one drachm of Herrmann's fifth-century group 3 D.[74] The final hoards to be treated are those regarded as the earliest ones on record as containing coins of Larissa. Both are large hoards whose contents can only be partially described at present, but their evidence is valuable.[75] Both hoards come from Thessaly, and neither contains any Macedonian regnal coinage. This absence of the coinage of the Macedonian kings is not a very precise chronological indication because no Macedonian coins appear in Thessalian hoards until the reign of Alexander.[76] Since the other Greek coinages in these hoards are not easily dated themselves, the mid-fourth-century date given these two hoards in *IGCH* must be regarded as tentative. Their date could be later in the century. In any case, both hoards exhibit a mixture of Larissa types in which A-M 168 appears to be the most numerous and, as a group, the least worn.[77]

[73] *IGCH* 371 (Macedonia, ca. 348) with one; *IGCH* 56 (Thessaly, ca. 350) with one or two (?). The contents and the date of the latter hoard are uncertain. The date for *IGCH* 371 rests on the presence of coins of the Chalkidian League and the absence of any coins of Philip II. See n. 100.

[74] *IGCH* 55 (Thessaly, ca. 350?).

[75] *IGCH* 52 (Larissa environs, before 350); 58 (Atrax, ca. 350). The latter hoard's contents are supplemented by *CH* 4, no. 21, and 5, no. 20.

[76] As the record stands now, the first Thessalian hoards to contain Macedonian regnal coins are *IGCH* 80, *CH* 2, no. 51 and *CH* 2, no. 52 (*CH* 6, no. 20). All of these hoards contain coins of both Philip II and Alexander III, and their dates are ca. 323–320 B.C.

[77] The following list identifies the types, as closely as can be determined from photographs, of all the coins that are illustrated in the publications of *IGCH* 52 and 58 according to Herrmann's classification as modified to include A-M and A-M 168 as separate categories.

IGCH 52 in *ADelt* 19 (1964), pt. 2, 1 *chronika*, pl. 1: 13 = group 4; 14–16 = F; 17 = A-M 168; 18 = A-M; 19 = N 1, Q or R; 20 = O or R. Hirsch 34, 21–22 Feb. 1963: 1187–89 = group 3H; 1190 = A (didrachm); 1191–95 = A-M 168; 1196 = A-M; 1197–98 = E; 1199 = O?; 1200 = D. Hirsch 35, 25–28 June 1963: 341–44 = A-M 168; 345–46 = E; 347 = F; 348 = O; 349–50 = O, Q or R; 351 = B.

IGCH 58 in *ArchAnAth* 2 (1969), pp. 106–7, figs. 1–2: 1 = group 6; 2–7, 9 =

The facing-head coins which consistently show signs of considerable wear are those belonging to Herrmann's series M 1, N, N 1, O, P, Q and R.[78] This evidence agrees with that of the other hoards surveyed and provides the basis for a realignment of the facing-head series. In this realignment, the earliest issues will be Q, one of those which Herrmann made the latest, and the latest issue will be A-M 168, a particular variety of two series, A and M, which, in my opinion, are in fact the same. Unfortunately the evidence of the hoards does not indicate precisely how to arrange the other series.

The most distinctive of the facing-head series is Q because it is the only one to have dolphins around the nymph's head on some examples (Plate 1, 1). Since these dolphins recall those of the late fifth-century Arethusa type of Syracuse on which the Larissa imitation is based, it makes sense to think that this particular detail was copied at Larissa on the mint's early copies of the prototype and was then omitted from later dies, perhaps because dolphins were an inappropriate accompaniment for the nymph who represented a landlocked city such as Larissa. These dolphins could mean that Q is at the beginning of Larissa's facing-head issues.[79]

Other indications help to confirm this view. First, the indented or scalloped neckline of the nymph on the coins of Q recalls the same detail on fifth-century issues of Syracuse with a profile head and facing-head issues of Motya from ca. 400 B.C.[80] Second, since the chlamys which the

A-M 168; 8, 10–12 = A-M; 13 = C; 14 = F; 15 = B; 16 = G; 17 = H; 18–19 = L; 20 = O or P; 21 = N; 22 = O; 23 = M 1, N, O or P; 24 = R.

[78] Notice, for example, in *IGCH* 52, Hirsch 35, nos. 348–50; in *IGCH* 58, *ArchAnAth*, fig. 2, nos. 23–24.

[79] An analogous situation exists in the appearance of a solitary dolphin beside the female facing head modeled after Arethusa which occurs on the coinage of the satrap Pharnabazos minted at Tarsos. The dolphin appears on what (to judge from the style) is perhaps the earliest issue of this type but then disappears on later issues of Pharnabazos and continues to be missing on the similar coins of Datames from the same mint. For these coins, see *SNGvAulock* 5916–24 (Pharnabazos) and 5934–42 (Datames). No. 5916 definitely has a dolphin. From the photographs, it is not possible to determine whether 5917–18 also have a dolphin or just a die break in the same area. On the imitation of the Syracusan Arethusa at Tarsos, see *ACGC*, pp. 118–19, 281–82.

[80] See n. 52.

nymph wears in Q and P, but not in later series, was a characteristically Thessalian garment which seems to be very rare in depictions of women and was therefore likely to attract notice, it could be explained as a detail introduced on early issues to emphasize that the lady was indeed Thessalian despite her resemblance to the Syracusan nymph and occasional representation in company with very un-Thessalian dolphins.[81] Once the nymph was familiar in her new facing-head pose, this rather mannish attribute could be dropped.

As for the reverse, it too is comfortable at the beginning of these issues because the straight-legged grazing horse resembles the horse on the obverse of the coins which Herrmann makes the very earliest issues of Larissa at the start of the fifth century.[82] More importantly, the legends which appear on coins of Q are those of the undeniably earlier issues of Larissa in Herrmann's groups 1–3 rather than the genitive plural ethnic spelled with omega of the issues like A-M 168 which belong at the end of the coinage of Larissa.[83] Some specimens have ΛΑΡΙ

[81] Others beside Thessalians of course wore the chlamys, but the garment's nickname ("Thessalian wings") attests its particular association with Thessaly. The chlamys is worn by the youths who appear on fifth-century coins of Larissa as participants in the Thessalian sport of bull-leaping (e.g., Herrmann, pl. 3, 16–23). On bull-leaping, see *RE*, Ser. 2, 9, s.v. "ταυροχαθάψια," cols. 24–27 (Ziehen). The chlamys was a male garment only rarely shown on female figures in art. See *RE* 6, s.v. "χλαμύς," cols. 2343–45 (Amelung); *DarSag* 1, s.v. "chlamys," pp. 1114–16; Margarete Bieber, *Griechische Kleidung* (Berlin, 1928), pp. 22–24.

[82] Herrmann, p. 3, group 1, pl. 1, 1–3.

[83] The appearance in *IGCH* 52 and 55 as well as in the excavations at Olynthos of worn specimens of group 3 confirms the early date of these coins. For *IGCH* 52, see n. 77; for *IGCH* 55, see *BCH* 84 (1960), pl. 7, 2; for Olynthos, see David M. Robinson and Paul M. Clement, *Excavations at Olynthos*, pt. 9 (Baltimore, 1938), p. 242, pl. 32, 14.

Herrmann's groups 1 and 3 have ΛΑΡΙΣΑΙΟΝ as one of their legends, but this form of the genitive plural ethnic is distinguished from the later form by the use of omicron instead of omega. The legend in group 6, which Herrmann dates to the start of the fourth century, is reported to be ΛΑΡΙΣΑΙΩΝ, but none of the examples I have seen has the inscription sufficiently well preserved to show whether omega is in fact used. The spacing of the letters in the legend of group 6 is so close that omicron would appear to fit better than the wider letter omega. See Herrmann, pl. 4, 17–18; *BMCThessaly*, pl. 5, 13; *ArchAnAth* 2 (1969), p. 106, fig. 1, 1. It may be relevant that the local script of Thessaly, which did not have omega, continued

as their legend, thereby recalling groups 1, 2 and 3.[84] Those with ΛΑΡΙ-ΣΑΙ recall group 3.[85] On the basis of these characteristics of the coins of Q in combination with the evidence of the hoards (e.g., a worn specimen in *IGCH* 386; several worn specimens in *IGCH* 52 which are Q or related series), I would make series Q the first of the facing-head issues of Larissa. The coins of Q which have dolphins on the obverse are probably the first of this series.

Like those of Q, the coins of series M 1, N, N 1, O, P and R are over-all the most worn of the facing-head issues in the hoards.[86] It is therefore probable that these series also belong at the early end of the facing-head issues. Unfortunately, the evidence of the hoards is not sufficient to demonstrate the order in which these series should be placed. I can only suggest that the types of P may be likely candidates for placement in a very early series because they closely repeat characteristics already familiar from Q, in particular the scalloped neckline with a chlamys on the obverse and a straight-legged horse on the reverse with the legend ΛΑΡΙΣΑΙ (Plate 1, 12). Moreover, the elongated facing head with straggling hair beside the neck seen in P resembles the distinctive style of the nymph in Q. At the present time it is only possible to say that series M 1, N, N 1, 0 and P, in an unknown order, represent as a whole the early series of the facing-head issues after series Q. The evidence will not yet allow a more precise alignment. Fortunately, there is one piece of evidence which provides a basis for placing this group of series in relation to the remaining series. An obverse die link connects series R to series K.[87] In conjunction with the hoard evidence, this link

to be used until at least the later part of the fifth century in inscriptions. See L. H. Jeffrey, *The Local Scripts of Archaic Greece* (Oxford, 1961), p. 98.

[84] The coins with the legend ΛΑΡΙ which Herrmann, p. 36, calls group 4b do not in fact belong to group 4, in my opinion. See n. 90.

[85] ΛΑΡΙ and ΛΑΡΙΣΑΙ may both be shortened forms of the early legend ΛΑΡΙΣΑΙΑ found spelled out in groups 3 and 4.

[86] Of course, an occasional specimen from these series can survive in an excellent state of preservation. The coin of O or R shown in *ADelt* 19 (1964), pt. 2, 1, *chronika*, pl. 1, 20, is said to be FDC (p. 9).

[87] Herrmann, p. 45, coin K gamma, p. 48, coin R beta. It must be pointed out that the reverse of coin R beta bears a resemblance to the reverse of a coin whose authenticity worried Herrmann (see n. 50). However, since there is no reason to doubt the authenticity of coin K gamma and Herrmann personally examined coin R beta in

furnishes important confirmation of the relative chronology of the earlier series already described and the later series such as K which are distinguished in part by the horse with bent legs on the reverse. K in turn is associated with I by the general appearance of the obverse and reverse types as well as the inscription ΙΔ or ΔΙ found in both these series.[88]

The remaining series except for A and M again cannot be put into a secure chronological order as a result of the paucity of evidence. For the moment it will suffice to say that the individual series K and I, followed by B, C, D, E, F, G, H and L in an unknown order, represent the "middle" of the over-all series between the earlier series and the series A-M, a single group which can be placed with confidence at the end of the facing-head issues of Larissa. The hoard evidence for the placement of A-M is consistent, and the obverse and reverse types are appropriate as well for this chronology. The style of the head of the nymph has became standardized, with wavy hair that generally fills the space around the head more uniformly and completely than did the more straggly strands of some of the earlier heads. The horse has bent legs which give it a distinctive posture that is usually a deeper crouch than the similar posture seen on earlier series. The legend is the full genitive ethnic plural, ΛΑΡΙΣΑΙΩΝ, divided so as to fit above and below the horse (Plate 1, 2–4). Some of the A-M series coins have small symbols (plant, trident) below the belly of the horse, and it is possible that these coins may belong earlier rather than later in this group.[89] The final coins of A-M are those which I have called A-M 168, on which the head on the obverse is always three-quarters left and the horse on the reverse is always right.[90]

Berlin, it is reasonable to believe that both coins are genuine and that the die link is a reliable and important piece of evidence.

[88] Herrmann, pp. 44–45, 54. I cannot agree with Herrmann's opinion, pp. 52–53, that a conspicuous break in the style of the obverse from "beautiful" to "not beautiful" occurs between I and K.

[89] Martin (above, n. 19), pp. 75–76.

[90] It should be pointed out that the unusual legend ΛΑΡΙ (above) ΠΛΕΙ (below) which appears in Herrmann's series A and in his profile-head group 4b (Herrmann, p. 36) does not constitute an argument for placing series A at the start of the facing-head isues and therefore closer in time to the earlier profile-head issues. This legend is reported for only one drachm in 4b; otherwise the coins in this group are triobols. But this drachm is in fact not a profile-head piece as reported by Herrmann but rather

So far, this discussion has concerned only the drachms of the facing-head coinage of Larissa, the denomination which served as the mint's largest denomination in almost all periods, in typical Thessalian fashion.[91] Hoard evidence is largely lacking for smaller denominations, which must therefore be left out of consideration. It is possible, however, to say something about the one issue of didrachms known from Larissa. On these coins, the obverse type is the stylistically fully developed facing head three-quarters left, while the reverse features either a prancing horse wearing a bridle or collar, or the familiar crouching horse, both to the right (Plate 1, 13). The legend is the full genitive plural ethnic. Herrmann placed these didrachms with the "most beautiful" drachms of series A.[92] I agree that these coins belong with the later rather than the earlier series of drachms, but it is difficult to determine exactly where this larger denomination belongs because the hoard evidence is of little help. Didrachms in worn condition are found in hoards both of the middle of the fourth and the middle of the third century B.C.[93] The fully developed head and the slightly crouching horse would be appropriate in series A-M, while the prancing horse type with legend distributed around the flan should be somewhat earlier. All one can say is that the didrachms, or at least some of them, should be earlier than the middle of the fourth century.

ABSOLUTE CHRONOLOGY

The didrachms provide an appropriate transition to the meager evidence available for the dates which should be assigned to the various

a standard facing-head type of series A. For the coin, see Mionnet, *Supplément*, vol. 3 (Paris, 1829), p. 293, 192. (A second example can be found in *NC* 1923, pp. 219–20, no. 14, pl. 9.) That the triobols assigned to 4b have a profile head does not mean that these coins must necessarily be early because these smaller denomination pieces could have been minted with an older obverse type even while contemporary drachms were showing a more modern type, the facing head. I suspect that 4b does not belong with 4a and 4c at all, a suspicion heightened by the differences in the style between the profile head of 4b and those of 4a and 4c.

91 For the coinage of Thessaly, see *ACGC*, pp. 115–20.

92 Herrmann, p. 51.

93 *IGCH* 52 (before 350); 71 (ca. 350–325); 371 (ca. 348); 162 (ca. 250).

facing-head issues of Larissa. Pherae was apparently the only other Thessalian mint to issue didrachms.[94] Two types are known, one with a profile head and the other with a female facing head whose flowing locks of hair are vaguely reminiscent of Kimon's Arethusa.[95] A resemblance to the female facing head of the coins of Larissa is also discernible (Plate 1, 14). In the light of the appearance of the unusual denomination of didrachm with a facing head at both Larissa and Pherae and of the traditional rivalry between the two cities, it would be surprising if their facing-head didrachms were not roughly contemporary. Fortunately, at least an approximate date can be given to the facing-head didrachms of Pherae because they are inscribed with the name of Alexander, the nephew and successor of Jason of Pherae. Alexander ruled, it seems, from 369 to 358 B.C.[96] This was a period of increased military activity in Thessaly as Alexander tried to achieve dominance and the Aleuads at Larissa tried to block him.[97] Since cavalry was a national specialty in Thessaly and a cavalryman's pay at this time was most likely exactly one didrachm of the Aeginetan standard per day, the mints of Larissa and Pherae could have begun to issue didrachms as a convenient and attractive denomination to use in the competitive recruiting and payment of mounted troops.[98] This new mint practice may have begun with Alexander's predecessor at Pherae, and it has been suggested that the profile-head didrachms of Pherae belong to Jason's rule, which extended from ca. 385 to 370 B.C.[99] The change

[94] To judge from the varieties listed by Herrmann and in *BMCThessaly*.

[95] For these coins, see *ACGC*, p. 118, pl. 21, 387–88. The nymph is identified as Hypereia rather than Hekate by Erhart (above, n. 28), pp. 248–49.

[96] Westlake (above, n. 42), pp. 128–29, 156; Sordi (above, n. 38), pp. 193, 230. It is an interesting coincidence that one sees on coins of Perdikkas III from this same period a horse in the striking pose with right front and left rear legs raised (prancing or trotting) which also appears on some of the didrachms of Larissa. For Perdikkas' coins, see *ACGC*, p. 144, pl. 28, 508, to which compare pl. 21, 396, of Larissa. For the dates of Perdikkas' coins as 368–359 B.C., see Hammond (above, n. 37), p. 192.

[97] For the events of this period, see Westlake (above, n. 42), pp. 126–59; Sordi (above, n. 38), pp. 191–234.

[98] For the Thessalian emphasis on cavalry, see, for example, Westlake (above, n. 42), pp. 108–9. For the rate of pay, see Xen. *Hell.* 5.2.21.

[99] Kraay, *ACGC*, p. 118, suggests the coins are Jason's. For the dates, see Sordi (above, n. 38), pp. 156–61, 187. Jason built his power with substantial forces of cavalry, a number of whom were mercenaries. See Xen. *Hell.* 6.1.18–19, 4.28.

from profile to facing head on the didrachms of Pherae perhaps took place under the influence of the facing head on the coinage of Larissa because the latter city's mint, which had produced facing-head issues before the didrachms, clearly had this type before Pherae did. In fact, Pherae retained the profile head on its drachms throughout this period. Based on these observations, a date of ca. 370 B.C. would seem reasonable for the didrachms of Larissa, with a considerable margin of approximation clearly understood. This dating receives some support from the appearance previously noted of a worn didrachm in *IGCH* 371, a hoard which is plausibly dated ca. 348 B.C., and the report of some didrachms in *IGCH* 52, a hoard perhaps no later than 350 B.C.[100]

The hoards are otherwise not very helpful at present with absolute chronology because we cannot yet establish precise dates for hoards with coins of Larissa which do not also include Macedonian regnal issues.[101] It is not necessarily safe to date hoards such as *IGCH* 52, 55 and 58 to ca. 350 B.C. on the grounds that they do not include any coins of Philip II because his coins do not otherwise turn up in hoards in Thessaly until late in the 320s B.C.[102] And the only Macedonian hoard to contain a coin of Larissa beside the hoards which also have coins of Philip is *IGCH* 371.

There is, however, some small help to be found in the reports of the excavations at Olynthos. Two silver coins of Larissa were found there, a worn trihemiobol of group 3a DE (i.e., earlier than the facing-head

[100] *IGCH* 371 consisted of at least four tetradrachms of the Chalkidian League and one didrachm of Larissa. It is usually assumed that the coinage of the Chalkidian League ceased in 348 B.C. when Philip captured and plundered the League's capital city and mint, Olynthos. See Robinson and Clement (above, n. 83), pp. 112, 133–34, 162–63. This view is supported by the hoard evidence. Chalkidian coinage appears in fifteen fourth-century hoards, but in only one of these are there any coins of Philip (*IGCH* 385 of ca. 337/6 B.C. with 136 tetradrachms of Philip and one Chalkidian tetradrachm). The other fourteen hoards are plausibly dated 348 B.C. or earlier. For these hoards, see the index of mints in *IGCH*, s.v. "Chalcidian League." For the date of *IGCH* 52, see n. 25.

[101] Study of the Theban issues with magistrates' names may help to determine absolute dates for the hoards in which they occur. These issues appear to belong to the period ca. 371–338 B.C. See *ACGC*, pp. 113–14.

[102] See n. 76.

issues) and a worn drachm that could be O, P, Q or R.[103] Twelve bronze coins of Larissa are also recorded from these excavations, and their types are of interest. Ten of these coins have the type of the triobols of group 4b, the profile head on the obverse and a crouching horse on the reverse. The legend appears to be the full genitive plural ethnic distributed above and below the horse rather than the peculiar legend of 4b.[104] Only two of these bronzes have facing heads on the obverse and in both cases the reverse is a horseman like that on the drachms of G and H and the obols Herrmann tentatively assigned to A and B together (while admitting they could belong with later series).[105]

As a result of the scanty number of bronze coins of Larissa recorded in hoards, it is impossible to draw a certain correlation between the types of the facing-head silver and bronze issues, but it would be odd if there were not some connection. Therefore, the types of the bronze coins found at Olynthos at least confirm that the facing-head type was already in use by mid-century. However, they may also suggest that the production of the A-M types was not yet so common that it had been put on all small denominations. In general, the limited information from Olynthos confirms the other indications of chronology already surveyed, with perhaps the added hint that facing-head types were not yet so numerous in, say, the late 360s B.C. that they had migrated to Macedonia in large numbers.[106]

[103] Robinson and Clement (above, n. 83), p. 242, pl. 32, 14; David M. Robinson, *Excavations at Olynthus*, pt. 3 (Baltimore, 1931), pp. 24–25, pl. 4, 62. Robinson, p. 25, refers to Herrmann's pl. 8, 4–8, which is series Q, but he says the coin belongs to "Group I," which is presumably an error for "Group VII," because the page reference to Herrmann is given as p. 49.

[104] Robinson, pt. 3 (above, n. 103), p. 96, pl. 19, 794; Robinson, *Excavations at Olynthus*, pt. 6 (Baltimore, 1934), pp. 83–84, pl. 18, 739–43; Robinson and Clement (above, n. 83), p. 243, no. 3 (four specimens), pl. 32, 16.

[105] Herrmann, p. 42.

[106] Robinson's statistics (above, nn. 103–4), pt. 3, pp. 4–5, and pt. 6, p. 1, show that the great majority of the coins found in the Olynthos excavations belong to the period before 348 B.C. It is of course impossible to tell how long before that date the coins of Larissa made their way to Olynthos. The only coins of Larissa found in a hoard at Olynthos are Robinson, pt. 6, 739–40, the 4b type in bronze. See Robinson and Clement (above, n. 83), pp. 191–93, hoard no. 1 Æ.

There are virtually no other criteria for the determination of absolute chronology. We have already seen that the name Simos in series R is not a reliable indicator of chronology for those coins. The same can be said of the other abbreviated names and solitary letters that occasionally appear on other facing-head issues from Larissa. The name ΝΑΥΚ occurs in Q, ΙΔ and ΔΙ in K, Ι, Μ and Ξ on the obols assigned to A and B, and ΠΛΕΙ in A.[107] Only the last is inscribed in large letters and in the exergue. Under the arrangement I have proposed for these issues, "Nauk" comes at the head of the series (although it is not on the very earliest specimens of Q, those with dolphins), the following names and letters (including "Simos") occur on issues which follow one another somewhat later in the series, and "Plei" comes last of all. With the exception of "Plei," these inscriptions come at points in the series where the coins exhibit perceptible changes in style or type, and it is not out of the question that the inscriptions refer to the mint officials or die makers involved in implementing these changes.

But how is one to explain the great disparity between the appearance of these diminuitive letters in the field and that of the inscription "Plei" which is so large and displaces part of the normal ethnic legend in its position in the exergue? It is hard to believe that an artist could have aspired to such prominence on the civic coinage in the light of the local tradition in this matter. This distinctive and unique inscription perhaps reflects political circumstances of a special character. It is only a suggestion for thought, but the sort of episode described by Aristotle in which a special magistrate at the head of a military force whose job was to avert civil war actually became a tyrant would offer such special circumstances. When he seized power at Pherae, Alexander broke tradition by putting his name on Pherae's coins in large letters in place of the civic legend.[108] It is not out of the question that a tyrant in Larissa did the same for a brief period. This explanation cannot be proven,

[107] Herrmann, pp. 41–42, 44–45, 47.

[108] For Aristotle, see n. 45. ΠΛΕΙ could be the abbreviation for a name known in Thessaly such as Pleistarchos (*IG* IX, 2, no. 6, line 1; no. 24, line 5, from Hypata) or Pleistainos (*IG* IX, 2, no. 568, line 16, from Larissa). The archon appointed to settle factional strife would surely have had control of the mint as part of the necessary administration of the city's finances. Compare the comparable fourth-century situation at Pharsalos, Xen. *Hell.* 6.1.2, for which such power is specifically attested.

but it does have the virtue of suggesting why no names or letters occur on the very numerous examples of series A-M 168, which have only symbols as some sort of control mark. If the occurrence of "Plei" in the A-M series was associated with an episode of tyranny, the inscription of a name or even of letters from a name on coinage at Larissa would thereafter have been abandoned in order to avoid any association with the anti-traditional practices of a tyrant.[109]

I have argued elsewhere that the silver coinages of Larissa came to an end not long after 321 B.C. as a result of economic devastation after a period of famine, war and destruction in Thessaly.[110] It is unfortunately not possible to suggest a date for the beginning of the facing-head issues with equal confidence. Herrmann suggested ca. 395 B.C. because he put the didrachms first in the series and associated them with the victory of Larissa over Pharsalos in 395 B.C.[111] This hypothesis has no evidence to support it, and I think it more likely that the didrachms are not the earliest facing-head issue and that they are contemporary with the similar coins of Pherae. Too little is known about the events of Thessalian history in the fifth and early fourth centuries to settle upon a particular event as the catalyst for the change from the older types at Larissa to the facing head in imitation of Syracuse. And in

[109] Even if this explanation of ΠΛΕΙ is correct, it still does not help with chronology. The only possible hint is the report that Simos of Larissa was traveling around with the hetaira Neaira and came to Athens with her sometime before 374/3 B.C. See Dem. 59.24, 33, 108. If this is the Simos of Aristotle's story, he could have left Larissa as a result of the strife that led to the establishment of the tyrannical neutral archon. The date of the ΠΛΕΙ issues would then be ca. 375 B.C. This is only speculation, however.

[110] "The End of Thessalian Civic Coinage in Silver: Macedonian Policy or Economic Reality?" *Proceedings of the 9th International Numismatic Congress, Bern, September 1979.* (Luxembourg, 1982), pp. 157-64. In brief, the evidence for economic devastation is, first, the extraordinary gifts of grain to Thessalian cities including Larissa attested by M. N. Tod, *A Selection of Greek Historical Inscriptions*, vol. 2 (Oxford, 1948), no. 196. These gifts show that the problems of the 320s B.C. imposed grave agricultural and therefore financial losses on Larissa. Second, the Lamian or Hellenic War was contested in Thessaly during 323–322 B.C., with a final struggle in 321 B.C. The Thessalians resisted the Macedonians to the bitter end with obvious consequences. See Diod. Sic. 18.12–13, 15–18, 38.

[111] Herrmann, p. 50.

fact, the change may have had nothing to do with political or military history. The impetus for the change to a facing head from a profile head like those of Herrmann's group 4 may have been entirely aesthetic. The facing-head motif in a three-quarter view was extremely popular as a coin type by the end of the fifth century, and the mint officials at Larissa may simply have decided to adopt the most up-to-date style for their production.[112] The Thessalians were proverbially wealthy, and at least some entertained pretensions to the latest canons of taste and fashion.[113] The profile head, which had replaced the very local type showing the national sport of bull-leaping, was itself probably a response to current trends in numismatic art, and the facing head could well be explained in similar fashion.[114] But we simply cannot tell on present evidence when the facing-head types began at Larissa.[115]

If the date suggested above for the didrachms is valid, I would say that the early and middle series should be placed roughly in the first quarter of the fourth century, while series A-M extends over the period ca. 375–320 B.C. It is of course quite possible that the early and middle series did extend further down into the century. That the number of series is large in a relatively shorter period of time in the earlier part of the century is not a decisive objection against this chronology because these series seem to have been greatly outnumbered by the coins of A-M in terms of the amount of coinage produced. There are more than enough coins of this latter series to cover the period assigned to them. In any case, this new chronology must remain tentative as a result of the nature of the evidence on which it rests. I hope, however, that it will be helpful to have outlined the objections to Herrmann's chronology

112 See Erhart (above, n. 28), pp. 141–209, on the proliferation of this type in the last quarter of the fifth century.

113 For their wealth in the earlier part of the fourth century, see Isoc. 8.117. Simonides was only one of the poets who had worked for Thessalians (Pl. *Prt.* 339a), and the sophist Gorgias spent time in Thessaly, some of it in Larissa, it seems (Isoc. 15.155; Arist. *Pol.* 1275b26–31).

114 For the bull-leaping types, see Herrmann's groups 1–3. On the change to a profile head, see Herrmann, p. 37.

115 Kraay, *ACGC*, pp. 118–19, recalling the almost twenty-five year interval before the mint of Tarsos copied Kimon's Arethusa, points out that the change at Larissa need not have been made immediately after the appearance of the prototype.

and to have made a preliminary attempt at revising it. With further evidence, more secure progress may be possible in the future.[116]

KEY TO PLATE

1. Larissa, *BCH* 86 (1962), pl. 9, 6.
2. Larissa, ANS (*IGCH* 168).
3. Larissa, ANS (*IGCH* 168).
4. Larissa, ANS (*IGCH* 168).
5. Salamis, ANS (*IGCH* 168), Martin (above, n. 19), 495.
6. Miletos, ANS (*IGCH* 168), Thompson (above, n. 15), 107a.
7. Miletos, ANS (*IGCH* 168), Thompson (above, n. 15), 118b.
8. Syracuse, ANS.
9. Larissa, ANS.
10. Larissa, ANS.
11. Larissa, ANS.
12. Larissa, ANS.
13. Larissa, *ZfN* 35 (1924-25), pl. 5, 3.
14. Pherae, *ACGC*, pl. 21, 388.

[116] Thanks are due to Otto Mørkholm, Margaret Thompson, Hyla Troxell and Nancy Waggoner for helpful and valuable suggestions and for their care in reading drafts of this paper at various stages. They are not to be held responsible for any errors nor to be thought as necessarily in agreement with all the hypotheses presented here.

ANSMN 28 (1983)

ARSINOE'S NON-ERA

(Plates 2–10)

Hyla A. Troxell

The early posthumous portrait coins of Arsinoe II Philadelphus of Egypt, those struck by her brother-husband Ptolemy II and by his son Ptolemy III, are known in two denominations of silver and one of gold. All show on obverse Arsinoe's head. The gold octadrachms' and silver decadrachms' reverses show a double cornucopiae, the special emblem of Arsinoe Philadelphus; the silver tetradrachms' reverses bear the standard Ptolemaic eagle. All are inscribed ΑΡΣΙΝΟΗΣ ΦΙΛΑ-ΔΕΛΦΟΥ. Similar, but very rare, gold octadrachms are known from Phoenician, Palestinian, Cypriot, and other mints, but the chief gold mint and the only mint of the silver coins was presumably Alexandria.[1]

[1] For his very considerable help in and contributions to the preparation of this article, I thank the late Otto Mørkholm, a scholar whose knowledge was exceeded only by his generosity in sharing it. For their kindness in providing valuable information and material, I thank also Alain Davesne, Silvia Hurter, Georges Le Rider, Mando Oeconomides, and Martin Price.

Abbreviations used are

Benha — A. B. Brett, "The Benha Hoard of Ptolemaic Gold Coins," *ANSMN* 5 (1952), pp. 1-8. The hoard is *IGCH* 1694.

Kyrieleis — H. Kyrieleis, *Bildnisse der Ptolemäer*, Archäologischer Forschungen, Band 2 (Berlin, 1975).

Sv. — J. N. Svoronos, *Τὰ Νομίσματα τοῦ Κράτους τῶν Πτολεμαίων*, vols. 1–4 (Athens, 1904–8). Issue numbers with an added letter (e.g. 432a) and plates Α-Δ are in the supplementary section in vol. 4.

Thompson — D. B. Thompson, *Ptolemaic Oinochoai and Portraits in Faience* (Oxford, 1973).

These Alexandrian coins bear unusual issue marks on all 3 denominations: unusual in the first place because it is on the coins' obverses that they appear. No markings at all are found on the coins' reverses.[2] The markings are unusual in the second place because of their system of alphabetic numeration. By far the commonest Greek numbering system used the standard 24-letter alphabet increased to 27 by 3 extra letters, with Α-Θ standing for 1–9, Ι-ϟ for 10–90, Ρ for 100, and so on. Arsinoe's coins, however, are enumerated by another system. The decadrachms, the longest series, are known with all but 3 of the letters through 2 standard 24-letter alphabets, and the first 2 letters of a third.[3] With Α-Ω, ΑΑ-ΩΩ, Ⲁ (= ΑΑΑ), Ɓ (= ΒΒΒ), and 1 unmarked die whose style clearly places it first in the series, 51 decadrachm issues are known or presumed to have existed. The gold octadrachms are known from 3 dies without letters, again to be placed at the head of the series, and from all but 2 of the 14 letters Α through Ξ, where they stop. The tetradrachms are known from the 6 letters Α through Ζ.

From these pieces Svoronos in 1904 deduced an "Era of Arsinoe," with the coins' obverse letters denoting years of an era starting with Arsinoe's death on July 9, 270 B.C.[4] He equated the obverse dies with no letter with 271/0; Α with 270/69; Β with 269/8, and so on. In such an era, Ω would be 247/6 B.C., the last full year of Ptolemy II's reign (he died in January 246); ΑΑ would be 246/5, the first year of Ptolemy

[2] Except for the Χ between the eagle's legs on the tetradrachm reverses, which appears on all dies but the first.

[3] The alphabetic marking system of the Arsinoe coins is found also on some other coinages of Ptolemy II, although never exceeding one single alphabet, and always in the normal position on the coins' reverses: e.g. the bronzes included in Sv. 408–519, and Sv. 558–98. Alphabetic numbering systems were also used in the west on certain Italian and Roman coinages which have received a good deal of scholarly attention: see, most recently, H. B. Mattingly, "Coinage and the Roman State," *NC* 1977, pp. 201–2, and A. Burnett, "The Coinages of Rome and Magna Graecia in the Late Fourth and Third Centuries B.C.," *SNR* 1977, p. 119. The *way* the latters were used in the west, however, differed from the Arsinoe pattern (cf. Crawford pp. 138–39 and 584 for the Roman usage), and Burnett is surely correct in denying any connection between the Egyptian and western systems.

[4] Sv. 408–519.

III's reign; and ϡ would be 221/0, his last year. Ω (247/6 B.C., according to Svoronos) is notable not because it was the last letter of one alphabet, but because it is also the last letter of a series of similarly marked bronzes which Svoronos associated with Arsinoe's portrait coins[5]—and which Svoronos suggested were discontinued at Ptolemy II's death. The end of the decadrachm series in ϡ , which Svoronos equated with the last year of Ptolemy III's reign, seemed to provide another confirmation of the "Era of Arsinoe."

This supposed era has been more or less accepted, with more or less skepticism, for the past three-quarters of a century. Growing distrust has appeared in recent years,[6] although no serious rebuttal has yet appeared. This paper offers such a rebuttal.

The resources of the American Numismatic Society, its collection, library, and above all its invaluable photo file compiled from sale and auction catalogues, have allowed the study of 227 decadrachms, 41 tetradrachms, and 131 gold octadrachms of Arsinoe's early posthumous Alexandrian coinage. The only augmentation to the ANS material has been one tetradrachm in the author's possession, one cast furnished by Dr. Oeconomides, and the late Dr. Mørkholm's kind gift of his photographic record of the British Museum's holdings. How very far from a corpus this number of examples is can be seen from the extensive listings of specimens in Svoronos's great compilation. Yet the 399 coins include every previously known issue and a number of new ones, and provide quite enough material to disprove Svoronos's Era of Arsinoe. In conjunction with ANS records of the Phoenician and Palestinian octadrachms of Arsinoe, firmly dated by regnal years, these 399 coins also provide at least a partial alternative chronology, and a number of consequences for other early Ptolemaic coinages.

Mørkholm has suggested that the letters on Arsinoe's coins are merely die numbers.[7] This seems at first to be so, as in virtually every case there is but one known die for each obverse letter in each denomination.

[5] See n. 3, above.

[6] E.g. Mattingly (n. 3, above); Kyrieleis, p. 79: and O. Mørkholm, "The Hellenistic Period. Greece to India," p. 87, in *A Survey of Numismatic Research 1972–1977*, ed. by R. Carson, P. Berghaus, and N. Lowick (Bern, 1979).

[7] See n. 6, above.

Yet, even after allowing for the inevitable forgeries,[8] there remain three cases where the obverse dies do not correspond exactly with the letters.

One case is Σ in the decadrachm series. Coins which all look genuine are known from two Σ obverse dies (Plate 4, 2 and 3). On the stephane of the Σ[a] die (Plate 4, 2) is a flaw, found on two of the three coins located from this obverse; perhaps this break led to the die's premature abandonment and replacement by the Σ[b] die (Plate 4, 3). The second case is in the gold octadrachm series, where two I dies are known (Plate 7, 1 and 2). Here the genuineness of the I[a] die is proved by the reverse link between a Θ-obverse coin (Plate 6, 3) and one of the I[a] coins (Plate 7, 1). And the genuineness of the I[b] die is shown by the circumstance that produces our third case of non-correspondence between letters and obverse dies: die I[b] (Plate 7, 2) was recut to become die K (Plate 7, 3). The dotted border was filled in with a few extra dots, and two simple strokes (noticeably thinner than the upright I) transformed the I into a K. That the dies are the same is firmly established by the die breaks at the top of the head, just forward of the edge of the veil. Thus the obverse letters are not merely a means of identifying obverse dies; their significance, to which we shall return, went beyond the dies themselves.

Mattingly in 1977 noted that there was some sharing of dies between the octadrachms and tetradrachms, two denominations of approximately the same physical size.[9] Indeed, in every possible known case the obverse dies are shared; dies A, Δ, E and Ι of the gold (where B and Γ are not known) were used to strike the silver tetradrachms also, which stop at die Ι. If and when B and Γ octadrachms appear, they will undoubtedly be found to have been struck from the B and Γ tetradrachm dies.

More reverse die linkage between obverse dies is to be expected when a corpus of Arsinoe's coinage is eventually assembled, but the limited

[8] E.g. J. Schulman, 5 June 1930, 189 (ΘΘ decadrachm), and Naville 1, 4 Apr. 1921, 3234 (ΩΩ decadrachm). If the BB decadrachms Leu 20, 25 Apr. 1978, 178, and *de Hirsch* 1811 are genuine (and it is hard to imagine a coin that is not passing Bank Leu's scrutiny), they must be later strikings: the large flans, and the reverses' large lettering, cornucopiae tip style, and splayed-out fillet fringes all are quite unlike the coins here studied, but do bear resemblance to issues of, say, Ptolemy IV.

[9] See n. 3, above.

amount found among the 399 coins studied is probably sufficient to establish that the obverse dies were used in order from start to finish. No reverse links at all were found among the decadrachms: not surprising, as the 227 decadrachms located were from no fewer than 173 reverse dies. But the octadrachms (131 coins, 73 reverse dies) and the tetradrachms (41 coins, 12 reverse dies) furnish a number of reverse links in each series, in addition to the I[b]-K obverse recutting already described. Of the 11 reverse links and 1 obverse recutting, 10 are between contiguous letters, and the remaining 2 between letters only one apart.

In the following table summarizing die linkage, NL indicates dies with no obverse letters. The bracket to the left represents the I[b]-K recutting; brackets to the right indicate reverse links; and horizontal lines show obverse links between the two denominations. No coins are known for the letters in parentheses. All links are illustrated.

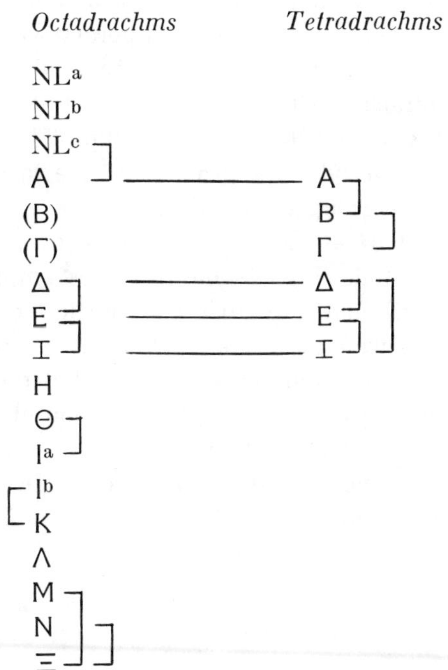

The stylistic progression of the coins also shows that the obverse dies were used in order, or at least roughly so. At first glance the style of Arsinoe's gold and silver coins seems unvarying, boringly so. But a number of details change and successive stages can be objectively distinguished. Kyrieleis seems virtually the only author to have noted the most obvious change: the direction of the tip of the small horn of Ammon under Arsinoe's ear.[10] But there are other developments: on the obverses the shape of the chignon, and whether or not the stephane is indicated under the veil; and on the reverses the decoration of the tip of the cornucopiae.

Various changes in these details allow the division of the longest series, the decadrachms, into four different groups of approximately equal size, with a few transitional issues between groups. The octadrachms divide themselves into three groups of rather unequal size, each group corresponding in its stylistic details to a particular decadrachm group. The tetradrachms, of course, can be securely placed together with the octadrachms whose obverse dies they share.

The surprising discovery is that, contrary to all previous assumptions, the letters on the gold coins turn out not to be contemporary with the corresponding letters on the decadrachms. There is no gold which corresponds to the earliest decadrachms. The earliest gold octadrachms share the stylistic features of the second decadrachm group. The next gold issues are very like the third decadrachm group; and the last few gold issues correspond to the last group of decadrachms.

A full catalogue of Arsinoe's portrait coins will have to await the assembling of a corpus, but the following résumé of issues amplifies Svoronos's listings. As before, NL indicates dies with no letter, and parentheses are used for letters for which no coins are known. Svoronos numbers are given when possible. The number of coins and of reverse dies found in the present survey is given as a rough indication of relative issue size. Representative issues of each decadrachm group are illustrated here; all octadrachm and tetradrachm obverse dies are shown; and all known die links are illustrated. For decadrachm issues

[10] Kyrieleis, p. 79. Although noting that this change takes place at widely different places in the gold and silver alphabets, he fails to follow up on this fatal flaw in Svoronos's "Era."

not illustrated, a reference to a published example is given: to Svoronos, or to other publications when necessary or preferable.

Obverses (all denominations): Head of Arsinoe II Philadelphus r., wearing ribbon diadem, stephane, and veil, and with a small horn of Ammon under the ear; above, tip of a lotus-headed scepter whose shaft is seen below her chin; to l., letter or letters.

Reverses (octadrachms and decadrachms): ΑΡΣΙΝΟΗΣ ΦΙΛΑΔΕΛΦΟΥ Double filleted cornucopiae, holding fruits and cakes.

Reverses (tetradrachms): ΑΡΣΙΝΟΗΣ ΦΙΛΑΔΕΛΦΟΥ Eagle standing l. on fulmen; between legs, X (on all but the first die illustrated).

All coins are of Ptolemaic weight.

GROUP 1: DECADRACHMS

Obv. Letter	*Coins*	*Rev. Dies*	*Sv.No.*	*Plate, Number*
NL	3	3	409	2, 1
Α	5	5	420	2, 2
Β	4	3	428	Sv. B, 11
Γ	2	2	432	Sv. 15, 19
Δ	5	2	434a	Sv. B, 12
Ε	11	7	444	2, 3
Ι	1	1	455	Sv. 16, 1
Η	1	1	–	Gans 16, 19 Apr. 1960, 468
Θ	1	1	461	Sv. 16, 2
(Ι)	–	–	–	–
(Κ)	–	–	–	–
Λ	7	5	477	2, 4
(Μ)[11]	–	–	–	–

[11] Sv. 487, described with M on obverse, is known from a single example whose M Svoronos considered doubtful. Dr. Oeconomides has kindly sent a cast of the coin, and it clearly bears MM. No other M coins have been located in the present survey. The placement of the presumed M issue in Group 1 rather than with the transitional issues is of course purely arbitrary.

TRANSITIONAL: DECADRACHMS

Obv. *Letter*	*Coins*	*Rev.* *Dies*	*Sv.No.*	*Plate, Number*
N	3	3	488	Sv. 16, 4
Ξ	5	3	490	Sv. 16, 5

GROUP 2: OCTADRACHMS, DECADRACHMS AND TETRADRACHMS

OCTADRACHMS

NL[a]	1	1	408	3, 1
NL[b]	1	1	408	3, 2
NL[c] ┐	6	3	408	3, 3
A ┘	1	1	419	3, 4 (rev. die of 3, 3)
(B)	–	–	–	–
(Γ)	–	–	–	–
Δ ┐	1	1	434	3, 5
E ┘ ┐	4	3	443	3, 6 (rev. die of 3, 5); 3, 7
I ┘	3	1	454	3, 8 (rev. die of 3, 7)

DECADRACHMS

O	1	1	492[12]	4, 1
Π	4	3	495	Sv. B, 13 (obv. only)
P	5	4	496	Sv. 16, 7
Σ[a]	3	2	502	4, 2
Σ[b]	3	3	502	4, 3
T	4	4	503[13]	Helbing, 9 Apr. 1913, 765
Y	8	6	508	Naville 12, 18 Oct. 1926, 2595
Φ	4	3	512	Sv. 16, 9
X	2	2	513	Myers-Adams 5, 15 Mar. 1973, 288
Ψ	4	3	517	4, 4

[12] Svoronos's illustration for this issue (pl. 16, 6) erroneously uses a second reproduction of the reverse of Sv. 512 (pl. 16, 9).

[13] Svoronos's illustration for this issue (pl. 16, 8) is a coin whose obverse bears TT (Sv. 954); the right edge of the first T is clearly visible on the plate.

TETRADRACHMS[14]

Obv. Letter	*Coins*	*Rev. Dies*	*Sv.No.*	*Plate, Number*
A	2	1	421	4, 5 (without X on reverse)
B	17	5	429	4, 6 (rev. die of 4, 5); 5, 1
Γ	1	1	432a	5, 2 (rev. die of 5, 1)
Δ	10	4	435	5, 3; 5, 4
E	6	3	445	5, 5 (rev. die of 5, 3); 5, 6
I	5	3	456	5, 7 (rev. die of 5, 4); 5, 8 (rev. die of 5, 6)

TRANSITIONAL: OCTADRACHMS AND DECADRACHMS

OCTADRACHMS

H	5	4	459	6, 1
Θ	42	24	460	6, 2; 6, 3 (rev. die of 7, 1)

DECADRACHMS

Ω	1	1	518	6, 4
AA	10	6	937	6, 5
BB	11	8	938	6, 6

14 As mentioned above, the tetradrachms are struck from the obverse dies used for the lettered octadrachms A-I. No tetradrachms without obverse letters have been located by the present author, but two such supposed issues must be denied. Sv. 410 describes a tetradrachm issue with no letter on obverse: the illustration for the issue, however, shows a coin whose obverse letter E is not preserved (pl. 16, 13 = *BMC* p. 43, 7; pl. 8, 3 = our Plate 5, 5). And Sv. 936 (illustrated in vol. 1, p. σλ'), attributed to Ptolemy III, describes a single tetradrachm with no obverse letter and with, uniquely, the double cornucopiae reverse type of the octadrachms and decadrachms. The obverse die is the octadrachm die NL[c], and the reverse also seems to be known in the octadrachm series (see Coin Galleries, 20 Apr. 1961, 9). In light of the obverse die sharing of the octadrachms and tetradrachms, such an initial tetradrachm issue would be understandable, but the coin is not genuine. Dr. Oeconomides, Hélène Nicolet-Pierre, and Olivier Picard have all seen it at Athens and agree that it is a cast piece, evidently a silver cast of a gold octadrachm. I am most grateful to them for enabling the record to be set straight.

GROUP 3: OCTODRACHMS AND DECADRACHMS

OCTADRACHMS

Obv. Letter	Coins	Rev. Dies	Sv.No.	Plate, Number
I[a] ↑	1	1	471	7, 1 (rev. die of 6, 3)
⌈ I[b]	6	3	471	7, 2
⌊ K	32	17	475	7, 3
Λ	11	9	476	7, 4

DECADRACHMS

Obv. Letter	Coins	Rev. Dies	Sv.No.	Plate, Number
ΓΓ	2	2	938a	7, 5
ΔΔ	3	2	939	Sv. 28, 5
EE	19	15	940	7, 6
ΖΖ	1	1	941	Naville 1, 4 Apr. 1921, 3230
HH	11	9	942	Glendining, 7 Mar. 1957, 370
ΘΘ	4	4	943	Hirsch 14, 17 Nov. 1905, 589
II	10	5	944	Leu 2, 25 Apr. 1972, 305
KK	7	4	945	Sv. 28, 10
ΛΛ	5	3	946	Naville 5, 18 June 1923, 2921
MM	15	11	947	7, 7
NN	4	3	948	Naville 7, 23 June 1924, 1841
ΞΞ	3	3	949	Hirsch 29, 9 Nov. 1910, 850
OO	4	2	950	Sv. 28, 15

TRANSITIONAL: DECADRACHMS

Obv. Letter	Coins	Rev. Dies	Sv.No.	Plate, Number
ΠΠ	2	2	951	Sv. Γ, 15
PP	2	2	952	*SNGBerry* 1484

GROUP 4: OCTADRACHMS AND DECADRACHMS

OCTADRACHMS

Obv. Letter	Coins	Rev. Dies	Sv.No.	Plate, Number
M ⌉	3	3	486	8, 1
N ⌉	1	1	–	8, 2
Ξ ⌋ ⌋	13	6	489	8, 3 (illustration slightly oversized; rev. die of 8, 1); 8, 4 (rev. die of 8, 2)

DECADRACHMS

Obv. Letter	*Coins*	*Rev. Dies*	*Sv.No.*	*Plate, Number*
ΣΣ	2	2	953	8, 5
TT	1	1	954	Sv. 16, 8 (called T)
YY	3	3	955	*SNGBerry* 1485
ΦΦ	2	2	956	G. Hirsch 34, 21 Feb. 1963, 1329
XX	1	1	957	Vinchon, 22 Feb. 1971, 182
ΨΨ	3	3	958	8, 6
ΩΩ	6	4	959	Sv. 28, 22
Ἁ	1	1	960	Sv. 28, 24 (obv. only)
Β̔	8	6	961	8, 7

In the absence of a corpus, the totals of examples and dies found for the various denominations in the different groups may serve as a preliminary guide to the volume of the coinage.[15]

	Octadrachms			*Decadrachms*			*Tetradrachms*		
	Coins	*Obv. Dies*	*Rev. Dies*	*Coins*	*Obv. Dies*	*Rev. Dies*	*Coins*	*Obv. Dies*	*Rev. Dies*
Group 1				40	10	30			
Transitional				8	2	6			
Group 2	17	7	8	38	10	31	41	6	12
Transitional	47	2	28	22	3	15			
Group 3	50	3	30	88	13	64			
Transitional				4	2	4			
Group 4	17	3	8	27	9	23			
Totals	131	15	74	227	49	173	41	6	12

As the transitional coins should probably be considered as the initial issues of the groups which follow them, perhaps a clearer presentation of the size of the various groups would be as follows.

[15] The I^{b}-K die is counted as 1 only. Totals reflect shared dies.

	Octadrachms			Decadrachms			Tetradrachms		
	Coins	Obv. Dies	Rev. Dies	Coins	Obv. Dies	Rev. Dies	Coins	Obv. Dies	Rev. Dies
Group 1				40	10	30			
Transitional and Group 2	17	7	8	46	12	37	41	6	12
Transitional and Group 3	97	5	57	110	16	79			
Transitional and Group 4	17	3	8	31	11	27			
Totals	131	15	73	227	49	173	41	6	12

The stylistic features which distinguish the four groups will be discussed in turn. On the obverse they are the depiction of the chignon, whether or not the stephane is indicated under the veil, and the shape of the small horn of Ammon under Arsinoe's ear. On the reverses (of the decadrachms and octadrachms only, of course) the crucial feature is the degree of elaboration of the tip of the double cornucopiae.

Arsinoe's chignon is a coiled braid of hair. In Group 1 (Plate 2, 1–4) it is shown in a rather tentative fashion, hardly projecting from the head at all on the earliest dies. Both the right and left sides of the coil are often indicated sketchily, so that with a little effort the coil can be perceived as an oval. In Group 2 (Plates 3–5) the coil is seen completely in profile, its back edge straight, and the folds of the veil continue to the back edge without interruption. In Group 3 (Plate 7), especially on the earliest dies, the clinging veil clearly reveals the coiled braid, which is seen, as if slightly from the rear, as a complete oval. Of the decadrachms transitional between Groups 2 and 3, one (AA, Plate 6, 5) shows a clearly oval chignon; the following issue (BB, Plate 6, 6) returns to the flat chignon of Group 2. In Group 4 (Plate 8) a double row of four rather large lumps forms the chignon.

The continuation of the stephane under the veil is shown only on Group 3 (Plate 7), and, weakly, on the two transitional decadrachms AA and BB (Plate 6, 5 and 6).

The horn of Ammon in Group 1 (Plate 2, 1–4) curves all around the ear, the tip reaching to the lowest of the five sections of hair at the brow; and the lowest of the loose wisps of hair at the hairline ends in front of the upright portion of the horn. In Group 2 (Plates 3–5) the horn still curves around the ear, but its tip is not so high: it does not reach the lowest hair section, and the lowest loose wisp of hair ends above it. This treatment of the horn continues through the transitional issues on Plate 6. On all dies in Groups 3 and 4 (Plates 7 and 8), however, the horn curves downward.

On Arsinoe's reverse dies occur small but unmistakable changes in the elaboration of the tip of the cornucopiae. Figure 1 shows the portion below the lower ribbed sections of the bodies.

FIG. 1

1. 2. 3. 4.

In Group 1 (Plate 2, 1–4) the tip is shown as in Fig. 1, 1, a simple sphere above the terminal point. In Group 2 (Plates 3–5) a projection at either side above the sphere has been added, as in Fig. 1, 2: presumably this is a profile representation of a disc. On the transitional coins between Groups 2 and 3 (Plate 6) a short-lived intermediate form appears, as in Fig. 1, 3, where the disc is replaced by a calyx-shaped ornament. This calyx appears on the Ω decadrachms and on all known H and a very few of the Θ gold octadrachms (Plate 6, 1, 2, and 4). On the other transitional coins (Plate 6, 3, 5, and 6) and on all of Groups 3 and 4 (Plates 7 and 8) the cornucopiae ends in an elaborate tip, as in Fig. 1, 4, with calyx, disc, sphere, disc, and terminal point.

The four details just described furnish the clearest and most definitive criteria for dividing Arsinoe's coins into the four groups, but three other stylistic changes are also worthy of note. The two small central fruits on the cornucopiae, the two which sit on the invariably present small tray or "bridge" between the two cornucopiae, are not identifiable, at least by the present author, but one of them often shows vertical ribbing, dividing the fruit into three or four segments, and the other usually seems partially covered by three leaves or perhaps sections of a shell which leave a triangular open space in the center of the fruit (or nut?).[16] Fig. 2 shows a rough sketch of the two fruits.

FIG. 2

The significance of these fruits is that their relative positions as shown are those of the decadrachms from Ι on, and on all of the gold. Only on the decadrachms Α-Γ, on some of those with Ε (no clear examples of Δ have been located), and on the decadrachms with no letter are the fruits' positions reversed (e.g., Plate 2, 1–3), which would seem to confirm that the no-letter decadrachm die was indeed the first in its series.

Another change, which occurs gradually, is the degree of agitation of the cornucopiae fillet to the right. The fillet to the left follows the curve of the cornucopiae throughout the coinage, but, starting with the transitional issues on Plate 6, the right fillet on most dies becomes ever more sharply curved. The shape of the curves varies between the gold and silver, but coins in both metals show an increasingly agitated right fillet which, if straightened out, would be ever longer than the left fillet.

Finally, there is the general appearance of the portraits.[17] That of Group 1, and especially the earliest, no-letter decadrachm (Plate 2, 1) is of a heavy-featured woman, with the extremely wide, staring eye and barrel chin of the dynasty (cf. Plate 2, A). The portrait of Group 2 (Plates 3–5) is the finest, of course idealized, showing a thinner, finer, more youthful and quite lovely face, with the staring eye more gently treated. The head on Group 3 (Plate 7) is similar to that on Group 2, more attenuated, with a somewhat haughty expression and again a bulging eye. Group 4 (Plate 8), where the heads actually measure slightly larger than

[16] Scale seems unimportant in the depiction of cornucopiae contents: see the enormous ear of grain in Berenice's cornucopiae (Plate 10, B-C).

[17] On the portraits, see also pp. 61-62.

most earlier ones, shows a passive, full-featured woman of no great individuality; the obvious intelligence and forcefulness of the earlier portraits is gone.

To recapitulate: the first group of Arsinoe's portrait coins was of decadrachms only; the second of octadrachms, decadrachms, and tetradrachms; and the third and fourth of octadrachms and decadrachms. The letters found on the obverse dies of each denomination occur in order. The tetradrachms, with Α-Ι, must be contemporary with the similarly lettered gold octadrachms, as their obverse dies are shared. But there is no correlation between the octadrachms' obverse letters and those of the decadrachms. Twelve or so decadrachm issues appeared before the gold started to be struck; and the last of the 51 decadrachm issues were contemporary with the last of the 15 gold issues. This alone indicates that the letters cannot denote years of an era; and the chronology worked out below provides still more proof.

An examination of stylistic changes in the Arsinoe portrait gold octadrachms from the Phoenician and Palestinian mints of Tyre, Sidon, Joppa, Ace-Ptolemais, and Gaza furnishes the basis for an absolute dating of the main Arsinoe series at Alexandria. These eastern octadrachms are similar in every respect to the Alexandrian ones, except that they bear mint markings, subsidiary monograms, and, instead of obverse letters, reverse *dates*: the endearing Phoenician custom of dating coins resulted in these octadrachms being firmly dated by regnal years of Ptolemy II and III. The coins are extremely rare: only 42 of them have been located by this author. Their dates range from year 25 of Ptolemy II (261/0 B.C.) to year 6 of Ptolemy III (242/1 B.C.).[18] That

[18] Svoronos's Julian dates for the regnal years are not quite accurate. I follow T. C. Skeat, *The Reigns of the Ptolemies*, Münchener Beiträge zur Papyrusforschung und antike Rechtsgeschichte 39 (1954), p. 11. Regnal years started on the Egyptian New Year's Day, which at this period fell in late October. Ptolemy II's year 25 thus ran from October 261 to October 260, and his year 35 from October 247 until his death in January 246. Ptolemy III's year 1 then started immediately, lasting, however, only until the next New Year's Day in October 246, when his year 2 commenced. Year 6 thus spanned the Julian years 242 and 241.

A few Arsinoe octadrachms have been erroneously dated to years prior to 261/0 B.C. Sv. 794 (Joppa) was hesitantly dated by Svoronos to 263 B.C. because of its ΚΓ date. The coin, however, belongs with the similarly marked silver issues recently shown by Otto Mørkholm to belong instead to the twenty-third year of Ptolemy

this range is the full one, despite the gold's scarcity, is shown by the similarly dated and far more common accompanying ΠΤΟΛΕΜΑΙΟΥ ΣΩΤΗΡΟΣ tetradrachms from the same five mints, which all fall in precisely the same period.

Quite a few new issues have appeared since Svoronos's work was published, and a tabulation of the 42 coins located by the present author follows. Mint by mint, the listings give the years B.C., the coins' markings from left to right, and the Svoronos number for the issue. The next column, with F or O, U or D, and 1 or 2, is the important one. It indicates whether Arsinoe's chignon is flat, F, or oval, O; whether the tip of the horn of Ammon points up, U, or down, D; and whether the bottom of the cornucopiae is decorated with a simple disc, 1, or the calyx ornament, 2. These style changes will be discussed below. The coins are then numbered and listed, and die links indicated where ascertainable. Some dies are so close and Svoronos's plates often so poor that certainty was not always possible; but the links are not necessary to the arguments which follow.

All coins except 37 and 42 bear the date between the cornucopiae and the left fillet; all except 42 have the mint marking and any subsidiary markings between the cornucopiae and the right fillet.

TYRE

259/8	[monogram] [monogram]	—	FU1	1.[19] Numismatic Fine Arts 4, 24 Mar. 1977, 446 = Gans 16, 19 Apr. 1960, 464 = Hirsch 32, 14

III: see below, pp.66-67. An octadrachm with markings of club and Σ (Benha 15) was attributed by Brett to Tyre in 268 B.C., but the coin is of Salamis, and is later: see below, p. 63.

[19] On coin 1 are visible two markings, [monogram] at the very edge of the flan to lower left, and [monogram] to right. The right-hand marking is the mint marking, as discussed above, and in n. 21; thus the coin is of Tyre. The left-hand monogram is cut off by the edge of the flan, and should be completed as [monogram], or KI, year 259/8 B.C. Dates from KA through KH were almost invariably expressed in monogram form at all the Phoenician and Palestinian mints on the Arsinoe octadrachms and on the Ptolemy Basileos silver tetradrachms which preceded them, as well as the Ptolemy Soter tetradrachms which accompanied them.

					Nov. 1912, 594 = Hirsch 18, 27 May 1907, 2512
253/2	ΛΓ ⳨ Ⓝ	—	FU2	2.	Leu 25, 23 Apr. 1980, 194 (Plate 9, C). The calyx is small, but unmistakably present.
252/1	ΛΔ ⳨ Θ	680	FU2	3.	Sv. pl. 19, 26
			FU2	4.	Sotheby, 20 July 1914, 42 = Sotheby, 26 Apr. 1907, 32. Dies of 3
251/0	ΛΕ ⳨ Θ	685	FU2	5.	Sv. pl. 20, 3
			FU2	6.	ANS (Plate 9, D). Dies of 5
249/8	ΛΙ ⳨ Θ	—	FU2	7.	Benha 16. Obv. die of 5
			FU2	8.	ANS. Obv. die of 5; rev. die of 7
			OD1	9.	Stack's, 20 Jan. 1938, 131
248/7	ΛΗ ⳨ Θ	696	FU2	10.	Sv. pl. 20, 7
			FD2	11.	Auctiones 12, 29 Sept. 1981, 178
247/6	ΛΘ ⳨ Θ	699	FD2	12.	Sv. pl. Γ, 1. Obv. die of 10
			FD2	13.	Benha 17. Dies of 12
246	Α ⳨ Θ	1011	FD2	14.	Sv. pl. 31, 1
246/5	Β ⳨ Θ	1012	FD2	15.	Sv. pl. 31, 2. Dies of 14, the date recut
			FD2	16.	ANS (Plate 9, F). Obv. die of 14
244/3	Δ ⳨ Θ	1018	FD2	17.	Sv. pl. 31, 6 (London = *BMC*, p. 42, 4) (Plate 9, G)
			FD2	18.	Benha 21. Dies of 17

SIDON

256/5	Λ ΣΙ ΜΗ	—	FU1	19.	Münz. u. Med. 19, 5 June 1959, 582
			FU1	20.	Leu 18, 5 May 1977, 275 = Münz. u. Med. 25, 17 Nov. 1962, 493 (Plate 9, B). Rev. die of 19

253/2	ΛΓ	ΣΙ	ΔΙ	—	FU1	21. London. Obv. die of 20
250/49	ΛC	ΣΙ	[monogram]	747	FU2	22. Sv. pl. 21, 22. Perhaps obv. die of 20
249/8	ΛI	ΣΙ	ΔΙ	750	FU2	23. Sv. pl. 22, 3. Perhaps obv. die of 20
	ΛI	ΣΙ	[monogram]	752	FU2	24. Sv. pl. 22, 1. Perhaps obv. die of 20
248/7	ΛΗ	ΣΙ	[monogram]	754	FU2	25. Sv. pl. 22, 5 = Leu 13, 29 Apr. 1975, 340. Obv. die of 20
					FU2	26. Canessa 3, 28 June 1923, 94. Obv. die of 20; rev. die of 25
					FU2	27. Numismatic Fine Arts 6, 27 Feb. 1979, 430. Obv. die of 20; rev. die of 25
244/3	Δ	ΣΙ	[monogram]	1028	FU2	28. Sv. pl. 32, 4
243/2	Ε	ΣΙ	[monogram]	1030	FU2	29. Sv. pl. 32, 6
242/1	C	ΣΙ	[monogram]	1032	FU2	30. Sv. pl. 32, 9
					FU2	31. Glasgow = *Hunter*, vol. 3, p. 377, 22

ACE-PTOLEMAIS

251/0	ΛΕ	Ⲡ	Θ	779	OU2	32. Sv. pl. 25, 14
					OU2	33. Vinchon, 2 Dec. 1975, 180 (Plate 9, E). Dies of 32
					OU2	34. Hess-Leu, 4 Apr. 1963, 103 = Münz. u. Med. 11, 23 Jan. 1953, 87. Rev. die of 32
246/5	Β	Ⲡ	Α	1034	FU2	35. Sv. pl. 32, 12
242/1	C	Ⲡ	Θ	—	FU2	36. Leu 22, 8 May 1979, 176 = Münz. u. Med. 52, 19 June 1975, 239 = Münz. u. Med. 25, 17 Nov. 1962, 510 (Plate 9, H)

Joppa

261/0	ΠΙ Κ	—	FU1	37.[20]	Münz. u. Med. 52, 19 June 1975, 237 (Plate 9, A)
246	Α ΙΠΙ	—	FD2	38.	ANS = Benha 20
245/4	Γ ΙΠ Θ	1040	FD2	39.	Sv. pl. 32, 21
244/3	Δ ΙΠ Θ	—	FU2	40.	ANS
242/1	Ϲ ΙΠ Θ	—	FU2	41.	Münz. u. Med. 25, 17 Nov. 1962, 539

Gaza

257/6	Ⱥ ΚΘ	823	FU1	42.[21]	Sv. pl. 24, 4

These dated Phoenician and Palestinian octadrachms do not repeat every stylistic variation of the main Alexandrian series. The only changes which can be detected are the most obvious ones: whether the chignon is flat or oval, whether the horn of Ammon turns up or down, and whether or not the calyx is present on the cornucopiae tip (where it is not, the cornucopiae is ornamented with a simple disc, as on Series 2; as at Alexandria, no gold corresponds to the decadrachms of Group 1). I have been very conservative in indicating the substitution of an oval for a flat chignon, and the change from an up-turned to a down-turned horn: only definitely oval chignons, and only strongly down-turned horns have been so described. Further, the cornucopiae tip with calyx is not the same as that of Groups 3 and 4 at Alexandria: in Phoenicia and Palestine, as in Cyprus, the calyx is very rarely accompanied by the two discs above and below the sphere which are found with it in Egypt. The addition of the calyx ornament is, however,

[20] Coin 37 is the earliest known Phoenician or Palestinian octadrachm issue, and dates from the first year of the accompanying Ptolemy Soter tetradrachms. The form of its civic monogram is that of the Ptolemy Soter tetradrachm issue Sv. 795 of the same year (given erroneously in the text: see pl. 23, 2); and the placement of the octadrachm's date to upper right is the same as that of the tetradrachms—understandable on this initial gold issue.

[21] Coin 42, Gaza's sole known octadrachm, is the only octadrachm known to me of the period in question from Phoenicia, Palestine, or any of the Cypriot mints to bear the civic marking to the left of the cornucopiae: the wider space between the cornucopiae and the right-hand fillet was otherwise the invariable spot chosen for the coins' most important marking, the mint indication.

a decisive and easily spotted change: its appearance in Phoenicia and Palestine provides a terminus ante quem for its introduction at Alexandria, and thus for the introduction of Group 3.

The following table shows in convenient form when these three style changes occurred on the known Phoenician and Palestinian octadrachms. The abbreviations are those used in the listing of issues above.

As can be seen, the down-turned horn of Ammon is found only at Tyre, from 249/8 to 244/3, and at Joppa, from 246 to 245/4. The oval chignon appears only twice, at Ptolemais in 251/0 and at Tyre in 249/8. In contrast, the calyx ornament, once introduced in 253/2 B.C., is found on every known subsequent die but one (at Tyre, 249/8).[22] Group 3

		Tyre	*Sidon*	*Ace-Ptolemais*	*Joppa*	*Gaza*
261/0	ΚΕ				FU1 (Pl. 9, A)	
260/59	ΚϹ					
259/8	ΚΙ	FU1				
258/7	ΚΗ					
257/6	ΚΘ					FU1
256/5	Λ		FU1			
255/4	ΛΑ					
254/3	ΛΒ					
253/2	ΛΓ	FU2 (Pl. 9, C)	FU1 (Pl. 9, B)			
252/1	ΛΔ	FU2				
251/0	ΛΕ	FU2 (Pl. 9, D)		OU2 (Pl. 9, E)		
250/49	ΛϹ		FU2			
249/8	ΛΙ	FU2, OD1	FU2			
248/7	ΛΗ	FU2, FD2	FU2			
247/6	ΛΘ	FD2				
246	Α	FD2			FD2	
246/5	Β	FD2 (Pl. 9, F)		FU2		
245/4	Γ				FD2	
244/3	Δ	FD2 (Pl. 9, G)	FU2		FU2	
243/2	Ε		FU2			
242/1	Ϲ		FU2	FU2 (Pl. 9, H)	FU2	

[22] As it was on the Phoenician and Palestinian issues, so it was on all late posthumous octadrachms struck anywhere under Ptolemy III and his successors. The oval chignon was a short-lived phenomenon. The horn of Ammon is found on later issues turned either up or down. The calyx ornament, however, became an invariable feature of the cornucopiae not only on all late posthumous Arsinoe octadrachms, but also on the gold of later Ptolemaic rulers.

at Alexandria, where the calyx first appears, thus must have been being struck at least by 253/2 B.C. Although earlier data is scanty (four coins in all), the calyx's absence prior to 253/2, as well as on the Sidonian coin of 253/2, probably allows us to place the start of Group 3 in that year. Thus the change from Group 2 to Group 3, the approximate midpoint of the decadrachm dies, is to be dated ca. 253/2 B.C.

It is hard to believe that the Phoenician gold would have been introduced before that at Alexandria, and therefore the start of the Alexandrian gold, and of all of Group 2, may be put no later than 261/0 B.C. A likely occasion for the introduction of Arsinoe's gold coins would have been the recent receipt of the diverted revenues of the *ἀπόμοιρα*, the enormous one-sixth share of the produce of vineyards and orchards: in Ptolemy II's twenty-third regnal year, 263/2 B.C., these revenues were diverted from the cults of the native Egyptian gods to that of the goddess Arsinoe Philadelphus.[23] The amount of gold struck at Alexandria with Arsinoe's portrait was not extraordinary—only 17 obverse dies are known or presumed to have existed—and other gold was struck before and after hers, but the propaganda value for the recently created goddess would have been considerable, and may have helped to "sell" the diversion of the revenues.

Neither the transition from Group 3 to Group 4 nor the end of Group 4 can be dated with objectivity or precision. The present author does see, however, in the rather fat and bovine faces of Ptolemy III's eastern issues (Plate 9, F-H), and especially in those of the last three years, 244–241 B.C. (Plate 9, G-H) a strong similarity to those of the heavy, placid portraits of Group 4 (Plate 8). It seems likely that both reflect the plump features of the new queen, Berenice II (Plate 10, B-C, and G). We may perhaps then assume that Group 4 started early in Ptolemy III's reign, and ended at the time of the abrupt end of all the Phoenician and Palestinian issues of both Arsinoe octadrachms and Ptolemy Soter tetradrachms, in 241 B.C. No real proof, however, can be offered that this was the terminal date at Alexandria.

The start of the whole series, the decadrachms of Group 1, cannot be dated precisely, either. As the coins depict the queen with the

[23] B. P. Grenfell, *The Revenue Laws of Ptolemy Philadelphus* (Oxford, 1896), cols. 36–37.

attributes of a goddess, however, they can only have started after her death in July 270 B.C.

The new chronology suggested here may be summarized as follows.

270 B.C. or later–ca. 261/0 B.C.	Group 1:	AR	Decadrachms to M
ca. 261/0–253/2 B.C.	Transitional:	AR	Decadrachms N–Ξ
	Group 2:	AV	Octadrachms to Ι
		AR	Decadrachms O–Ψ
		AR	Tetradrachms A–Ι
ca. 253/2–246? B.C.	Transitional:	AV	Octadrachms H–Θ
		AR	Decadrachms Ω–BB
	Group 3:	AV	Octadrachms Ia–Λ
		AR	Decadrachms ΓΓ–OO
246?–242/1? B.C.	Transitional:	AR	Decadrachms ΠΠ–PP
	Group 4:	AV	Octadrachms M–Ξ
		AR	Decadrachms ΣΣ–ʹB

Hoard evidence is of little use, but does furnish some slight confirmation of this chronology. Two hoards are helpful. One is the Megalopolis 1947 Hoard (*IGCH* 180), which contained tetradrachms of Alexander III (lifetime and posthumous), Philip III, Lysimachus, and Ptolemy II (14 coins); and two decadrachms of Arsinoe, with obverse letters EE and ΣΣ. The hoard's burial date of ca. 225 B.C. is determined by the latest Alexander coins it contained; with this Svoronos's dates for the decadrachms of 242/1 and 229/8 B.C., during the reign of Ptolemy III, accord well. But while in general the presence in the Peloponnese of Ptolemaic silver from the reign of Ptolemy II is well attested (7 hoards; 101 coins), the presence there of silver struck under Ptolemy III is quite exceptional (1 hoard; 4 coins, not including the decadrachms in question).[24] On the dating here proposed for Arsinoe's coins, the EE and ΣΣ decadrachms would have been struck in the latter years

[24] See T. Hackens, "A propos de la circulation monétaire dans le Péloponnese au IIIe av. J.C.," *Antidorum W. Peremans sexagenario ab alumnis oblatum*, Studia Hellenistica 16 (Louvain, 1968), pp. 74–82.

of Ptolemy II's reign (the ΣΣ coin possibly in the first year or so of Ptolemy III's rule). This earlier dating brings them more into line not only with the 14 tetradrachms of Ptolemy II in the Megalopolis Hoard, but also with the strong pattern of Ptolemaic coins known from other Peloponnesian finds.

The other useful mixed hoard is the Gülnar 1980 Hoard.[25] This enormous deposit from Cilicia, over 5,200 pieces of silver in all, contained ca. 2,600 Alexanders, ca. 35 coins of later Macedonian rulers to Antigonus Gonatas, 144 Lysimachi, 62 Attalids, 246 Seleucids, and some 2,168 Ptolemaic coins—among which were 2 tetradrachms and 13 decadrachms of Arsinoe. The two latest decadrachms were of the OO and ΨΨ issues, dated 232/1 and 224/3 by Svoronos's "Era," but ca. 246–241 in the present paper. The preliminary hoard report suggests a burial date of ca. 225–220 B.C.—but so late a date is based in part on very rough estimates of the various non-Ptolemaic series' terminal dates, and in part on Svoronos's date for the ΨΨ decadrachm. At the moment of the writing of the present article, however (June 1983), further examination of the separate series is leading the hoard's publishers to favor an earlier date, ca. 240 B.C.[26] The final publication of this important deposit is eagerly awaited: but from current information it appears to provide solid confirmation that the Arsinoe decadrachms ceased earlier than Svoronos believed, and thus that his Era cannot be.

The chronology proposed in the present paper also shows that the letters cannot denote years. To take the decadrachms, the longest series, and the basic one: if they started promptly in 270 B.C., the year of Arsinoe's death, and if the change from Group 2 to Group 3 (probably the best documented date in the new chronology) occurred ca. 253/2, then the maximum number of years between these two points is 19 (270–252, inclusive). Yet the number of decadrachm issues to the end of Group 2 is 23 (A-Ψ) or, if we count the issue with no letter, 24. Clearly the letters cannot denote years, even aside from the circumstance that

[25] E. Laroche and A. Davesne, "Les Fouilles de Meydandjik près de Gülnar (Turquie) et le trésor monétaire hellénistique," *CRAI* 1981, pp. 356–70 provides a preliminary report.

[26] Correspondence from A. Davesne and G. Le Rider, to both of whom I am extremely grateful for their generous sharing of both information on the hoard and their present thoughts about its burial date.

quite different letters were used concurrently on the decadrachms and octadrachms. The letters can only be issue numbers of some sort, assigned separately to the different metals.

These issues seem to have varied greatly in size, especially the gold ones, where Θ and K alone account for well over half of the known coins and reverse dies: the single Θ die is, even in this preliminary survey, found coupled with no fewer than 24 reverse dies, only one of which is shared with another obverse die. But the definition of the issues remains obscure: they conceivably represented sporadic half-years, months, or some other chronological unit; or perhaps they simply marked certain amounts of bullion ordered to be struck from time to time. We cannot tell, but in any case the obverse letters on Arsinoe's coins are not year dates, but simply issue numbers.

Arsinoe was obviously a highly capable and energetic woman who took an active role in affairs. She is credited by modern scholars with having contributed greatly to the eventual success of the First Syrian War, 276–273 B.C. The Chremonidean Decree of 266 B.C. makes the remarkable statement that Ptolemy II in regard to the affairs of Greece "followed the policy of his ancestors and that of his sister."[27] Many queens of Macedonian blood were noted for their active participation in affairs, but this is the first official recognition given to any of them as a formulator of state policy. The immense popularity of the dead queen's cult is too well known to need description here: Egyptians, Greeks, and Macedonians paid her honor in both private and public ways. It is a pity that we know no details of her activities.

The portrait of Ptolemy I was continued on the Ptolemaic coinage until the dynasty's end, emphasizing the unbroken continuity and divinity of the ruling house. Helmut Kyrieleis has recently made an eminently sensible and long-needed statement urging that Arsinoe's coin portraits, the only other ones to last through many successive reigns, should be considered in the same way. It was not personal considerations—as so often suggested today—which led Ptolemy II to place her portrait on the coins; not a mere desire to honor the dead queen as an

[27] *IG* II[2], 687: *ὁ τε βασιλεὺς Πτολεμαῖος ἀκολούθως τεῖ τῶν προγόνων καὶ τεῖ τῆς ἀδελφῆς προ[α]ιρέσει φανερός ἐστιν σπουδάζων . . . .*

individual, or to promote her cult. It was, rather, his taking advantage of the actively earned popularity of his full sister and co-ruler to strengthen his own position as a member of the ongoing and divine Ptolemaic dynasty.[28] That the Arsinoe portrait coins were not marked by an "Era of Arsinoe" but simply with issue marks strongly supports this view of the Arsinoe coinage.

COMMENTS ON SOME RELATED PTOLEMAIC COINAGES

The new chronology and interpretation of the early posthumous portrait coinage of Arsinoe Philadelphus forces a reconsideration of a number of related Ptolemaic series. Some of these are provincial or late posthumous Arsinoe portrait issues; others are associated issues. Comments on some of these related Ptolemaic coinages follow, in approximately chronological order.

1. Ptolemy II: Ptolemy Soter Tetradrachms with X on Reverse[29]

The tetradrachms have X between the eagle's legs just as on Arsinoe's tetradrachms, and no letter, B, Γ or Δ to the left of the obverse head as on Arsinoe's coins. As the letters on Arsinoe's different denominations are independent of each other and occur at different times, these Soter tetradrachms cannot be dated by their obverse letters. The X on reverse, however, would seem to associate them with the Arsinoe Group 2 tetradrachms, similarly marked, and thus these Soter tetradrachms would appear to have been struck ca. 261/0–253/2 B.C.

2. Ptolemy II: Bronzes with No Letter, or A to Ω on Reverse[30]

Eight denominations of bronze coins of standard Ptolemaic types, with letters between the eagle's legs on reverse, were dated by Svoronos according to the "Era of Arsinoe." Even approximate dating by the

[28] Kyrieleis, p. 155.
[29] Sv. 411, 430, 433, 436.
[30] Scattered throughout Sv. 408-519.

reverse letters is impossible for the reason given above—that letters on Arsinoe's different denominations occur at different times. The occurrence of the letters on the bronzes' reverses would seem in any case to show no necessary connection with the obverse lettering of Arsinoe's portrait coins. These bronzes may well be later than Svoronos thought.

3. Ptolemies II-V(?): Gold Theon Adelphon Octadrachms, Tetradrachms, and Smaller Coins[31]

The coins bear on reverse jugate portraits of Ptolemy II and Arsinoe II, with inscription ΑΔΕΛΦΩΝ; and on obverse jugate portraits of their parents Ptolemy I and Berenice I, with inscription ΘΕΩΝ (see Plate 2, A). They were struck by several successive Ptolemies, but papyri show that it was Ptolemy II who initiated the series, probably somewhere in the decade of the 260s.

The papyri are two from the archives of Zenon, estate manager to Apollonios, Ptolemy II's chief finance minister.[32] One is a letter from Demetrios, seemingly the director of the mint at Alexandria, dated in October 258 B.C. Demetrios speaks of restriking the old *τρίχρυσα* (gold pentadrachms) into the "new" money. This new money was the gold now struck as octadrachms, and could, of course, have been either the Theon Adelphon octadrachms or the earliest Arsinoe octadrachms. The second Zenon papyrus is an account of a bank deposit listing specific numbers of coins: *τρίχρυσα* (gold pentadrachms), *μναιεῖα* (pieces of 100 drachms: gold octadrachms), and *πεντηκοντάδραχμα* (pieces of 50 drachms: gold tetradrachms). This papyrus bears no date, but has been dated on internal evidence to 258/7 or 257/6; its importance lies in the mention of the *πεντηκοντάδραχμα*, which can only be the tetradrachms of the Theon Adelphon series, the earliest Ptolemaic gold

[31] Sv. 603–6, 613–14, 616a, 618, 621, 934, 1229, 1247–48 (most illustrations confuse obverse and reverse). The exceedingly rare issue 934 varies the placement of portraits and inscriptions.

[32] P. Cairo Zenon 59021 and 59022: C. C. Edgar, ed., *Catalogue général des antiquités égyptiennes du Musée du Caire: Zenon Papyri*, vol. 1 (Cairo, 1925). See also W. Schubart, "Die ptolemäische Reichsmünze in den auswartigen Besitzungen unter Philadelphos," *ZfN* 1922, pp. 68–92.

of this denomination. Thus the Theon Adelphon coins were in use at least by the early 250s, and their introduction would not have been far from the date of Arsinoe's death—but whether before or after it is impossible to guess.

The present down-dating of the start of Arsinoe's portrait gold to ca. 261/0 B.C. now leaves ample room for the Theon Adelphon coins earlier, either preceding or accompanying the earliest Arsinoe decadrachms, those of Group 1. The resemblance between Arsinoe's portraits on these earliest decadrachms and those on the Theon Adelphon coins is striking (compare the reverse of Plate 2, A, with Plate 2, 1). These early decadrachms are rarely pictured or discussed; it is the handsomer portraits of Groups 2 and 3, in both silver and gold, that one usually finds taken as Arsinoe's likeness.[33] The heavy-featured, wide-eyed, barrel-chinned woman of Group 1, however, is as close as she can possibly be to the portrait on the Theon Adelphon gold.

Kyrieleis regards the Theon Adelphon coins as worthless for identifying Arsinoe's sculpture portraits, stating that the Arsinoe head on the coins' reverses differs in no way from the portrait of Berenice on their obverses.[34] It actually does vary in one significant way: Arsinoe virtually always has short wisps of hair escaping along the browline from the pulled-back hair sections—precisely as on the Arsinoe portrait coins—whereas Berenice virtually always does not.

Thompson draws a clear distinction between portraits of Arsinoe the woman and Arsinoe the goddess. She sees the woman, not the goddess, on the Theon Adelphon coins, and on the well known portrait oinochoai. "The receding forehead is rounded; the eyes, wide open; the nose long and slightly retroussé . . . . The small mouth is sinuous and pursed, set off from the little round chin by a marked groove. The neck is ringed by a prominent 'collar of Venus'."[35] This is a description of

[33] E.g. Kyrieleis, pl. 70, 1 (BB decadrachm) and 70, 2 (Λ octadrachm); Thompson, pl. 73, a (Δ tetradrachm) and 73, b (Σ decadrachm); G. H. Macurdy, *Hellenistic Queens* (Baltimore, 1932), pl. 12, 3 (Θ octadrachm); Newell, *Royal Greek Portrait Coins* (New York, 1937), pl. 15, 1 (Θ octadrachm) and 2 (AA decadrachm).

[34] Kyrieleis, p. 80. Kyrieleis illustrates only two exceptional coins of the Theon Adelphon series: one of Sv. 934 (see above, n. 31), pl. 8, 1–2; and one of a coin struck under, probably, Ptolemy V, pl. 8, 3.

[35] Thompson, p. 82.

Arsinoe's portraits on the faience oinochoai which Thompson proceeds quite rightly to say resemble those of the Theon Adelphon issue. But the description fits also the portraits on the earliest decadrachms, which one then expects show a relatively true likeness of the woman Arsinoe.

Thompson goes on to suggest that the portrait on the Arsinoe portrait coins (as opposed to the Theon Adelphon coins) shows Arsinoe the goddess, idealized, finer, and more beautiful. She makes an important distinction here, but the comment applies only to the portraits of Groups 2 and 3, as her illustrations of the portrait coins reveal.[36] On these groups we may well see Arsinoe the goddess, as opposed to Arsinoe the woman.

4. Ptolemies II and III: Arsinoe Octadrachms from Citium, Paphos and Salamis

Svoronos assigned the Cypriot gold to the years immediately following Arsinoe's death,[37] but this dating is no longer tenable. A number of Cypriot issues have appeared since Svoronos's time, and a compilation of these rare coins known to the present author follows. All can be roughly dated by the criteria used above: whether the chignon is flat or oval, whether the horn of Ammon turns up or down, and whether or not the calyx ornament is present.[38] Although only 13 coins have been found for the 3 mints, these criteria place some at each mint in the time of Alexandrian Group 2, ca. 261/0–253/2 B.C., and others at Citium and Salamis in the time of Group 3 or 4, ca. 253/2–241? B.C. The Cypriot gold thus would seem to cover a good deal if not all of the same time span as did the Phoenician and Palestinian issues.

The format of the following listings is similar to that used above for the Phoenician and Palestinian strikings. All markings are between the cornucopiae and the right fillet, except for the star of coin 13, which is placed between the cornucopiae and the left fillet.

[36] Thompson, p. 83. See n. 33, above.

[37] Vol. 1, pp. ϱξβ′-ϱξγ′ and Table Γ.

[38] See above, pp. 46-47. As elsewhere, no Cypriot gold is known without either disc or calyx on the cornucopiae tip—that is, no gold which can be dated as early as the Group 1 decadrachms of Alexandria.

CITIUM

Corresponding to Group 2

KI	522	FU1	1. Sv. pl. 15, 4
		FU1	2. Münzhandlung Basel 4, 1 Oct. 1935, 982. Dies of 1

Corresponding to Group 3 or 4

Fulmen over K	523	FU2	3. Sv. pl. 15, 5
		FU2	4. *MFA Suppl.* 321 = Münz. u. Med. 11, 23 Jan. 1953, 86 = *Jameson* 1810. Dies of 3
		FU2	5. Benha 12. Dies of 3
Ꝁ I over fulmen	—	FU2	6. ANS = Benha 13

PAPHOS

Corresponding to Group 2

Π	520	FU1	7. Sv. pl. 15, 1[39]
		FU1	8. Numismatic Fine Arts 10, 17 Sept. 1981, 254 = Naville 1, 4 Apr. 1921, 3227. Dies of 7

SALAMIS

Corresponding to Group 2

Club over Σ	—	FU1	9. Benha 15[40]
Caduceus over **Σ**	—	FU1	10. Leu 25, 23 Apr. 1980, 199[41]
ΣΑ	—	FU1	11. Leu 18, 5 May 1977, 274

39 Sv. pl. 15, 2 (another illustration of Sv. 520) is a coin with calyx ornament, but of such poor style that it must be later than our Groups 3 and 4.

40 Brett in publishing the Benha Hoard took the club as the mintmark of Tyre, and the Σ as an alphabetic date, assigning the coin to Tyre in 268 B.C. Such an early date is impossible; and the placement of the date to the right of the cornucopiae, where the Σ is, would be most exceptional (see above, p. 50). The coin's similarity of format to no. 12 makes it virtually certain that it is the letter and not the symbol that is no. 11's mint marking: the coin is of Salamis.

41 The monogram was read as Σ in the sale catalogue, but it is clearly **Σ**. The coin was assigned to the reign of Ptolemy V, but the cornucopiae terminating with the simple disc as ornament places it earlier.

Corresponding to Group 3 or 4

ΣA	521	FD2	12. Sv. pl. 15, 3
Star, ΣA	—	O ?U2	13. Benha 11

5. Ptolemy III: Arsinoe Double Octadrachm

This remarkable issue first appeared in 1978[42] (Plate 10, A). The obverse, with letter A, is handsome and very close indeed to those of our Group 2, where the A octadrachms occur. One subtle but significant feature differs, however. The pronounced fold in the veil at the top of the head, midway between the chignon and the front edge of the veil, is concave *toward the rear*: a seemingly minor feature, but one which is never found on the regular coinage of Arsinoe discussed in this article, although it is standard in Berenice II's portraits (Plate 10, B-C).

The reverse of the double octadrachm, however, provides the surest indications that the coin may not belong with Arsinoe's other obverse-lettered coinage. The treatment of the cornucopiae's tip is unclear (a disc with drooping edges?), but the presence of symbols in the field is unknown in Arsinoe's regular coinage. And the symbols, laurel-wreathed piloi and stars, are precisely those which occur on many of Berenice's coins (Plate 10, B-C). Above all, the fillet on the octadrachm, its two straight ends hanging together to the right of the cornucopiae, is not Arsinoe's but Berenice's (Plate 10, B-C).

The largest known Ptolemaic silver coin, a dodecadrachm of Phoenician weight, bears Berenice's name and portrait; so do the hitherto largest known Ptolemaic gold issues, decadrachms of Attic weight.[43] It would seem that this spectacular double octadrachm was later than the early posthumous portrait coinage of Arsinoe discussed in this article, and that it was struck under Ptolemy III.

6. Ptolemy III: "Berenice-type" Arsinoe Octadrachms[44]

This unusual issue of octadrachms (Plate 10, G) has long been accepted as presenting the portrait of Berenice II in the guise of Arsinoe. Svoro-

[42] Leu 20, 25 Apr. 1978, 174, 55.55 g.

[43] Silver: Sv. 988; gold: Sv. 972, 986.

[44] Sv. 1061–62.

nos assigned the issue to Berytus, because of the trident symbol which a few examples bear, but there has been no clear indication of date.

There are also known rare octadrachms in Berenice's name (Plate 10, E) which show a lovely youthful head on obverse, but one which is recognized as merely an idealized Greek head, not a true portrait.[45] The single cornucopiae on the reverse does not show Berenice's standard cornucopiae contents of, from left to right, 1) grapes, sitting precariously unsupported at the edge of the cornucopiae, 2) pomegranate, 3) pyramidal cake, and 4) oversized grain ear (see Plate 10, B-C). Instead, this issue's reverse is still highly influenced by Arsinoe's cornucopiae contents: it retains the two hanging grape clusters, and the small round fruit to left; and keeps the pomegranate in the right-hand position. Added, however, at the left is the oversized ear of grain which, shifted to the right, becomes an unvarying prominent feature of Berenice's standard cornucopiae contents.[46]

The bee on the reverse has led to an attribution to Ephesus, a city which was reclaimed for Egypt by Ptolemy III in 245 B.C., early in his reign. This time and place would seem a very likely attribution for the striking of this issue, with its Greek-style portrait, perhaps executed before the arrival of any example of Berenice's official portrait, and its only partial change of the cornucopiae contents from Arsinoe's to Berenice's standard assortment.

A new Berenice issue which has just appeared on the market[47] (Plate 10, F) now makes a rather surprising connection between the early Ephesian Berenice coins (Plate 10, E) and the "Berenice-type" Arsinoe issue (Plate 10, G). The new octadrachm's obverse lacks the stephane (as do the Ephesian coins), but in all other respects is extremely close to that of the "Berenice-type" coins; the lumpy chignon, the arrangement of the veil's folds, the dots along the browline, and one unique, non-natu-

[45] Sv. 899–900.

[46] Interestingly enough, Thompson notes (p. 32) that in the contents of the cornucopiae carried by Arsinoe and Berenice on the faience oinochoai, the pyramidal cakes "grow thinner and thinner until in the time of Berenice they are displaced by the long yellow stalks [the oinochoai were painted, of course] which appear to represent grain, though the heads are not represented . . . . " Grain was evidently a part of Berenice's official iconography and not of Arsinoe's.

[47] Leu 30, 28 Apr. 1982, 224.

ralistic detail—the four thin, closely spaced, almost parallel lines which form the lower portion of the veil seen to the right of the neck.

On the new coin's reverse to lower right is what may be a bee symbol, but whether or not this is the correct identification, the cornucopiae's contents and their arrangement are precisely those of the Ephesian issue—and of no others. The new octadrachm would thus seem to suggest that some at least of the "Berenice-type" Arsinoe tetradrachms were struck in Ephesus, and fairly early in Ptolemy III's reign.

7. Ptolemy III: Phoenician and Palestinian Arsinoe Octadrachms of 225/4 B.C.

The monogram  (sometimes ) distinguishes a coherent but rather puzzling group of Ptolemy Soter tetradrachms and Arsinoe octadrachms from the five eastern mints. Svoronos knew silver from Tyre, Sidon, Ace-Ptolemais and Gaza; and gold from Ace-Ptolemais and Joppa.[48] The coins bear other markings as well, among which appears occasionally the date ΚΓ, and Svoronos's catalogue placed the dated coins in Ptolemy II's twenty-third year, or 263 B.C.; but this early date is quite impossible, and Svoronos's text reveals his serious doubts.[49]

Otto Mørkholm has recently collected and published the silver tetradrachms, including also an issue of Joppa, and shown that all belong to the twenty-third year not of Ptolemy II, but of Ptolemy III, in 225/4 B.C.[50] To Svoronos's two gold octadrachms of this  group can now be added another issue of Ace-Ptolemais and one of Sidon, all of which would have been struck in this brief unexplained resumption of minting in 225/4 B.C.

Coin 4's obverse is indistinct, but on the other three, while the lotus-head scepter tip is shown atop Arsinoe's head, there is, quite excep-

48 Sv. 701–4, 757, 785–87, 794, 821.

49 In vol. 1, pp. *ροδ′* and *ροζ′-ροη′*, he hesitantly assigns the issues to various dates around 263/2 and 261/0 B.C. Earlier, he had evidently not considered them Ptolemy II's at all: in *Τὰ χρυσᾶ νομίσματα τῶν Λαγιδῶν τοῦ τύπου 'Αρσινόης τῆς Φιλαδέλφου*," *JIAN* 3 (1900), he placed the dated Joppa octadrachm on his plate of coins of Ptolemy III and later rulers (pl. Δ, 8: there is no accompanying text).

50 O. Mørkholm, "A Group of Ptolemaic Coins from Phoenicia and Palestine," *INJ* 4 (1980), pp. 4–7.

tionally, no depiction of the scepter's shaft: the lines to the right of the neck belong to the veil because, if extended, they lie far to the rear of the scepter tip. The forms of the civic monograms differ from those used earlier, and the placement of the markings is erratic.

The format of the listings below is that used elsewhere in this article. The first marking listed for each coin is placed to the left of the cornucopiae; all others are to the right.

Sidon

[monogram] ΣΙ	—	FD2	1. Leu 30, 28 Apr., 1982, 225 (Plate 10, D)

Ake-Ptolemais

[monogram] [monogram] over Ω	785	FD2	2. Sv. pl. 25, 2
[monogram] [monogram]	—	FD2	3. Rollin et Feuardent, 9 May 1910, 675

Joppa

[monogram] [monogram] over ΚΓ	794	FD2	4. Sv. pl. 23, 1

8. Ptolemies VI-VIII: Arsinoe Octadrachms with Κ on Obverse[51]

Any lingering belief that these obverse Κs signify dates of any sort should be dispelled by the demonstration that the letters on the early posthumous coins were not dates but simply issue markings. It may well be that tradition required that a "proper" Arsinoe coin have a letter on obverse, but that any letter would do. The Κ issue was the last large issue in the early posthumous coinage (second only to Θ in the number of reverse dies known); and one suspects that the Κ on the late coins represents nothing more than successive rote copyings of an earlier Κ coin.[52]

[51] Sv. 1241–42, 1374, 1498–99, 1726, 1841. For the attribution to Ptolemies VI and VIII see E. T. Newell, *Two Recent Egyptian Hoards*, ANSNNM 33 (New York, 1927), pp. 16 and 26–27.

[52] See especially Sv. pl. 40, 23 (an example of Sv. 1242), whose obverse seems a direct copy of the original Κ die.

KEY TO PLATES

Numbers identify coins in the early posthumous Arsinoe coinage from Alexandria; letters are used for all other coins.

At the bottom of the plates, brackets above coin numbers indicate obverse die links; brackets below, reverse die links.

PLATE 2: Theon Adelphon Octadrachm (A) and Group 1 Decadrachms (1–4)

A. Florange, 10 Feb. 1923, 64
1. Numismatic Fine Arts 8, 6 June 1980, 379 = Schulman, 29 Oct. 1953, 2137
2. New Netherlands-Seaby, 14 Nov. 1973, 25 = Egger 40, 2 May 1912, 1229
3. Naville 13, 27 June 1928, 939
4. Ciani, 18 Dec. 1924, 301 = Bourgey, 7 June 1909, 362

PLATE 3: Group 2 Octadrachms

1. Naville 4, 17 June 1922, 981 = Hirsch 25, 29 Nov. 1909, 3188 = Hamburger, 24 Oct. 1898, 56
2. Sv. pl. 15, 6
3. Bullowa, 12 June 1953, 497
4. Athens = Sv. pl. 15, 7
5. Glasgow = *Hunter*, vol. 3, p. 363, 8 = Sv. pl. 15, 8
6. Stack's, 9 Nov. 1946, 11 = Naville 17, 3 Oct. 1934, 624
7. Naville 7, 23 June 1924, 1833 = Hirsch 21, 16 Nov. 1908, 4483
8. London = Glendining, 18 Apr. 1955, 42 = Münzhandlung Basel 4, 1 Oct. 1935, 979

PLATE 4: Group 2 Decadrachms (1–4) and Tetradrachms (5–6)

1. ANS = Stack's, 20 Jan. 1938, 135 = Naville 12, 18 Oct. 1926, 2594
2. Coins and Antiquities 1972, FPL 2, G151 = Stack's, 20 Jan. 1938, 136 = Naville 13, 27 June 1928, 940.
3. ANS
4. ANS
5. Coin Galleries, 20 Apr. 1961, 163 = Stack's, 4 May 1960, 154 = Stack's, 20 Jan. 1938, 137
6. Glendining, 21 Feb. 1961, 2794 = *SNGLockett* 3408 = Naville 7, 23 June 1924, 1831 = Egger 40, 2 May 1912, 1228 = Rollin et Feuardent, 9 May 1910, 678

PLATE 5: Group 2 Tetradrachms

1. J. D. Bishop and R. R. Holloway, *Wheaton College Collection of Greek and Roman Coins*, ANSACNAC (New York, 1981), 293 = Stack's, 9 Nov. 1946, 256 = Morgenthau 342, 26 Nov. 1934, 172

2. Münz. u. Med. 54, 26 Oct. 1978, 397
3. Private coll.
4. *SNGBerry* 1473
5. London = *BMC* p. 43, 7 = Sv. pl. 16, 13 (Sv. 410, described as without obverse letter)
6. ANS = Hirsch 29, 9 Nov. 1910, 846
7. Kricheldorf FPL 11, July-Aug. 1956, 451
8. London = *Weber* 8243 = Sv. pl. 16, 16

PLATE 6: Transitional Octadrachms (1–3) and Decadrachms (4–6)

1. Naville 17, 3 Oct. 1934, 625
2. Naville 17, 3 Oct. 1934, 626
3. Münz. u. Med. 19, 5 June 1959, 581
4. Stack's, 9 Nov. 1946, 255 = Naville 1, 4 Apr. 1921, 3226
5. Stack's, 27 June 1952, 1259 = Cahn 66, 9 May 1930, 470 = Hess, 25 Mar. 1929, 465 = Hamburger, 24 Oct. 1898, 57
6. Hess-Leu, 16 Apr. 1964, 254

PLATE 7: Group 3 Octadrachms (1–4) and Decadrachms (5–7)

1. Vinchon, 23 Apr. 1976, 200
2. Numismatic Fine Arts 8, 6 June 1980, 380 = *MFA Suppl.* 320
3. ANS
4. Sotheby, 21 Feb. 1929, 98
5. Naville 15, 2 July 1930, 1174
6. Vinchon, 3 Mar. 1975, 83
7. Glendining, 21 Feb. 1961, 2800 = *SNGLockett* 3415

PLATE 8: Group 4 Octadrachms (1–4) and Decadrachms (5–7)

1. Benha 8
2. Münz. u. Med. 11, 23 Jan. 1953, 88
3. Hess-Leu 28, 5 May 1965, 312 (illustration slightly over-sized)
4. Leu 18, 5 May 1977, 273 = Stack's, 30 Apr. 1964, 24 = Münzhandlung Basel 4, 1 Oct. 1935, 981
5. Stack's, 20 Jan. 1938, 190 = Naville 14, 2 July 1929, 461
6. Leu 7, 9 May 1973, 303 = Bourgey, 23 May 1910, 143
7. ANS

PLATE 9: Palestinian and Phoenician Octadrachms

See coin listings, pp. 50-53.

PLATE 10: Miscellaneous Arsinoe (A, D, G) and Berenice II (B, C, E, F) Strikings. All are octadrachms except A, double octadrachm; B, silver Attic 2 1/2 drachm; and C, gold Attic decadrachm.

A. Leu 20, 25 Apr. 1978, 174
B. ANS = Florange, 16 Oct. 1923, 66
C. Glendining, 21 Feb. 1961, 2801 = *SNGLockett* 3416
D. Leu 30, 28 Apr. 1982, 225
E. Leu 20, 25 Apr. 1978, 175
F. Leu 30, 28 Apr. 1982, 224
G. In trade, 1981

ANSMN 28 (1983)

COINAGE OF THE ARMENIAN KINGDOMS OF SOPHENE AND COMMAGENE

(PLATES 11–12)

PAUL Z. BEDOUKIAN

Certain types of coins which have on the obverse a characteristic headdress (called the Armenian tiara by Babelon, Langlois, Blau, and others) were struck in southwestern Armenia during the first three centuries before Christ. Although the existence of these coins has long been known, a systematic study of them has not been made because of the paucity of specimens and the lack of historical evidence for their proper attribution. Recent excavations at Nemroud Dagh[1] have shed much light on the history of this region—especially of Sophene and Commagene. In addition, much new material has surfaced, making it now possible to attempt a chronological attribution of the coinage of these two Armenian kingdoms.

Historians have generally acknowledged that Armenian and Greek tribes entered Asia Minor from Europe in the eighth century B.C. and gradually spread eastward toward the highlands of historic Armenia. By the sixth century B.C., Armenians were already settled over the lands of the Urartuan kingdom and were in close contact with the Medes.

During the rise of the Achaemenid empire, Armenia constituted a distinct province governed by satraps. Often these satraps were native rulers who had allied themselves with the Persian kings and partici-

[1] F. K. Dorner and T. Goell, *Arsameia am Nymphaios: Die Ausgrabungen im Hierothesion des Mithridates Kallinikos von 1953–1956* (Berlin, 1963) L. Jalabert and R. Mouterde, *Inscriptions Grecques et Latin de la Syrie* (Paris, 1929), 1, pp. 2–42.

pated in their military expeditions. For example, in the year 612 B.C., an Armenian ruler, Paruir, took part in the sack of Nineveh and was rewarded by being recognized king of Greater Armenia. Several centuries later, King Orontes of Armenia joined the Persian army with a contingent of 40,000 infantrymen and 7,000 horsemen in the battle of Arbela (331 B.C.) which resulted in the total victory of Alexander over Darius. The Orontid kingdom, however, was never conquered by Alexander. Its rulers were descended from the Achaemenid royalty and for a time controlled all of historic Armenia, including Sophene and Commagene.

Sophene, situated between the Euphrates and the Tigris rivers, separated the Hittites from the Urartuans. After Alexander's victory over Darius, it became the first region exposed to Greek influence and adopted some aspects of Greek culture. Around the third century B.C., the Seleucids forced its separation from historic Armenia and allowed it to form an independent kingdom. The rulers of Greater Armenia apparently did not issue coins, but the Armenian kingdom of Sophene, which included Commagene initially, followed the western custom of issuing coinage.

Perhaps the greatest single obstacle in studying the coinage of Sophene and related Armenian principalities has been the prevailing opinion that Sophene and Greater Armenia were governed by the same family of rulers.[2] Both Toumanoff and Lang presented us with a sequence of rulers of Armenia which included not only the kings of Sophene but also six Orontid kings who ruled over Greater Armenia. Because the names of the rulers of both Sophene and Greater Armenia were mixed together, it was hitherto impossible to correctly attribute the coinage of Armenia from the fifth to the first century B.C.

The excavations of the tumulus of Antiochus Theos of Commagene at the beginning of the twentieth century changed the picture and provided us with much information on the Orontids and on Sophene. They established that Sophene was a distinct and different Armenian kingdom. The recently published Armenian encyclopedia clearly diffe-

[2] C. Toumanoff, *Studies in Christian Caucasian History* (Washington, 1963), pp. 282, 293–94; David M. Lang, *Armenia, Cradle of Civilization* (London, 1970), p. 121.

rentiates the kingdom of Sophene at the start of the third century B.C from that of Greater Armenia.[3]

The inscriptions of Nemroud Dagh list the ancestors of Antiochus I and connect his lineage with the Orontids of Armenia and the Achaemenid house. They also list the kings of Sophene, who were closely related to the ruling dynasties of Armenia and Persia. We are thus able to study the coinage of Sophene as that of a dynasty separate from Greater Armenia.

It has been noted that Armenians named their cities after the rulers who founded them.[4] This custom prevailed in Greater Armenia and in Sophene as well. A number of cities around Mount Ararat were named after the Artaxiad kings, and hundreds of miles southwest, we find another set of cities named after the rulers of Sophene.

Our present knowledge and the numismatic material now available make it possible to present the following chronology of the rulers of Sophene and of Commogene and their coinage.

SOPHENE

SAMES (ca. 260 B.C.)

Toumanoff[5] writes that the city of Samosata was first mentioned in the year 245 B.C. by Erasthenes who stated that Ziaelas of Bythinia took refuge in that city in 260 B.C. It seems justifiable to conclude that its founder, Sames, ruled around that time. Although no historical record exists concerning the rule of Sames, his coins were described as early as 1754.[6] Somewhat later, Belley[7] gave a fuller description of the

[3] *Haikakan Sovetagan Hanrakidaran* [Soviet Armenian Encyclopedia] (Erevan, Arm. S.S.R., 1970), vol. 5, s.v. "Sophene," pp. 139–41 (B. Haroutunian).

[4] H. A. Manandian, *The Trade and Cities of Armenia in Relation to Ancient World Trade*, trans. Nina G. Garsoian (Lisbon, 1965), e.g. pp. 34 and 37.

[5] Toumanoff (above, n. 2), p. 280.

[6] E. Froelich, *Armenia Regum Numismatum. . .* (Vienna, 1754), pp. 89–91.

[7] L'Abbe Belley, *Mémoires de l'Académie des inscriptions et belles-lettres*, vol. 26 (Paris, 1840), pp. 355, 380.

coins and attributed them to Sames. Subsequently, other numismatists have accepted this attribution.[8]

In his treatise on the coinage of ancient Armenia, Langlois[9] mentions the single specimen found in the Vienna Museum. Both Langlois and Babelon[10] considered this coin to be Commagenian. This is incorrect because at that time Commagene was part of the kingdom of Sophene, and the coin was issued by Sames of Sophene.

Sames initiated a style of coinage (Plate 11, 1) with the pointed headdress which, as mentioned above, underwent a gradual change and led to the tiara seen on the coins of the Artaxiads of Greater Armenia.[11] On the obverse, the king's head is turned right: he is wearing a tall, conical cap with a diadem, ending in a bow in the back and long strands falling down the neck. On the reverse are the names of the king and Thyrse of Dionysos, with interlaced cornucopiae. At least six examples of the coins of Sames have been found in various collections.

ARSAMES I (ca. 240 B.C.)

It is interesting that two cities were named after Arsames, Arsamosata and Arsameia. Dittenberger[12] and Jalabert and Mouterde[13] examined the chronological sequence of the rulers of this dynasty and reached the conclusion that there were two kings named Arsames. Although Toumanoff[14] disagrees with this conclusion, numismatic evidence (the existence of two types of coins bearing the name Arsames) strongly supports the argument in favor of two rulers named Arsames.

[8] J. Eckel, *Catalogue du Musée de Vienne*, p. 252; T. E. Mionnet, *Descriptions des medailles antiques, greques et romaines*, vol. 4 (1807), p. 454; E. Q. Visconti, *Iconographie Ancienne, Iconographie Greque*, vol. 2 (Paris, 1811), pp. 345–64.

[9] V. Langlois, *Numismatique de l'Arménie dans l'Antiquité* (Paris, 1859), p. 9.

[10] E. Babelon, *Rois de Syrie, d'Armenia et de Commagene* (Paris, 1890), p. ccviii.

[11] P. Z. Bedoukian, *Coinage of the Artaxiads of Armenia*, RNS Special Publication 10 (London, 1978), p. 4.

[12] W. Dittenberger, *Orientis grecci inscriptiones selectae* 1 (Leipzig, 1903), p. 611.

[13] L. Jalabert and R. Mouterde, *Inscriptions Greques et Latin de la Syrie* (Paris, 1929), p. 28.

[14] Toumanoff (above, n. 2), p. 281.

Some Arsames coins (Plate 11, 2–4), the obverses of which are remarkably similar to those of Sames, certainly belong to the first Arsames. On the reverse is a horseman galloping right, holding a spear in his right hand. A figure in front of the horse may represent a foot soldier. This reverse type appears on a coin that Morkholm[15] attributed to Ariarathes III of Cappadocia who ruled in that period. A variant of the reverse has two foot soldiers facing the armed horseman and a fallen soldier beneath the horse's feet. Two denominations of this coin were struck.

Arsames II (ca. 230 B.C.)

Arsames II is reported to have offered asylum to Antiochus Hierax, the viceroy of Asia Minor and brother of Seleucus II. Antiochus, by setting himself up as an independent king, had incurred the wrath of his brother. The obverse design on the coins of Arsames II is different from that of the preceding king. Instead of being conical, the tiara now resembles a cap and does not have the sharp point (Plate 11, 5–8). It sits lightly on the head with the diadem circling the forehead and ending in a bow in the back, then hanging down the neck. On the reverse of the large coppers, under the legend, is a horseman with a cap and floating robes, holding a spear in his right hand, galloping to the right. The larger copper coins of Arsames II have been described by Visconti, Langlois, Babelon[16] and others.

The obverse of the smaller copper coins is identical to the large coppers, with the head of the king turned right and the same type of tiara. There are a number of variations in the reverse design, however, perhaps suggesting that this king ruled over a longer period than his predecessor. On one type is a nude figure, standing and facing, with the right arm extended from the elbow, the left holding a club. A second type shows an eagle turned left holding a bolt of lightening. The third

15 O. Mørkholm, "The Classification of Cappadocian Coins," *NC* 1969, p. 22, pl. 5.

16 Visconti (above, n. 8), pp. 345-64; Langlois (above, n. 9), p. 12; Babelon (above, n. 10), p. 211.

type shows the caps of dioscuri along with the legend found on the others.[17]

XERXES (ca. 220 B.C.)

Xerxes was the son of Arsames and succeeded his father to the throne. A passage from Polybius[18] sheds considerable light on the events during his rule. It appears that Antiochus IV Epiphanes resolved to subdue Sophene and besieged Xerxes in his city of Arsamosata. Unable to resist such a powerful adversary, Xerxes sued for peace. It was granted on condition that he pay the tribute owed to Antiochus by Arsames. The payment is said to have consisted of 300 talents, 1,000 horses, and 1,000 mules with their harnesses. As a gesture of amity, Antiochus gave his sister in marriage to Xerxes.

The Nemroud Dagh inscriptions do not list Xerxes as one of the ancestors of Antiochus I of Commagene. However, as Toumanoff[19] has pointed out, not all the inscriptions have survived. The existence of coinage issued by Xerxes is ample proof that he was a ruler of this dynasty. Moreover, judging from the fabric and style of his coins, he was either the son or the successor of Arsames II.

The coinage of Xerxes (Plate 11, 9–10, 13–14; Plate 12, 15) shows the continued evolution in the design of the headdress of the kings of Sophene. The cap-like headdress is placed lightly on the head, with the diadem around the head and hanging in the back. The coins of Xerxes show the tiara folded, and open on the side. Unlike his predecessor, the king is heavily bearded, but as on all the coins of this dynasty, he is facing right. Several types of coins, in two denominations, are known to have been struck by Xerxes.

The earliest example of a chalcus of this king was described by Froehlich[20] and later, by Langlois, Babelon and other writers. On the reverse of this coin is a representation of victory standing left, holding a crown or wreath in her extended right arm, with the left hand resting

[17] NFA 10, 17 Sept. 1981, 227–28.

[18] Polybius, 8.23.

[19] Toumanoff (above, n. 2), p. 283.

[20] E. Froelich (above, n. 6), pp. 91–100.

on the belt of her tunic. Other examples show Athena holding the crown and resting her left arm on a shield. Zeus appears on the reverse of a third variety, seated, holding Nike in his right hand, the left resting on a shield.

ABDISSARES (ca. 210 B.C.)

No information has survived from early historians to establish the genealogical position of this king. However, the striking similarity of his coins (Plate 12, 16–17) to those of Xerxes leaves little doubt that Abdissares was his successor. On the obverse, the king is turned right and is lightly bearded. The reverse of the larger coppers shows an eagle standing right. A similar eagle appears on the smaller versions of this coin. A horse's head, turned right, is on a second variety of the smaller denomination.

Visconti[21] was apparently the first to note the similarity between the coins of this king and those of Xerxes and to conclude that they belonged to a king of Arsamosata. Subsequently, de Saulcy[22] published an article on the coinage of Abdissares. Other numismatists, including Langlois[23] and Babelon[24] mentioned the existence of several types of coins struck by this king.

ZARIADRES (ca. 190 B.C.)

It appears that the Seleucids had extended their power over Sophene at the beginning of the third century B.C. and had appointed Zariadres (Zareh) as the strategus of Sophene. In the battle of Magnesia (189 B.C.), the Romans crushed the power of the Seleucids. Taking advantage of the situation, Zariadres declared his independence and was later recognized as king by Rome. It is interesting that the strategus

[21] Visconti (above, n. 8), p. 329.

[22] M. de Saulcy, *Bulletin archéologique de l'Athenaeum français* (1855), no. 12, p. 101.

[23] Langlois (above, n. 9), pp. 15–18.

[24] Babelon (above, n. 10), p. cxciv.

of Greater Armenia, Artaxias, likewise declared his independence and established the Artaxiad dynasty.

These events have been described in some detail by Strabo.[25] Strabo made a significant remark to the effect that the political situation resulted in the formation of two independent countries whose people spoke the same language. Historians made the same statement a hundred years later when Tigranes the Great joined Sophene and adjacent lands to his empire. There seems to be no doubt that both Sophene and Commagene at that time were inhabited by Armenian people.

Friedlander[26] was the first to describe a coin with the legend ΔΣΑΡΙ (Plate 12, 18) which he attributed to a ruler in Armenia. Blau,[27] in discussing the coin in the Berlin Museum, attributed it to Zariadres of Sophene. His views were shared by Babelon; however, Regling considers this coin an issue of Anissa.[28]

Strabo indicated that Zariadres controlled territories beyond Sophene. Perhaps the establishment of a new realm justified a change from the type of coinage issued by the preceding kings of Sophene. On the obverse, we again see the king's head turned right, wearing a tiara. The headdress, however, is somewhat different, with the flaps under the chin. The different styling of the reverse prompted Babelon to suggest the possibility that this coin was struck outside of Sophene. On the reverse is a deity (Anaitis?) facing, with the right hand raised and holding a flower. At her feet are two sphinxes back to back and facing.

MORPHILIG (ca. 150 B.C.)

Friedlander[29] described a coin similar to that of Zariadres in the Berlin Museum, with a deity (Anaitis) standing, holding a flower. The letters ΜΟΡΙ can be expanded to ΜΟΡΙΦΙΛΙΟΣ, as there is no space on the flan for the entire name.

[25] Strabo 11. 14. 5, 15.

[26] J. Friedlander, "Satrapenmünzen," *ZfN* 4 (1877), pp. 266–67.

[27] O. Blau, "Die Herron von Sophene und deren Münzen," *NZ* 9 (1877), p. 104.

[28] Babelon (above, n. 10), p. cxcviii; K. Regling, "Dynastenmünzen von Tyana, Morima und Asisa in Kappadokien," *ZfN* 1932, p. 10, no. 11 (Berlin).

[29] J. Friedlander (above, n. 26), pp. 266–67.

Morphilig and Zariadres fit into the historical frame of the period. The headdress design on the coins of both kings bears marked similarities to that on the contemporary coins of Cappadocia.

ARTANES (ca. 110 B.C.)

According to Strabo,[30] Artanes, a descendant of Zariadres, was the last king of Sophene. He lost his kingdom in 95 B.C. No coins bearing his name are extant. The discovery of such a coin would do much to clarify the end of the coinage of the Sophene dynasty. There exists the possibility that a coin mentioned by LeRider with the incomplete legend ...ABANOY (Artabanes?) belongs to this king.[31]

ARSACES (ca. 90 B.C.)

On the evidence that Tigranes, upon adding Sophene to his empire, placed a certain Arsaces as governor of that region, de Sallet[32] suggested that certain coins with the legend ΒΑΣΙΛΕΩΣ/ΑΡΣΑΚΟΥ be attributed to this viceroy.

When Pompey in 69 B.C. signed a peace treaty with Tigranes the Great, he gave Sophene to Ariobarzanes of Cappadocia. As a result, this territory gradually became hellenized and became part of the Roman empire.

COMMAGENE

It was mentioned above that the Seleucids succeeded in detaching Sophene from Greater Armenia and allowed it to become an independent kingdom. This action probably secured the northern mountainous

30 Above, n. 25.

31 G. Le Rider, "Monnaies grecques acquises par le Cabinet des Médailles en 1959," *RN* 1959-1960, p. 21, no. 28 (Paris).

32 A. de Sallet, "Die ältesten Tetradrachmen der Arsaciden," *ZfN* 1 (1874), p. 312; see also P. Cl. Sibilian, "Drei sehr seltene Münzen armenischer Dynasten," *NZ* 2 (1870), pl. 8, 3.

frontier and at the same time placed the territory, through which passed a major trade route, under the control of the Seleucids. Later, through the intervention of the Seleucids, Commagene detached itself from Sophene and also became an independent kingdom. The circumstances are not clear, but Diodores of Sicily stated that around 163 B.C., Ptolomaeus, the satrap of Commagene, declared his independence and even captured Melitene from the king of Cappadocia.[33]

Numismatists, in discussing the coinage of Commagene, have not considered this country as part of the Armenian kingdom. Historical evidence, however, shows clearly that its language and population was Armenian. It was, in effect, an Armenian kingdom separated from Greater Armenia for political reasons. It lost its connection with Armenia some one hundred fifty years later.

PTOLOMAEUS (ca. 163 B.C.)

We do not have any coins bearing the name of this ruler, which is a little surprising, as one would expect that a ruler beginning a dynasty would have taken pains to issue coins in his name.

MITHRADATES I CALLINICUS (96–70 B.C.)

Several coins (Plate 12, 20–21, 23) have been attributed to this king. It is curious that he ruled during the period when Tigranes had gained control of both Sophene and Commagene. It may be that Mithradates was allowed to strike coins even though he recognized the overlordship of Tigranes. The same situation seems to have occurred with his successor, Antiochus.

A few coins of Callinicus are similar to the ones issued by the kings of Sophene, portraying on the obverse the king's head with the pointed Armenian tiara. Three examples have been described in the literature by Babelon and Troxell.[34] On one type, Athena is standing left with

[33] Toumanoff (above, n. 2), pp. 281–82: E. Honigmann, *Kommagene*, pp. 980, 983.

[34] Babelon (above, n. 10), p. 217, pl. 30, 2–4; H. Troxell, "Greek Accessions, Asia Minor to India," *ANSMN* 22 (1977), pp. 21–22, pl. 4, 8–10.

extended right hand, the left supporting a spear, with a shield at her feet. A second type attributed to this king shows on the reverse Pegasus with curled wing. The legend is incomplete. Troxell has attributed to Callinicus a third type with Pegasus on the reverse.

Other coins with the inscription ΒΑΣΙΛΕΩΣ/ΜΙΘΡΙΔΑΤΟΥ which do not portray the king on the obverse must be attributed to Callinicus. The obverse shows an eagle turned right with a palm branch under its left wing. This may represent the coat of arms of Tigranes who had extended his power over Commagene. On the reverse is the king's name, ΚΑΛΛΙΝΙΚΟΥ, with a palm branch upwards to right, The obverse of another example has an eagle and a winged caduceus. and its reverse has the legend ΒΑϹΙΛΕΩϹ/ΜΙΘΡΑΔΑΤΟΥ/ΚΑΛΛΙΝΙ-ΚΟΥ. A fourth class of coins shows the king with a pointed tiara on the obverse and Pegasus on the reverse. The legends are unclear or missing.

ANTIOCHUS I THEOS (60–34 B.C.)

The accepted date for the beginning of the reign of this king coincides with the defeat of Tigranes at the hands of Pompey. For some reason, the few coins of Antiochus I which have reached us (Plate 12, 25, 27) bear on the obverse the portrait of the king wearing a tiara identical with the tiara seen on the coins of Tigranes.[35] This has prompted some discussion.[36] Were these coins struck for some years before the defeat of Tigranes, indicating the peaceful acceptance of the suzerainty of Tigranes by Antiochus, or were they struck after Tigranes lost control over Commagene? If the latter is true, then Antiochus must have adopted the Armenian tiara to stress the legitimacy of his succession as a descendant of the Armenian Orontid house which in turn was related to the Achaemenid house. The answer to these questions must be left to the historians, but it is clear that Antiochus, by placing the Armenian tiara on his coins, was either declaring himself to be a vassal

[35] *BMCCappadocia*, p. 102, pl. 14, 4.

[36] P. Z. Bedoukian, "A Coin of Tigranes the Great of Armenia, Struck in Commagene," *NC* 1970, pp. 19–22; R. D. Sullivan, "Diadochic Coinage in Commagene after Tigranes the Great," *NC* 1973, pp. 18–39.

of Tigranes the Great or was claiming that he had the same dynastic lineage as Tigranes.

In any event, after Antiochus, Commagene became a Roman province and the coins of the succeeding kings are entirely different in style and fabric. They are in effect Roman coins, indicating the termination of Commagene as an Armenian state.

Until recently only one type of coin of Antiochus I Theos was known. On the obverse is the portrait of the king wearing the Armenian tiara, and on the reverse, the lion of Commagene walking right, with the legend ΒΑΣΙΛΕΩΣ/ΑΝΤΙΟΧΟΥ. Recently the author acquired a second type of copper (Plate 12, 26) struck by this king, which appears to be overstruck on an unidentifiable coin. On the obverse is the familiar youthful portrait of the king turned right. On the reverse is an eagle, standing right on a branch with the legend ΒΑΣΙΛΕΩΣ/ΑΝΤΙΟΧΟΥ.

SOPHENE

Sames (ca. 260 B.C.)

Two Chalci

1. *Obv.*: Head of Sames r. wearing pointed tiara with ends of diadem hanging at back of neck; behind head, a laurel branch; border of dots.

   Rev.: Thyrsos of Dionysos, between two cornucopiae interlaced; to l. upward ΒΑΣΙΛΕΩΣ/ΣΑΜΟΥ; to r. upward ΘΕΟΣΕΒΟΥΣ/ΚΑΙΦΙΚΑΙΟΥ.

   Bibliothèque Nationale, 4.80 g, 4.15 g; Paul Bedoukian, 7.69 g, 7.56 g (Plate 11, 1); Hunterian Museum, one specimen; Mechitarian Museum, Vienna, one specimen; Hermitage, 6.14 g.

Arsames I (ca. 240 B.C.)

Two chalci

2. *Obv.*: Head of Arsames r. wearing pointed tiara with drapes covering neck.

Rev.: Horseman advancing r. with spear in r. hand and pointed at foot soldier or soldiers facing him with shield and spear; sometimes below horse, a fallen soldier; above horseman ΒΑΣΙΛΕΩΣ/ΑΡΣΑΜΟΥ.

Paul Bedoukian, 6.45 g (Plate 11, 2a), 5.87 g (Plate 11, 2b); British Museum, 4.51 g; Jack Guevrekian, 4.25 g.

One chalcus

3. *Obv.*: As 2.
Rev.: As 2.

Paul Bedoukian, 3.18 g, 2.92 g (Plate 11, 3).

4. *Obv.*: As 2.
Rev.: Winged thunderbolt; to l. upward ΒΑΣΙΛΕΩΣ/ΑΡΣΑΜΟΥ; to r. uncertain.

American Numismatic Society, 3.61 g (Plate 11, 4).

ARSAMES II (CA. 230 B.C.)

Two chalci

5. *Obv.*: Head of king r. wearing tiara with flat top like a cap; a diadem encircles the head, ends in bow, and hangs down neck.
Rev.: Horseman advancing r. holding spear in r. hand and wearing similar headdress; above horseman ΒΑΣΙΛΕΩΣ/ΑΡΣΑΜΟΥ.

Paul Bedoukian, 8.35 g (Plate 11, 5); Bibliothèque Nationale, 6.59 g; Mechitarian Museum, Vienna, one specimen.

6. *Obv.*: As 5.
Rev.: Nude figure standing and facing, r. arm extended from elbow and l. arm holding long club; to r. downward ΒΑΣΙΛΕΩΣ; to l. downward ΑΡΣΑΜΟΥ.

Paul Bedoukian, 6.41 g, 5.37 g (Plate 11, 6); Jack Guevrekian, 7.68 g; British Museum, three specimens.

One chalcus

7. *Obv.*: As 5.

Rev.: Eagle standing r. holding thunderbolt; legends as 6.

Paul Bedoukian, 5.27 g (Plate 11, 7), 3.87 g; Mechitarian Museum, Vienna, one specimen.

8. *Obv.*: As 5.
Rev.: Caps of dioscuri; legends as 6.

Paul Bedoukian, 3.25 g (Plate 11, 8).

XERXES (CA. 220 B.C.)

Two chalci

9. *Obv.*: Bearded head of king r. wearing folded tiara; diademed with ribbon hanging behind head; in l. field, monogram ¥.
Rev.: Victory standing l. holding crown in extended r. hand, l. hand resting on belt of tunic; in field monogram ꓠK; to r. downward ΒΑΣΙΛΕΩΣ: to l. downward ΧΕΡΧΟΥ.

Paul Bedoukian, 5.43 g (Plate 11, 9); Bibliothèque Nationale, 5.42 g; Berlin Museum, 4.97 g; Mechitarian Museum, Vienna, one specimen.

10. *Obv.*: As 9, no monogram.
Rev.: Athena seated holding a figure (Minerva?) in extended r. hand; l. hand resting on large shield; legends as 9, no monogram.

British Museum, 4.51 g (Plate 11, 10).

One chalcus

11. *Obv.*: As 10.
Rev.: As 9, monogram H.

Bibliothèque Nationale, 1.90 g.

12. *Obv.*: As 11.
Rev.: As 9, monogram Z.

Rollin collection (see Langlois).

13. *Obv.*: As 11.
Rev.: As 9, monogram N.

British Museum, 1.89 g (Plate 11, 13).

14. *Obv.*: As 9.
Rev.: As 10.

Bibliothèque Nationale, 1.90 g (Plate 11, 14) Hermitage Museum, one specimen.

15. *Obv.*: As 9.
Rev.: Athena standing l. holding crown in extended r. hand and resting l. arm on shield.

Bibliothèque Nationale, 2.52 g (Plate 12, 15); Mechitarian Museum, Vienna, one specimen; Hermitage Museum, one specimen.

ABDISSARES (CA. 210 B.C.)

Two chalci

16. *Obv.*: Head of king r., lightly bearded, wearing folded tiara; diademed, with, ribbon hanging behind head; beaded border.
Rev.: Eagle standing r; to r. downward ΒΑΣΙΛΕΩΣ; to l. downward ΑΒΔΙΣΣΑΡΟΥ.

American Numismatic Society, 6.73; Paul Bedoukian, 5.71 g (Plate 12, 16a); Bibliothèque Nationale, 7.40 g; Berlin Museum, 9.44 g (Plate 12, 16b), 7.25 g; Jack Guevrekian, 7.77 g.

One chalcus

17. *Obv.*: As 16.
Rev.: As 16.

American Numismatic Society, 2.18 g; British Museum, 2.99 g (Plate 12, 17); Bibliothèque Nationale, 2.15 g, 1.85 g; Mechitarian Museum, Vienna, one specimen.

ZARIADRES (CA. 190 B.C.)

18. *Obv.*: Head of king r., wearing a tiara with flaps tied under chin.
Rev.: Deity (Anaitis?) standing facing; r. hand raised, holding

flowers: at feet two sphinxes, seated, back to back and facing; to r. downward ΑΝΙΣΑ/ΔΩ; to l. downward ΔΣΑΡΙ.

British Museum, 5.42 g (Plate 12, 18); Berlin Museum, one specimen.

MORPHILIG (CA. 150 B.C.)

19. *Obv.*: Head of king turned r., wearing pointed tiara with flaps tied under chin.

Rev.: Deity (Anaitis?) standing; to r. downward ΔΣΑΡΙ [ΑΔΡΙΟΣ]; below deity ΜΟΡΙ[ΦΙΛΙΟΣ].

Berlin Museum, one specimen.

ARTANES (CA. 70 B.C.)

No known coins.

ARSACES (after 70 B.C.)

No known coins, but see A. de Sallet, "Die ältesten Tetradrachmen der Arsaciden, *ZfN* 1 (1874), p. 312, and P. Cl. Sibilian, "Drei sehr seltene Münzen armenischer Dynasten," *NZ* 2 (1870), pl. 8, 3.

COMMAGENE

PTOLOMAEUS (ca. 163 B.C.)

No known coins.

MITHRIDATES CALLINICUS (96–70 B.C.)

Two chalci

20. *Obv.*: Head of Mithridates r., beardless, wearing pointed tiara with flaps down and behind neck.

Rev.: Athena wearing helmet and long chitan, standing l.; r. hand extended while l. hand supports spear; large shield rests at her feet; to r. downward ΒΑϹΙΛΕΩϹ; to l. downward, ΜΙΘΡΑΔΑΤΟΥ/ΚΑΛΛΙΝΙΚΟΥ.

American Numismatic Society, 8.47 g; Bibliothèque Nationale, 6.55 g; Hunterian Museum, 7.52 g; Paul Bedoukian, 5.72 g (Plate 12, 20), 5.56 g, 5.53 g, 5.49 g, 5.41 g, 5.33 g.

One chalcus

21. *Obv.*: As 20.
Rev.: As 20.

Paul Bedoukian, 4.54 g (Plate 12, 21); Berlin Museum, 4.77 g; British Museum, 3.88 g.

22. *Obv.*: Head of king r. wearing tall pointed tiara, with ties ending in bow at back of head and long strands falling down over back of neck.
Rev.: Pegasus with curved wings l.; below, sword; above ΒΑΣΙ-ΛΕΩΣ; below ΜΙΘΡΑΔΑΤΟΥ.

American Numismatic Society, 3.47 g (Plate 12, 22).

23. *Obv.*: Eagle turned r. and holding palm branch under left wing.
Rev.: Palm branch upward and curving right; to l. upward ΒΑ-ϹΙΛΕΩϹ/ΜΙΘΡΑΔΤΟΥ; to r. upward ΚΑΛΛΙΝΙΚΟΥ.

Bibliothèque Nationale, 3.85 g, 3.39 g; British Museum, 4.52 g (Plate 12, 23).

24. *Obv.*: As 23.
Rev.: Winged caduceus; to r. downward ΒΑϹΙΑΕΩϹ; to l. downward ΜΙΘΡΑΔΑΤΟΥ/ΚΑΛΛΙΝΙΚΟΥ.

American Numismatic Society, 4.51 g (Plate 12, 24); Bibliothèque Nationale, 3.95 g.

Antiochus Theos (69–34 B.C.)

Two chalci

25. *Obv.*: Head of beardless king r. wearing tiara of Tigranes the Great, having eight pointed star and eagles back to back facing.

Rev.: Lion walking r.; above ΒΑΣΙΛΕΩΣ; below ΑΝΤΙΟΧΟΥ.

Paul Bedoukian, 7.55 g, 7.26 g, 6.52 g, 5.88 g (Plate 12, 25), 5.55 g; British Museum, one specimen.

26. *Obv.*: As 25.
Rev.: Eagle standing on branch r.; legends as 25.

Paul Bedoukian 6.00 g (Plate 12, 26).

One chalcus

27. *Obv.*: As 25.
Rev.: As 25.

Paul Bedoukian, 2.95 g, 2.93 g (Plate 12, 27).

ANSMN 28 (1983)

THE AUTONOMOUS TETRADRACHMS OF LAODICEA AD MARE

(PLATES 13–19)

OTTO MØRKHOLM

Laodicea ad Mare was founded by Seleucus I at the beginning of the third century B.C.[1] It soon became an important seaport, and a Seleucid mint was operating there down to about 200 when it was closed during the reign of Antiochus III.[2] In the second century so-called municipal bronze coins were struck under Antiochus IV (175–164) and Alexander Balas (150–145),[3] but apart from these few issues the mint was apparently idle.

Toward the end of the second century a number of cities in the Seleucid empire acquired their independence. Their autonomy was generally celebrated by the issue of civic silver coins. In 109/8 Seleucia Pieria was declared free, and soon her autonomous tetradrachms, struck on the Aradian standard, became an important part of the monetary circulation in northern Syria. With the accession of Tigranes to the Seleucid throne in 82 B.C., Seleucia, in determined opposition to the new king, lost most of her economic importance. Her silver coinage came to an

[1] Together with Antioch, Seleucia and Apamea it formed the famous Syrian tetrapolis. On the foundation by Seleucus I, who named the city after his mother, see Strabo 16.2.4 (C 750). Cf. V. Tscherikower, *Die hellenistischen Städtegründungen*, *Philologus*, suppl. 19 (1927), p. 62.

[2] For the Seleucid coinage down to Antiochus III, see E. T. Newell, *WSM*, pp. 180–91, with the additions in the second edition, pp. vi-vii.

[3] *BMCSeleucids* p. 41, 82, and p. 57, 66–67, all with Poseidon as reverse type.

end, and Laodicea, favored by a grant of autonomy from Tigranes, eagerly assumed the function as the most important seaport on the Syrian coast, a position which she (under the name of Latakia) has preserved to the present day.[4]

THE TYPES

As was the case with other cities, autonomy (granted most probably in 81/0 (below, n. 12), soon led to the production of civic tetradrachms. The types were the same throughout the period of minting.

Obv. Bust of Tyche r., wearing turreted crown and veil; fillet border.

Rev. Zeus seated l. on throne, holding on extended r. hand Nike who offers him a wreath; the whole within laurel wreath.

The obverse type, the turreted bust of Tyche, is common to the autonomous city coinages of this region. It first appeared on the issues of Aradus from 138/7 and, undoubtedly influenced by the prolific coinage of this city, the bust of Tyche was adopted by Seleucia Pieria and Laodicea as well as the two small Cilician mints of Aegeae and Elaeusa for their issues of civic tetradrachms.[5] However, while the obverse was encircled by a line of dots at Aradus, the other mints used the Seleucid fillet border.

The reverse type of the seated Zeus Nicephorus is more surprising. During the second century Poseidon seems to have been the main god of Laodicea (see n. 3). As far as I can see, the choice of Zeus for the reverse was influenced by the contemporary coinage of the Syrian

[4] On the vicissitudes of Seleucia and Laodicea during this period, see H. Seyrig, "Sur les ères de quelques villes de Syrie," *Antiquités syriennes* 4 (1953), no. 42 (= *Syria* 27 [1950]), pp. 92–98 (hereafter, Seyrig, "Ères").

[5] For the common issues of Aradus and Seleucia see, for instance, the relevant volumes of *BMC*. The four known tetradrachms of Aegeae are listed by H. Bloesch, "Tetradrachms of Aegeae (Cilicia)," *Essays Thompson* (Wetteren, 1979), pp. 1–7; on p. 2 with n. 2, mention is made of the three known specimens from Elaeusa.

capital, Antioch on the Orontes. Here the seated Zeus became the constant reverse type on the royal and pseudo-royal silver coinage since ca. 105.[6] He also occupied the reverse on most of the local Antiochene bronzes, issued from 92/1 onwards. The laurel wreath surrounding the type and inscription is again derived from the royal issues of Antioch, where it had been a permanent feature since 121/0. The same device was used at Aradus (in imitation of Antiochus VII?), Seleucia, and the two Cilician mints.

INSCRIPTIONS

The main inscription on the tetradrachms of Laodicea appears on the reverse in two lines and in three different forms:

a. ΛΑΟΔΙΚΕΩΝ/ΤΗΣ ΙΕΡΑΣ; to l., ΑΥΤΟΝΟΜΟΥ
b. ΛΑΟΔΙΚΕΩΝ/ΤΩΝ ΠΡΟΣ; to l., ΘΑΛΑΣΣΗ
c. ʹΟΥΛΙΕΩΝ/ΤΩΝ ΚΑΙ; to l., ΛΑΟΔΙΚΕΩΝ.

The first form of the inscription, with the epithets "sacred" and "autonomous" added to the name of the citizen body, is not special to Laodicea. A similar formula occurs on the silver tetradrachms of Seleucia Pieria, Tripolis and Elaeusa, issued between 105 and 65. It also occurs on bronzes of the first century from Aegeae and Mopsus in Cilicia and Apamea in Syria. The Aradians placed only their own name on their silver, while the southern Phoenician cities of Tyre and Sidon preferred the adjectives "sacred" and "inviolable," ΙΕΡΑΣ ΚΑΙ ΑΣΥΛΟΥ.[7] Our formula thus seems to occur within a limited geographical area comprising the former Seleucid districts of Syria and Cilicia.

The second inscription is more neutral, providing only the geographical information necessary to distinguish this Laodicea from the other

[6] E. T. Newell, *The Seleucid Mint of Antioch* (New York, 1918), p. 105, nos. 405 ff. For the dating of the beginning of Antiochus VIII's fourth series to ca. 105 instead of 108 see H. Seyrig, *Trésors du Levant anciens et nouveaux* (Paris, 1973), p. 102.

[7] On the meaning of this formula, see H. Seyrig, "Les rois Séleucides et la concession de l'asylie," *Antiquités syriennes* 3 (1946) (= *Syria* 20, 1939), pp. 1–5.

Seleucid foundations of the same name.[8] The third inscription refers to an important event in the history of the city, its refoundation by Caesar in 47 under the new name of Julia-Laodicea. This great honor was to a certain degree neutralized by the fact that from this time all reference to the city's autonomy disappears from its coinage.

CONTROL MARKS

The issues were also differentiated by control marks and dates. The control marks commonly found on Hellenistic coins, consisting of monograms, initials or small symbols, served to identify the officials responsible for the various issues.[9] At Laodicea two or three different persons were involved. Ordinarily officials placed their mark below the throne, but sometimes (when more than one was active) also in the left field. The letters in the exergue seem to have a somewhat different function. Some of them can be followed over many years—KA for instance from year 11 to year 31, and ΣΕ from year 12 to year 30—while the most frequent monogram placed under the throne, [monogram], only occurs from year 11 to year 17. An explanation might be that the place under the throne was used by ordinary mint officials, while the exergue was reserved for a kind of shop or officina designation, the administrative subdivision of the mint being represented by its head of staff.[10] The number of subdivisions might change according to the

[8] This was the inscription on the municipal bronzes of the second century (above, n. 3).

[9] Recent attempts at reading another meaning into these marks are not convincing. Identifications with historical persons are, as a rule, quite arbitrary, and the theory of Thomas Fischer, "Johannes Hyrkan I auf Tetradrachmen Antiochos' VII?" *Zeitschrift des Deutschen Palästina-Vereins* 91 (1975), p. 195, that the monograms might indicate the source of the bullion or payments of taxes from individuals and communities ("Die Beizeichen der hellenistischen Münzen könnten m. E. die Herkunft des Silbers bzw. der Prägung angeben, ob es sich um eine Liturgie, einen Tribut oder sonst eine Zahlung einer Person oder Gemeinde handelt") is quite unacceptable as a general principle.

[10] A division into officinae has been suspected at Aradus. See G. F. Hill in *BMC-Phoenicia*, pp. xxxiii–xxxiv, and H. Seyrig, *Notes on Syrian Coins*, ANSNNM 119 (1950), p. 23.

needs of production. For most of the period between years 12 and 31 of the first era two officinae were used, but in years 17, 23, 24 and 31 their number was increased to three. Even in these cases, however, the whole production was controlled by one official, who placed his monogram below the throne. In favor of the officina theory we might add that the obverse dies tend to stay within one officina. Exceptions are few (obverse dies 19, used with ΚΑ and ΣΕ; 21, with ΙΩ and ΣΕ; and 22, occurring with ΚΑ and ΝΙ). At the beginning, the different style of the obverse dies suggests that each officina used its own die engraver. Thus one engraver produced obverse dies 7, 11, and 13, all used exclusively with ΚΑ (see Plates 14, 8–11, and 15, 15–17), while dies 9, 10, and 12, showing a quite different style, appear at the ΣΕ officina (Plate 14, 12–14). It is only with the increased production during year 17 that this distinction breaks down. Obverse die 14 (Plate 15, 18) is of typical ΣΕ style, but was nevertheless used by the ΚΑ officina.

THE DATES

In the left field of the reverse are one or two letters used as numerals. They are commonly assumed to indicate years reckoned by a civic era, and, in view of the predilection throughout the Syro-Phoenician region for dating the various coin issues during the hellenistic period, this seems a priori the most likely explanation.

However, it soon appears that two different eras were used. The tetradrachms with inscription *a* show the dates 1, 4, 6–7, 10–13, 15–18, 20, 23–27, 30–31 and 33. The few tetradrachms with inscription *b* are all dated to year 1, and the issues with the third form of inscription carry the numerals 2–3, 5, 9, 18–19 and 29–32. This last series is the easiest to deal with. The coin legend shows, by the title ΙΟΥΛΙΕΩΝ, that the coins must be dated by a Caesarian era, and an inscription of A.D. 221 provides evidence that the era started in the year 48/7.[11]

[11] *IGLS* 4 (1955), pp. 26–29, no. 1265. Cf. Seyrig, "Ères," p. 93, with n. 1 (wrongly giving the date of the inscription as A.D. 211).

Consequently the coins with inscription *c* can be securely dated between 47/6 (year 2) and 17/6 (year 32).

The other era used has been identified by H. Seyrig with an era of independence, starting in 82/1 or, more probably, in 81/0, reckoning backward from the introduction of the Caesarian era.[12] In this paper the first year of the civic era has been equated with 81/0 and the following dates read accordingly, but it should be noted that in theory these dates may all be a year too late, although I find it rather unlikely.

A problem is left regarding the coins dated year 1. They show two different forms of inscriptions (*a* and *b*), and might be thought to belong to the very beginning of the series, 81/0. However, their officina designation and other control marks clearly relate them to the coins inscribed Julia-Laodicea (legend *c*). Moreover, one obverse die (no. 26) was carried over from year 1 (issue 21a) to the issues with legend *c*, dated years 2–9, showing beyond any doubt that this first year also belongs to the Caesarian era and must be equated with 48/7. We thus get the following progression. After the news of the battle of Pharsalus (June 48) had reached Syria, the old civic era of Laodicea was replaced by the Caesarian. At some point during the troubled year 48/7, doubt about the autonomous status of the city under the new political circumstances was apparently raised, resulting in an issue with the neutral and inoffensive designation "Laodicea on the Sea" (issue no. 21b).[13] During Caesar's visit to Syria in 47 the problems were settled, and Laodicea received the honor of being allowed to rename herself, adding the name of the dictator to her own and henceforth appearing as "Julia-Laodicea." This title becomes permanent on her coins from the second year of the Caesarian era, 47/6.

WEIGHTS AND DIE POSITION

I have registered a total of 136 weights, but apparently two different weight standards were used. From year 5 of the Caesarian era (44/3)

[12] Seyrig, "Ères," pp. 93–94.

[13] The place of this issue *between* the coins inscribed with legend *a* and legend *c* was already perceived by G. F. Hill, *NC* 1925, pp. 15–16. For another use of the "neutral" legend *b* in 42/1, see H. Seyrig, "Ères," p. 96.

the coins of Laodicea were struck according to the Ptolemaic weight standard with a tetradrachm of ca. 14.30 g. This was the weight standard also used at Tyre, Sidon and Ascalon for their autonomous issues of the second and first centuries. There are only 14 coins approximating this weight: the two heaviest weigh 14.16 g and 14.01 g, while all the others are well below 14.00 g. The weights of the 122 coins struck before 46/5 are presented in Fig. 1.

FIG. 1. Frequency Table of Laodicean Coins

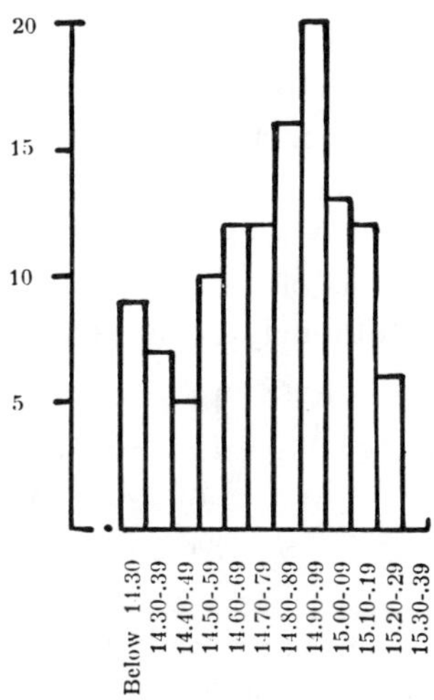

The peak of the frequency table occurs in the interval 14.90–.99 g which, with the addition of ca. 1%, gives a standard weight of the tetradrachm of ca. 15.10 g. This is the weight standard used by Aradus for her civic tetradrachms from 138/7. It was imitated by Seleucia Pieria, Tripolis and Elaeusa as well as by Laodicea. At Aradus and Tripolis the weight standard was ca. 15.30 g, while Seleucia used the same, slightly lighter variant as Laodicea.[14]

[14] On the Aradian coin standard see O. Mørkholm, "The Attic Coin Standard in the Levant during the Hellenistic Period," *Numismatica antiqua Paulo Naster oblata* (Louvain, 1982), pp. 144–45 where I have argued that it should be regarded as a separate standard, not just called "reduced" Attic.

The die position of the coins is upright or twelve o'clock. This indicates the use of fixed or adjusted dies, a technical feature that seems to have been first used in the Levant and from there to have spread to the other parts of the hellenistic world.

THE DIES

In the appendix all the variant monogram combinations on the tetradrachms known to me are listed. The individual obverse dies used have been identified and numbered consecutively from 1 to 34. The reverse dies are much more numerous and have not been recorded individually. In the column farthest to the right, the number of specimens known to me has been noted for each variant. It appears that 145 specimens are recorded, struck from 34 obverse dies, giving a ratio of obverse dies to specimens of nearly 1:4.3. The distribution is, however, very uneven. The total may be broken up in to three subdivisions:

Years 4–20	(78/7–62/1)	18 obv. dies,	47 spec.	1:2.6
Years 23–33, 1–9	(59/8–40/39)	10 obv. dies,	89 spec.	1:8.9
Years 18–32	(31/0–17/6)	6 obv. dies,	9 spec.	1:1.5
		34 obv. dies.	145 spec.	

From these figures it becomes apparent that this material is much more representative for the middle period than for the beginning and the end of the series. We may assume with some confidence that the record of obverse dies is practically complete for the years 59/8–40/9, where the index figure of specimens per obverse die is 8.2. For the other periods with their low index figures new obverse dies and even new variants may still be expected to turn up.[15] The considerable increase in recorded specimens for the middle period is due to the fact that all the known hoard material shows a strong concentration within these years.

[15] On the statistical background for the index figure see Wayne E. McGovern, "Missing Die Probabilities, Expected Die Production and the Index Figure," *ANSMN* (1980), pp. 209–23.

Another interesting question is the long life of some of the obverse dies. Obverse die 7 was used in years 11, 12 and 15, obverse die 13 in years 17, 18 and 20. Obverse dies 19 and 25 were striking coins in years 23 and 25 and in years 31 and 33 respectively. While these instances can be paralleled by material from other coin series, the issues of Laodicea contain two examples of exceptionally long-lived dies. Obverse die 22 appears in years 24–27 and 30-31, that is to say it was in active use over a period of eight years. As far as we know, coin production at Laodicea was stopped in two of these years, 28 and 29, but nevertheless the lifetime of this die is quite extraordinary. Just as astonishing is the longevity of obverse die 26 which we find in years 1–3, 5 and 9 of the Caesarian era. Again there are some breaks in the annual sequence, years when the mint presumably was not functioning, but again a life span of nine years for an obverse die is something of a record.

In another paper dealing with the lifetime of obverse dies in other hellenistic coin series[16] I have come to the rather obvious conclusion that the longevity of the obverse dies depended on the production rate at the mint in question. When the mint was small and coinage not necessarily produced every year, only a single pair of dies was used. The obverse die might then be retained for several years. The longevity of certain obverse dies thus becomes an indication of small and sporadic minting during these years. The lifetime of the obverse dies is in inverse relationship to the production rate of the coinage in question.

CIRCULATION

Tetradrachms from Laodicea have been found in three hoards.

IGCH 1581. This hoard had more than 70 tetradrachms from years 76/5 to 44/3. Seventeen specimens were acquired by the American Numismatic Society and four by the British Museum. According to *IGCH* they were found with silver coins of Seleucia Pieria, Aradus and

[16] O. Mørkholm, "The Life of Obverse Dies in the Hellenistic Period," *Studies in Numismatic Method* (Cambridge), pp. 11–21.

Tyre. It is, however, remarkable, not to say peculiar, that the series of the two last named cities according to the record stop in 61/0 and 63/2 respectively. This might be taken to indicate that Noe was after all right in regarding these coins as deriving from two different hoards one comprising the coins of Laodicea, and the other, buried nearly 20 years earlier, the remaining coinage.[17] The find place of the first lot was, most probably, Latakia itself.

IGCH 1582 = Seyrig, *Trésors du Levant* no. 36. Two tetradrachms of Laodicea (year 31 of civic era, year 2 of Caesarian era) were found at Tartus (Antaradus) with 16 coins of Aradus, the last of which was struck in 44/3.

Coin Hoards 6, no. 50. In 1980 a hoard of Laodicean silver began to appear on the market. It was said to have been found somewhere in Syria in 1979 and to have contained ca. 200 specimens. As far as I know, the dates ranged from year 11 to year 30 of the civic era (71/0–52/1).[18] No other coinages are known to belong to the same find.

The information from these three hoards is not very exciting. The find places indicate a local circulation and the use of the Aradian weight standard would have tended to keep the coins within a rather narrow circulation area comprising northern Phoenicia, Syria Seleucis, and eastern Cilicia.

CONCLUSION

We may now attempt to draw a general picture of the production of autonomous tetradrachms in the late second and first centuries within the former Seleucid kingdom and, on the basis of the preceding detailed discussion, try to place the silver coinage of Laodicea in its proper context.

[17] S. P. Noe, *A Bibliography of Greek Coin Hoards*, 2nd ed., ANSNNM 78 (1937), nos. 604 and 871. The distinction between the two hoards is also found in a letter of July 1927 from the dealer Roupen Ezadjian, Beirut, who sold coins from both lots to the ANS.

[18] I have listed a total of 49 coins as probably deriving from this hoard; year 11, 2; year 12, 1; year 17, 5; year 18, 1; year 20, 3; year 23, 18; year 24, 3; year 25, 7; year 26, 2; year 30, 7. This includes the 16 specimens listed in *Coin Hoards* 6.

In 138/7 Aradus started producing a prolific series of autonomous tetradrachms, struck on a local standard of ca. 15.30 g. In 126/5 Tyre was rewarded with the privilege of striking civic silver coins, but adopted the Ptolemaic weight with a tetradrachm of ca. 14.30 g. The same standard was used by Sidon, after she obtained her autonomy in 112/1. Down to this time the royal issues of Antioch and other Seleucid mints maintained an Attic standard of ca. 16.80 g for the tetradrachm although with a tendency towards a slight and gradual further reduction. In 109/8 Seleucia Pieria was declared autonomous, and her first silver tetradrachms appeared in year 4 (105/4), struck on a somewhat light Aradian standard of ca. 15.10 g. At about this time the royal issues of Antioch were suddenly reduced to ca. 16.30 g for the tetradrachms.[19] More important is the fact that precisely during the years 107/6 to 101/0 the production at Aradus seems to have stopped or, at least, to have been reduced dramatically.[20] This may have induced the Pierians to start their own production in order to fill the void. Apparently, the Aradian silver had already proved useful and acceptable within the region.

Some time between 105 and 95 Tripolis became autonomous. Her civic tetradrachms, dated between year 3 and year 32 of her local era, were struck on the full Aradian standard. The few and undated civic tetradrachms of Elaeusa in Cilicia were struck on the same standard. They belong most probably to the first decades of the first century. The era of Ascalon started in 104/3. Her tetradrachms, with complimentary portraits of Egyptian rulers, are dated between year 20 (85/4) and year 66 (39/8), the last with a splendid portrait of Cleopatra VII.[21]

[19] See n. 14.

[20] For Aradus I have consulted *BMCPhoenicia;* Babelon, *Les Perses achéménides;* D. C. Baramki, *The Coin Collection of the American University of Beirut Museum. Palestine and Phoenicia* (Beirut, 1974); J. Rouvier's list in *JIAN* 3 (1900), pp. 237ff.; as well as the collections in Copenhagen and New York. According to this material during the years 107/6 to 101/0 (Aradian era 153 to 159) there was no minting of tetradrachms except a single specimen from 103/2 (Aradian era 157) recorded by Rouvier under no. 272 as from his own collection. Rouvier's collection was acquired by E. T. Newell, but the coin seems not to be at the ANS now.

[21] For the coinage of Ascalon see A. Baldwin Brett, "A New Cleopatra Tetradrachm of Ascalon," *AJA* 41 (1937), pp. 452–63.

Naturally, these coins were struck on the Ptolemaic standard also used at Tyre and Sidon.

With the advent of Tigranes in 83 political and economic changes occurred. Seleucia was hostile to the Armenian king and closed its gates against him.[22] Its production of silver coins came to an end precisely in year 26 (84/3). At Tripolis there is a gap in the silver coinage between years 18 and 30 which may correspond approximately to the reign of Tigranes. On the other hand, Aradus and Tyre continued their minting on a quite extensive scale. And, as already mentioned, Laodicea eagerly took over the position of Seleucia as the leading seaport on the Syrian coast. Having received a grant of autonomy from Tigranes in 81/0 she began coining her tetradrachms in year 4 (78/7). The first coinages seem to have been rather small, but from year 12 (70/9) two officinae were functioning. The weight standard used was the light Aradian standard of Seleucia Pieria. During the same time the Attic weight tetradrachms of Tigranes, struck at Antioch, dropped to ca. 15.60–16.00 g, i.e. they were still recognizably heavier than the coins of Aradian weight.[23]

In spite of the fact that the opposition of Seleucia to Tigranes recommended the city strongly to Pompey when he organized the Syrian province in 64–63,[24] it had no effect on the monetary situation. Seleucia did not resume the minting of silver coins, while Laodicea in 65/4 increased her production, using for the first time five obverse dies and three officinae during a single year.

Down to year 33 (49/8) coin production was fairly continuous at Laodicea. In years 23 (59/8, 24 (58/7) and 31 (51/0) three officinae were used, but the longevity of some obverse dies, especially no. 22, suggests that only a limited amount of coin was actually struck. During the 20 years from 59/8 to 40/39, the period when the coinage is best represented (see above, p. 96), 10 obverse dies were used: not a very impressive number, which again indicates a rather small production.

[22] On Tigranes in Syria see the positive statement of Justinus 40.1.4. Strabo 16.2.8 (C 751) mentions the opposition of Seleucia to his rule.

[23] See my article mentioned in n. 14. The weights of the coins of Tigranes from Antioch are recorded by P. Z. Bedoukian, *Coinage of the Artaxiads of Armenia* (London, 1978), pp. 49–54, nos. 17–42.

[24] Strabo 16.2.8 (C 751).

Caesar's victory in the civil war had important repercussions in Syria. During the year after Pharsalus, 48/7, Laodicea first adopted a new era and then changed the coin inscription. The proud designation of the city as "sacred and autonomous" was dropped in favor of the colorless geographical description "on the sea." It is a natural inference that some loss of favor with the Roman government was incurred or feared. However this may be, the political situation soon changed for the better. During his stay in Syria in 47 Caesar allowed the city to add his own family name to her old name, a singular distinction which may have amounted to a refoundation of the city.[25] From year 2 of the Caesarian era (47/6) the silver tetradrachms were issued in the name of the inhabitants of Julia-Laodicea.

Further troubles, however, were looming ahead. In 44/3 Aradus issued the last of its long series of tetradrachms,[26] and in the same year Laodicea changed to the Ptolemaic standard. Thus the Aradian standard disappeared completely after having served as a regional coin standard for nearly 100 years. The Ptolemaic standard continued as did a reduced Attic standard at the mint of Antioch.[27] The changes must bear some relationship to the unsettled political conditions after the murder of Caesar. In the spring of 43 Laodicea was besieged and captured by Cassius, while the Caesarian Dolabella killed himself.[28] Issue 24 of Laodicea, the first to be struck on the Ptolemaic standard, was in all probability issued by Dolabella. It is a tempting hypothesis to connect the burial of the Latakia hoard (see above, p. 97-98) with the siege and capture of the city in this very year. Moreover, a bronze coinage of year 7 (42/1), inscribed "Laodicea ad Mare," has convincingly been

[25] On Caesar in Syria and Cilicia see *Bellum Alexandrinum* 65–66.

[26] The issue of tetradrachms at Aradus became quite sporadic after 60/9. Only one specimen of 44/3 (Aradian era 216) is known: cf. H. Seyrig, *Trésors du Levant anciens et nouveaux*, p. 107, trésor 36, no. 15.

[27] On the provincial silver coinage of Antioch between ca. 60 and 20 see E. T. Newell, "The Pre-Imperial Coinage of Roman Antioch," *NC* 1919, pp. 69–113; A. R. Bellinger, "Crassus and Cassius at Antioch," *NC* 1944, pp. 59–61: Seyrig, "Ères," pp. 81–82. The weight standard was still well above the former Aradian standard for the coins struck before 37.

[28] Appian, *Bell. civ.* 4.60–62; Strabo 16.2.9 (C 752); a report from the siege in Cicero, *ad fam.* 12.13.4.

ascribed by Seyrig to a time when the city was still under the authority of Cassius who would hardly have allowed the continued use of the dead dictator's name.[29]

After the eventful year 44/3 there is a gap in the silver coinage until year 9 (40/9), when it was resumed under the rule of Mark Antony. It is worthy of notice that the obverse die used for this issue (no. 26) had been used since year 1 of the Caesarian era and appears in all the intervening years from which a silver coinage is known. As already mentioned, the lifetime of this die is extraordinary.

After 40/9 the issue of silver at Laodicea becomes sporadic. Two issues of years 18 (31/0) and 19 (30/9) may be connected with the establishment of Octavian's rule in the East. Finally four issues of years 29–32 (20/9–17/6) mark the end of the series of silver tetradrachms of Laodicea. The first year, significantly, is the one which Augustus himself spent in the East, dealing with the frontier problems and receiving the Roman standard from the Parthians. Why the issues continued for three more years is difficult to surmise.[30] Already during the 30s the silver coinages of Sidon and Ascalon had come to an end. The only civic silver coinage in the Levant which continued further into the Imperial period was that of Tyre. Its prolific series lasted until about A.D. 60, well into the reign of Nero.

[29] Seyrig, "Ères," p. 97.

[30] The provincial silver of Antioch probably also came to an end in 17/6. See E. T. Newell, "The Pre-Imperial Coinage of Roman Antioch," *NC* 1919, p. 113.

APPENDIX

Variant	Year		L. Field	Below Throne	Exergue	Obv. Die Nos.	No. of Specimens
Legend *a*							
1	4	(78/7)	Δ	⊙	ΘΕ	1–2	2 (Plate 13, 1–2)
2a	6	(76/5)	ϛ	[monogram]	?	3	1 (Plate 13, 3)
b	6	(76/5)	[monogram] ϛ	[monogram]	ΣΕ	3	1 (Plate 13, 4)
3	7	(75/4)	Ζ	[monogram]	?	4	1 (Plate 13, 5)
4	10	(72/1)	Ι	ΑΣ	ΘΕ	5–6	3 (Plate 13, 6-7)
5	11	(71/0)	ΑΙ [monogram]	[monogram]	ΚΑ	7	5 (Plate 14, 8)
6a	12	(70/9)	ΙΒ	[monogram]	ΚΑ	7	2 (Plate 14, 9)
b	12	(70/9)	ΙΒ	[monogram]	ΣΕ	8	1 The Hague
7	13	(69/8)	ΓΙ	[monogram]	ΣΕ	9	1 (Plate 14, 12)
8a	15	(67/6)	ΕΙ	[monogram]	ΚΑ	7	2 (Plate 14, 10)
b	15	(67/6)	ΕΙ	[monogram]	ΣΕ	10	1 (Plate 14, 13)
9a	16	(66/5)	ϛ Ι	[monogram]	ΚΑ	11[a]	2 (Plate 14, 11)
b	16	(66/5)	ϛ Ι	[monogram]	ΣΕ	12	1 (Plate 14, 14)
10a	17	(65/4)	ΖΙ	[monogram]	ΚΑ	13–15	8 (Plate 15, 15, 18)
b	17	(65/4)	ΖΙ	[monogram]	ΣΕ	16	2 (Plate 15, 19)
c	17	(65/4)	ΖΙ	[monogram]	ΑΣ	17	7 (Plate 15, 21)
11a	18	(64/3)	ΗΙ	ΑΣ	ΚΑ	13	2 (Plate 15, 16)
b	18	(64/3)	ΗΙ	ΑΣ	ΣΕ	16	1 (Plate 15, 20)
12	20	(62/1)	Κ	[monogram]	ΚΑ	13; 18	4 (Plate 15, 17)

Variant	Year		L. Field	Below Throne	Exergue	Obv. Die Nos.	No. of Specimens
13a	23	(59/8)	ΓΚ	[monogram]	ΚΑ	19–20	14 (Plate 16, 22, 25)
b	23	(59/8)	ΓΚ	[monogram]	ΣΕ	19	10 (Plate 16, 23)
c	23	(59/8)	ΓΚ	[monogram]	ΞΩ	21	3 (Plate 16, 26)
14a	24	(58/7)	ΔΚ	[monogram]	ΚΑ	22	3 (Plate 16, 28)
b	24	(58/7)	ΔΚ	[monogram]	ΣΕ	21	2 (Plate 16, 27)
15a	25	(57/6)	ΕΚ	[monogram]	ΚΑ	22	7 (Plate 17, 29)
b	25	(57/6)	ΕΚ	[monogram]	ΣΕ	19	2 (Plate 16, 24)
16	26	(56/5)	ϛΚ	[monogram]	ΚΑ	22	2 (Plate 17, 30)
17	27	(55/4)	ΙΚ	[monogram]	?	22	3 (Plate 17, 31)
18a	30	(52/1)	Λ ΙΣ	[monogram]	ΚΑ	22	10 (Plate 17, 33)
b	30	(52/1)	Λ ΙΣ	[monogram]	ΣΕ	23–24	7 (Plate 17, 32)
19a	31	(51/0)	ΑΛ ΙΗ	[monogram]	ΚΑ	22	2 (Plate 17, 34)
b	31	(51/0)	ΑΛ ΙΗ	[monogram]	ΝΙ	22	1 (Plate 17, 35)
c	31	(51/0)	ΑΛ ΙΗ	[monogram]	ΑΝ	25	3 (Plate 18, 36)
20a	33	(49/8)	ΓΛ ΙΗ	[monogram]	ΑΝ	25	1 New York
b	33	(49/8)	ΓΛ	ΙΗ	ΑΝ	25	1 (Plate 18, 37)

Variant	*Year*	*L. Field*	*Below Throne*	*Exergue*	*Obv. Die Nos.*	*No. of Specimens*
21a	1 (48/7)	Α [monogram]	[monogram]	ΚΔ	26	1 (Plate 18, 40)
Legend *b*						
21b	1 (48/7)	Α Ι/Η	[monogram]	ΚΔ	27–28	5 (Plate 18, 38, 39)
Legend *c*						
22	2 (47/6)	Β Δ	[monogram]	ΚΔ	26	2 (Plate 18, 41)
23	3 (46/5)	Γ ΑΣ	Δ	ΚΔ	26	4 (Plate 18, 42)
24	5 (44/3)	Ε ΑΛ	[monogram]	ΚΔ	26	2 (Plate 19, 43)
25	9 (40/9)	Θ ΕΥ	ΘΕ	ΔΙ	26	3 (Plate 19, 44)
26	18 (31/0)	ΗΙ ΘΕ	ΜΕ	ΛΥ	29	1 (Plate 19, 45)
27	19 (30/9)	ΘΙ ΖΩ	ΜΕ	ΛΥ	30	1 Vienna
28	29 (20/9)	ΘΚ ΔΙ	ΘΕ	ΓΛ	31	1 (Plate 19, 46)
29	30 (19/8)	Λ ΔΙ	ΘΕ	ΓΛ	32	4 (Plate 19, 47)
30	31 (18/7)	ΑΛ ΔΙ	ΘΕ	ΓΛ	33	1 (Plate 19, 48)
31	32 (17/6)	ΒΛ ΜΕ	ΑΠ	ΓΛ	34	1 (Plate 19, 49)

[a] Obverse die 11 may be a recut version of obverse die 7.

KEY TO PLATES

Most variants are illustrated as well as all obverse dies except nos. 8, 15, 18, 24 and 30.

Plate,	*No.*	*Varient*	*Obv. Die*	*Location*
13.	1.	1	1	Vienna 27777
	2.	1	2	Paris 1064
	3.	2a	3	New York, ANS, ex Latakia hoard (*IGCH* 1581)
	4.	2b	3	Paris, du Clercq 274
	5.	3	4	Paris 1065
	6.	4	5	Paris 1066
	7.	4	6	Paris, Delepierre 2983
14.	8.	5	7	Münz. u. Med. 429, Jan. 1981, 22
	9.	6a	7	London, *BMCGalatia*, p. 247, 4
	10.	8a	7	London, BM acq. 1926
	11.	9a	11	Paris 1067
	12.	7	9	Vienna 36344
	13.	8b	10	New York, ANS
	14.	9b	12	New York, ANS
15.	15.	10a	13	Münz. u. Med. 267, August 1966, 4
	16.	11a	13	Brussels, *Coll. de Hirsch* 1730
	17.	12	13	New York, ANS
	18.	10a	14	New York, ANS
	19.	10b	16	Berlin, ex Löbbecke 1906
	20.	11b	16	New York, ANS
	21.	10c	17	Munich
16.	22.	13a	19	Copenhagen, ex 1979 hoard
	23.	13b	13	New York, ANS
	24.	15b	19	Copenhagen, ex 1979 hoard
	25.	13a	20	B. Peus Sale 303, Oct. 1981, 288, ex 1979 hoard
	26.	13c	21	Paris R.1681
	27.	14c	21	Copenhagen, ex 1979 hoard
	28.	14a	22	Copenhagen, ex 1979 hoard
17.	29.	15a	22	New York, ANS, ex Latakia hoard (*IGCH* 1581)
	30.	16	22	Bonham/Vecchi 1, May 1980, 207, ex 1979 hoard
	31.	17	22	Copenhagen, ex 1979 hoard
	32.	18b	23	Paris R.1683

	33.	18a	22	Copenhagen, ex 1979 hoard
	34.	19a	22	New York, ANS, ex Latakia hoard (*IGCH* 1581)
	35.	19b	22	New York, ANS, ex Latakia hoard (*IGCH* 1581)
18.	36.	19c	25	London, *BCMGalatia*, p. 247, 7
	37.	20b	25	New York, ANS, ex Latakia hoard (*IGCH* 1581)
	38.	21b	27	Paris 1060
	39.	21b	28	New York, ANS, ex Latakia hoard (*IGCH* 1581)
	40.	21a	26	New York, ANS, ex Latakia hoard (*IGCH* 1581)
	41.	22	26	Paris R.1684
	42.	23	26	London, BM acq. 1924, ex Latakia hoard (*IGCH* 1581); *NC* 1925, p. 14, 47
19.	43.	24	26	London, BM acq. 1924, ex Latakia hoard (*IGCH* 1581); *NC* 1925, p. 15, 48
	44.	25	26	Berlin, ex Imhoof-Blumer 1900
	45.	26	29	Paris 1081
	46.	28	31	Paris 1080
	47.	29	32	*SNGCop* 36, 325
	48.	30	33	New York, ANS
	49.	31	34	Berlin, ex Fox 1873. Pierced

ANSMN 28 (1983)

ROME AND ALEXANDRIA: THE MINTING OF EGYPTIAN TETRADRACHMS UNDER SEVERUS ALEXANDER

(Plate 20)

Andrew Burnett and Paul Craddock

In the past it has usually been assumed that a coin which bears a city's name was minted in that city from dies produced by the engravers at that city's mint, but in the last decade or so there have been a number of studies which have shown that, even though a coin may appear to come from a particular mint, the evidence of style or die links may suggest that it was in fact minted elsewhere. Kraft,[1] for instance, drew attention to the numerous links of dies and style between the obverses of "Greek Imperials" from different cities and interpreted these as showing that most of the imperial civic coinage of Asia Minor was made at only a few centralized mints. Analogously, Baldus[2] pointed out that the Syrian tetradrachms of the Roman emperor Philip fall into two stylistic groups: one group of local style have the name ANTIOXIA on the reverse, and the other, with the name MON VRB, have a finer style, like that of the antoniniani and denarii of the mint

[1] K. Kraft, *Das System der kaiserzeitlichen Münzprägung in Kleinasien* (Berlin, 1972).

We would like to thank R. Preston for taking the samples of the coins. P. C. is responsible for the scientific content of this paper and A. B. for the numismatic.

[2] H. R. Baldus, *MON(eta) VRB(is)—ANTIOXIA: Rom und Antiochia als Prägestätten syrischer Tetradrachmen des Philippus Arabs* (Frankfurt, 1969).

of Rome. Baldus argued that MON VRB (= Moneta Urbis, the mint of Rome) coins were struck at Rome and then shipped out to Syria.

The idea of coins being made in one place and then transported to another to be issued into circulation has not won immediate or universal acceptance, and scholars have suggested other explanations for the phenomena noted by Kraft and Baldus. The die links between "Greek Imperials," for instance, might show only that obverse dies travelled from city to city, perhaps taken by the itinerant artists who produced them. Similarly the dies of the MON VRB tetradrachms might have been engraved at Rome, then taken to Antioch and only there used to strike coins.[3] There are many other cases where a similar alternative explanation is possible, but here we wish to consider only one case, since it allows us to conclude with certainty that coins, and not dies, were shipped.

This case concerns the Egyptian tetradrachms minted by Severus Alexander (A.D. 222–35) in the fourth, fifth and seventh[4] Alexandrian years of his reign. Since Dattari[5] first drew attention to these coins in 1903, scholars[6] have been aware that the coins of these years fall into two groups, each of which has a number of distinctive features.

First, one group continues the style and appearance of tetradrachms minted by Elagabalus and by Alexander in his early years (Plate 20, 1–3; cf. 7). The other group consists of coins of a finer style, and the portrait of the emperor is exactly like that on denarii minted at Rome (Plate 20, 4–6; cf. 8).

3 E.g. A. Johnston "New Problems for Old," *NC* 1974, p. 205, and "The Intermittent Imperials," *NC* 1980, pp. 206–7 and 209; I. Carradice and M. Price in R. A. G. Carson, P. Berghaus and N. M. Lowick, eds., *A Survey of Numismatic Research 1972–77* (Berne, 1979), p. 118; D. R. Walker, *The Metrology of the Roman Silver Coinage* 3, BAR S40 (Oxford, 1978), Appendix 3.

4 There are no relevant coins of the sixth year, rather surprisingly. One can reject the idea that "seventh" is a mistake for "sixth," since the types of the seventh year include Julia Mamaea. She was replaced by Orbiana in the sixth year, and only returned to the Egyptian coinage in the seventh.

5 G. Dattari, "Appunti di Numismatica Alessandrina: XVI," *RIN* 1903, pp. 292–94.

6 J. G. Milne, "Some Alexandrian Coins," *Journal of Egyptian Archaeology* 4 (1917), p. 178; J. Vogt, *Die Alexandrinischen Münzen* (Stuttgart, 1924), pp. 184–85; Walker (above, no. 3), p. 159.

Second, the regnal years on Egyptian style coins are expressed as LΔ, LEL and Z, but on Roman style coins as L TETAPTOV, LΠEM-ΠTOV and LEBΔOMOY (Plate 20, 1–6).

Third, the busts and legends vary. On Egyptian style coins we find: 4th year, A KAI MAP AV(P) CEVHP AΛEΞANΔPOC-EVCEB, unbearded bust, draped and cuirassed from rear (Plate 20, 1); 5th year, A KAI MA AVP CEV AΛEΞANΔPOC EV, bust as before (Plate 20, 2); 7th year, A KAI MAP AV CEV AΛEΞANΔPOC EV, lightly bearded bust, cuirassed and seen from front (Plate 20, 3). The Roman style coins of all three years, however, have: A KAI M AVP CEOVHP AΛEΞANΔPOC EVCEB, lightly bearded bust, draped and seen from rear (Plate 20, 4–6). As well as the differences in legends and busts, the spelling[7] and letter forms[8] also vary.

Fourth, the reverse types diverge: although most of the types used on Roman style coins occur (even if rarely) on Egyptian style coins, the latter have many more which are not found on Roman style coins.[9] Even when a type is common to both groups it can be seen to be of quite different style (cf. Plate 20, 4 and 9).

These four stylistic features leave no doubt that there are two distinct groups of coins. One continues the style of earlier Alexandrian issues, while the other is quite different from them, but very similar to coins minted at Rome.

One never finds a combination of the two styles on different sides of the same coin, and there are also a number of physical differences in the way the coins were made. First, Egyptian style coins have a fixed

[7] CEVHP as opposed to CEVOHP.

[8] On Egyptian style coins the Ξ has a vertical upright, but on Roman Style coins a curved one.

[9] Roman style coins have, in year 4, a bust of Mamaea, a bust of Sarapis, Sarapis standing left, Sarapis seated left and a head of Zeus Ammon; in year 5, a bust of Mamaea, a bust of Orbiana, and the three Sarapis types; in year 7 the same types as year 4 except that the Sarapis bust is not recorded. Alexandrian coins of years 4 and 5 have most of these types, although Mamaea is usually, and Orbiana always, shown as a separate obverse. Many other types occur on Egyptian style coins of these years (see e.g. J. G. Milne, *Catalogue of Alexandrian Coins* [Oxford, 1971]), but in year 7 these are replaced with a new set of types, which have nothing in common with the Rome style coins.

die axis of 12 o'clock (or occasionally 11:30), but Roman style coins have an axis which is usually about 12 o'clock (varying between 11 and 1) or sometimes 6 o'clock (varying between 7 and 5),[10] i.e. the same as denarii minted at Rome. Second the coins are of different sizes. The Egyptian style coins are thicker and have a smaller diameter, as Fig. 1 shows. The weights, however, appear to be the same, as Fig. 2 shows, although the weights of the Roman style coins were less strictly controlled.[11] Finally the metallic composition of the two groups is slightly, but noticeably, different as is shown by the analyses in the Appendix. The Roman style coins contain small, but measurable, quantities of tin and zinc, the Egyptian have none; and the Roman style coins have a little more lead.

So although the two groups have almost exactly the same fineness (6%), the trace elements suggest that they were made from different stocks of metal.

These physical differences leave little doubt that the two groups were made in different places. One group continues the practice of Alexandria, the other shares a common style and die axis with the mint of Rome. We conclude that one group was made at Alexandria, and the other at Rome.[12] Both, however, were put into circulation in Egypt.[13]

This conclusion raises a number of general questions of interpretation. It is natural to ask, in the first place, how common it was for silver coins to be minted in one place and issued elsewhere. This is something a of crux in contemporary numismatics.[14] In the case of Egypt, the Roman style coins of Alexander stand out from the run of the mint, one of the most prolific minting operations of the ancient world, so it seems probable that it was exceptional for the Rome mint

[10] See J. Vogt (above, n. 6).

[11] Compare Dattari (above, n. 5), Walker (above, n. 3).

[12] Both Vogt and Walker seem to envisage the possibility of a section of the Roman mint working in Alexandria, but the different metallic composition of the two groups of coins rules this out.

[13] The billon tetradrachm only circulated in Egypt, where coins of both groups are found: see e.g. the hoard discussed below (n. 16).

[14] See e.g. M. Weder, "Zu den Arabia-Drachmen Trajans," *SM* 107 (Aug. 1977), pp. 47–61, A. Burnett, "Catalogues, Coins and Mints," review-article *JRS* 68 (1978), pp. 174–75, Carradice and Price (above, n. 3).

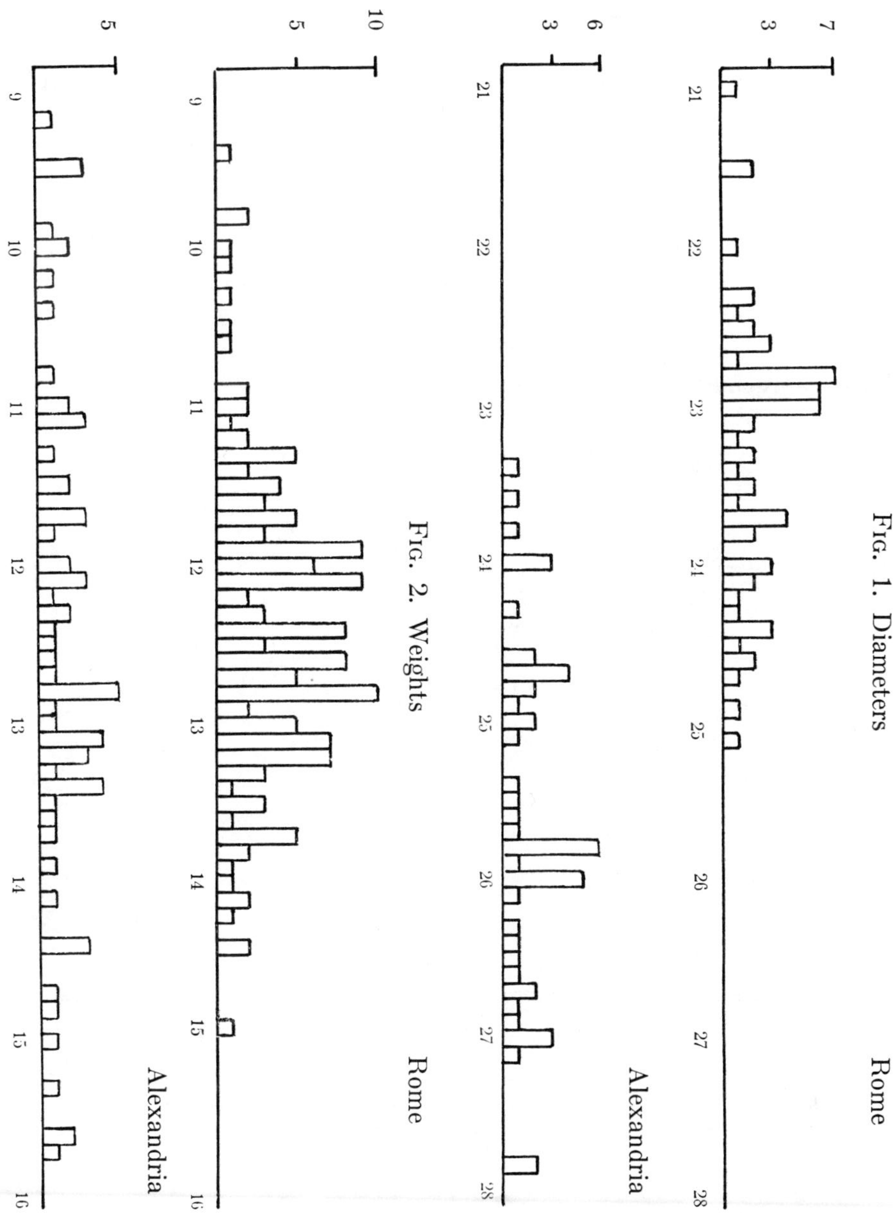

Fig. 1. Diameters

Fig. 2. Weights

to "help" the Alexandrian in this way. This case tends to support Baldus's interpretation of the MON VRB tetradrachms (as minted at Rome), and they again represent an exception to the history of the Antioch mint. We should see the problem not just in terms of Rome and the provincial mints, since one provincial mint could similarly mint coins for another province.[15] Probably the output of the big mints like Antioch and Alexandria was supplemented by other mints only occasionally. On the other hand, the smaller and more isolated issues of provincial silver may normally have been produced elsewhere (e.g. the Cretan, Cyrenaic and perhaps Arabian drachms of Trajan).

The second question is why Rome should have made tetradrachms for Egypt. To answer this one should look at the fluctuating quantities of tetradrachms produced under Alexander, as suggested by the Armenian cemetery hoard reported by Breccia.[16]

Year	*Number*
2:	41
3:	27
4:	59 + 8 Roman style
5:	51 + 16 Roman style
6:	28
7:	11 + 3 Roman style
8:	1
9:	0
10:	10
11:	28
12:	23
13:	17
14:	8

Sometimes it is possible to explain a prolific period of coinage by historical events, e.g. it has been suggested[17] that the high output of Alexan-

[15] Alexandria for Syria in Trajan's twelfth year: W. Wruck, *Die Syrische Provinzialprägung von Augustus bis Traian* (Stuttgart, 1931), no. 154.

[16] E. Breccia, "Un ripostiglio di monete imperiali alessandrine," *Bulletin de la Société Archéologique d'Alexandrie* (1920), pp. 230–50.

[17] J. G. Milne, *Catalogue of Alexandrian Coins* (Oxford, 1971), p. xxv.

dria from year 10 of Nero is connected with the use of Alexandria as a base for a proposed Ethiopian expedition and its subsequent use as a base during the Jewish revolt. The heavy coinage of the last years of Alexander's reign is presumably related to his journey to the east in 231 and the campaign against Ardaser (particularly so as he minted no tetradrachms from Antioch). The fairly high level of coining at the very beginning of his reign continues the pattern from the second year of Elagabalus, when the minting of silver in the east was switched from Antioch to Alexandria.[18] Yet even this volume is greatly increased in year 4, the year in which Rome first sent coins out to Egypt. Very little is known of the history of the period, but it is possible that this was the year of the sudden rise to power of Ardaser. The relevant text (of Herodian) is disputed[19] but may date to this year the sudden announcement of Ardaser's rise and the ensuing panic of the Roman governors in Syria and Mesopotamia. If it can be dated to this year, the sudden emergency may explain the decision to send extra funds out to Egypt, no doubt for military preparations.

A final question raised by the analyses of these tetradrachms, minted in the MONETA AVGVSTI celebrated on coins of Rome of this same year,[20] concerns the Roman conception of silver standards and debasements. The fineness of the Roman style tetradrachms is 6.35%, with a standard deviation of only 0.47: this is extraordinarily close to the fineness of the Eyptian style coins. Thus the mint of Rome had an exact knowledge of the fineness (and weight) of coins minted in Alexandria, and could produce coins extremely consistent with that standard. But the main effort of the Rome mint was in making denarii,

[18] Egyptian tetradrachms are exceedingly rare from the reign of Commodus until year 2 of Elagabalus. It was in 219 that the last tetradrachms were made at Antioch (A. R. Bellinger, *Syrian Tetradrachms of Caracalla and Macrinus*, ANSNS 3 [1940]) until the reign of Gordian III.

[19] Herodian 6.2.1. As received, the text says that Alexander had thirteen years of blameless rule, but in the fourteenth the emergency suddenly arose. As this is impossibly late, "fourteenth" has been emended to "tenth," but that emendation offers us no explanation of "thirteen." It has been suggested that the text originally read "three" and "fourth"; this makes good sense of both received numerals and would date the emergency to the fourth year of Alexander's rule. See C. J. Whitaker's Loeb edition of Herodian ad loc. for a discussion of the passage.

[20] *BMCRE* 6, 204.

where the degree of control over fineness was much lower: Walker records standard deviations between 4.18 and 9.22% during these years.[21] So although the mint could make coins to a very precise fineness it did not do so for denarii: as a result, no one in the Roman street could have had a very clear idea of how much silver a denarius of Alexander contained. If this was intentional (and the exactness of the tetradrachms' fineness suggests that it may have been), must we conclude that the mint hoped to disguise the silver standard of its coins by minting coins of identical types, some of which were more base and some more fine?

APPENDIX: ANALYSES

The coins all come from the British Museum collection and were analysed by atomic absorption spectroscopy, taking a sample by drilling a 1 mm hole in each coin's edge.[22] Two of the Egyptian style coins had twice the normal silver content, but we can think of no explanation for this. The summary therefore gives two sets of figures for the Egyptian style coins, the first including the two high ones, the second excluding them.

Mint	*No. Analyzed*	*Mean*	*Standard Deviation*	*Mean as Percentage of Cu*
Rome	12	6.35	0.47	7.1
Alexandria (1)	21	7.09	1.83	7.8
Alexandria (2)	19	6.59	0.86	7.2

There is no clear evidence for different standard deviations, if the two higher silver coins are omitted. This seems not unreasonable, given the small variation among the rest. There is a statistically significant correlation (0.8) between the lead and tin among the Roman style coins.

[21] Above, n. 3, pp. 27–29. It is hoped to publish soon some analyses of Macrinus which show an ever greater standard deviation.

[22] Dattari (above, n. 5) reports an analysis of one coin as 5.6% silver. He also distinguishes visually between the metals of the two groups of coins. For the method used here, see P. T. Craddock, A. Burnett and K. Preston in W. A. Oddy, ed., *Scientific Studies in Numismatics*, British Museum Occasional Paper 18 (1980), pp. 55–57.

ROMAN STYLE

YEAR 4

	Cu	*Pb*	*Sn*	*Ag*	*Fe*	*Sb*	*Ni*	*Au*	*Co*	*As*	*Cd*	*Bi*	*Zn*
BMC 1596	91.00	1.35	2.00	6.00	.190	.100	.065	.040	.000	.200	.000	.004	.300
BMC 1597	89.00	1.45	2.00	6.20	.300	.100	.070	.040	.000	.150	.000	.004	.300
BMC 1651	90.00	1.60	2.10	6.20	.075	.100	.055	.040	.000	.150	.000	.003	.300
BMC 1658	89.50	1.00	1.10	7.00	.120	.100	.050	.045	.000	.150	.000	.003	.200
BMC 1661	89.50	1.80	2.30	6.20	.060	.100	.050	.040	.000	.150	.000	.005	.350
1925–5–6–1[a]	89.00	1.35	2.10	6.10	.100	.030	.060	.045	.000	.100	.003	.003	.360

YEAR 5

	Cu	*Pb*	*Sn*	*Ag*	*Fe*	*Sb*	*Ni*	*Au*	*Co*	*As*	*Cd*	*Bi*	*Zn*
BMC 1662	91.00	1.45	2.00	5.60	.170	.050	.040	.045	.000	.100	.000	.004	.250
BMC 1663	90.00	1.20	1.70	5.40	.090	.070	.050	.040	.000	.100	.000	.003	.190
BMC 1664	90.00	0.65	2.10	6.00	.030	.100	.050	.045	.000	.100	.000	.005	.220

YEAR 7

	Cu	*Pb*	*Sn*	*Ag*	*Fe*	*Sb*	*Ni*	*Au*	*Co*	*As*	*Cd*	*Bi*	*Zn*
BMC 1598	88.50	1.40	1.90	6.40	.090	.100	.040	.045	.000	.100	.000	.002	.350
BMC 1665	90.50	1.10	1.80	6.60	.080	.050	.035	.045	.000	.150	.000	.003	.300
BMC 1660	89.50	1.30	2.00	7.20	.130	.100	.040	.050	.000	.250	.000	.005	1.50

EGYPTIAN STYLE

YEAR 4

	Cu	*Pb*	*Sn*	*Ag*	*Fe*	*Sb*	*Ni*	*Au*	*Co*	*As*	*Cd*	*Bi*	*Zn*
1950–10–6–90[b]	92.50	0.75	.000	5.50	.040	.050	.040	.050	.000	.170	.000	.003	.000
BMC 1606	89.00	1.45	.000	8.00	.000	.100	.000	.050	.000	.200	.000	.003	.000
BMC 1616	92.00	0.95	.000	5.40	.120	.020	.060	.055	.000	.100	.000	.015	.000
BMC 1629	92.50	0.60	.000	6.60	.000	.070	.080	.050	.000	.250	.000	.006	.000
BMC 1645	91.50	0.55	.000	7.40	.000	.020	.120	.025	.000	.350	.000	.015	.000
BMC 1694	91.00	0.74	.000	5.30	.000	.015	.035	.050	.000	.200	.000	.004	.000

YEAR 5

	Cu	*Pb*	*Sn*	*Ag*	*Fe*	*Sb*	*Ni*	*Au*	*Co*	*As*	*Cd*	*Bi*	*Zn*
BMC 1607	87.00	0.90	.000	12.00	.110	.030	.045	.100	.000	.130	.002	.004	.000
BMC 1617	92.00	0.70	.000	7.20	.000	.020	.020	.075	.000	.150	.000	.005	.000
BMC 1623	92.00	1.10	.000	6.90	.000	.050	.045	.060	.000	.100	.000	.006	.150
BMC 1630	91.00	0.80	.000	7.20	.000	.100	.040	.050	.000	.150	.004	.005	.000
BMC 1637	92.50	0.85	.000	6.20	.025	.050	.055	.055	.000	.150	.000	.002	.000

[a] Year TETAPTOV: Sarapis seated left.
[b] Year Δ: head of Zeus.

BMC 1646	91.00	0.80	.000	7.90	.025	.070	.050	.050	.000	.150	.000	.003	.000
BMC 1652	90.00	0.80	.000	7.40	.015	.015	.045	.060	.000	.100	.000	.003	.000
BMC 1673	92.00	0.90	.000	7.60	.085	.030	.040	.070	.000	.150	.000	.003	.000
BMC 1695	86.00	1.00	.000	12.50	.000	.010	.030	.065	.000	.130	.000	.003	.000
						YEAR 7							
BMC 1611	91.50	1.60	.000	6.60	.045	.080	.035	.075	.000	.100	.000	.004	.250
1950–10–6–93[c]	93.00	0.30	.000	5.30	.000	.050	.040	.055	.000	.070	.000	.004	.000
BMC 1666	91.50	0.65	.000	6.70	.080	.050	.045	.065	.000	.130	.000	.002	.000
BMC 1675	93.50	1.00	.000	6.40	.100	.070	.080	.055	.000	.150	.000	.005	.000
BMC 1677	91.50	0.40	.000	6.70	.400	.050	.045	.050	.000	.100	.000	.002	.000
BMC 1691	92.50	0.36	.000	6.80	.070	.050	.040	.075	.000	.130	.003	.004	.000

[c] Year Z: Dikaiosyne seated.

KEY TO PLATE

1. *BMCAlexandria* 1616
2. 1623
3. 1666
4. 1651
5. 1662
6. 1660
7. 1494
8. *BMCSevAlex* 262
9. *BMCAlexandria* 1652

ANSMN 28 (1983)

A COIN HOARD OF MAURICE TIBERIUS FROM ANEMURIUM, ISAURIA

(Plate 21)

James Russell

Since 1966 excavations have been carried out by a Canadian team at the city-site of Anemurium, situated on the east side of Cape Anamur, the southernmost point of Asia Minor.[1] The principal aim of this project has been to investigate some of the major public buildings and the cemetery of the Roman city, but in the process much light has been shed on the early Byzantine phase of the city's history. During this period many of the large buildings erected in the second and third centuries were reused for humbler purposes. In addition, several

1 The excavations at Anemurium began in 1966 under the direction of Professor Elisabeth Alföldi-Rosenbaum, University of Toronto. I assumed the direction of the project in 1971, since when the work has been sponsored by the University of British Columbia, Vancouver, and financed for the most part by research grants from the Canada Council and, since 1978, the Social Sciences and Humanities Research Council of Canada. For a description of the ruins of the city before excavation, E. Rosenbaum, G. Huber and S. Onurkan, *A Survey of Coastal Cities in Western Asia Minor* (Ankara, 1967), pp. 1–27. For summaries of the history and antiquities of the site on the basis of subsequent fieldwork, see J. Russell, "Anemurium—eine römische Kleinstadt in Kleinasien," *Antike Welt* 7:4 (1976), pp. 2–20, and "Anemurium: The Changing Face of a Roman City," *Archaeology* 33:5 (1980), pp. 31–40. Preliminary reports of excavations have been published in *Türk Arkeoloji Dergisi* since 1966 and shorter summaries have also appeared regularly in "Recent Archaeological Research in Turkey," *Anatolian Studies*, and M. J. Mellink, "Archaeology in Asia Minor," in *AJA*.

buildings, including two baths and four churches, erected for the first time in the early Byzantine period, have been excavated in whole or in part. During this work several hundred coins belonging to the fifth to seventh centuries have been found, a considerable proportion in significant contexts. These will be included in the general catalogue of coins from the site currently in course of preparation. Of special interest, however, is a hoard of thirty-seven copper coins of the late sixth century which was discovered in 1976 and, like all the other finds from the site, is now housed in the Museum at Alanya. Because of its numismatic and archaeological interest it merits separate and more detailed treatment.

CATALOGUE

In addition to the coin description, each entry contains, in parentheses, the acquisition number of the Alanya Museum followed by the excavation inventory number. Illustrated coins are asterisked. Additional references are to the following sources.

Bates	George E. Bates, *A Byzantine Coin Collection* (Boston, 1981).
Ismirlier	Y. Ismirlier, "Some Unpublished Byzantine Copper Coins," *NCirc* 77 (1969), pp. 318–22.
Metcalf	William E. Metcalf, "A Heraclian Hoard from Syria," *ANSMN* 20 (1975), pp. 109–37.
MIB	Wolfgang Hahn, *Moneta Imperii Byzantini*, vol. 1 (Vienna, 1981).
Seaby	David R. Sear, *Byzantine Coins and Their Values* (1974).
Waage	Dorothy B. Waage, *Antioch on the Orontes IV*, pt. 2, *Greek, Roman, Byzantine and Crusaders' Coins* (Princeton, 1952).

TIBERIUS II CONSTANTINE (578–82)

NICOMEDIA

M Above, cross

Armored bust facing, cross on crown

	g	*mm*				*yr.*	*date*	
1.	12.3	31	↓	NIKO	Off. A	II/II	578	*DOC* 27.2

(4648; AN 76/203). ꝺMTIbICONS TANTSP[

MAURICE TIBERIUS (582–602)

CONSTANTINOPLE

M Above, cross

Armored bust facing with shield, usually helmeted with plume

2.	15.2	33	↗	CON	Off. B	II/II	585/6	*DOC* 27b.

(4678; AN 76/233).]bЄRPPΔV Details of headgear unclear.

*3.	11.6	28	↑	CON	Off. Γ	II/II	585/6	

(4661; AN 76/216). ꝺNMΔVRC TIbЄRPPΔVI Headgear, crown with cross.

This headgear is not listed in *DOC* for year 4, nor in *MIB*.

4. 13.2 29 ↗ CON Off. Γ II/II 585/6 *DOC* 27c
(4660; AN 76/215).]ṂΔYṚ]ẸRPPΔ[Surface badly eroded, headgear unclear.

5. 12.2 32 ↙ CON Off. ϵ II/II 585/6 *DOC* 27e
(4646 ; AN 76/201).] ꙅIBERPPΔV Details of headgear unclear.

6. 11.8 31 ↙ CON Off. A ς 587/8 Bates 1503
(4667; AN 76/222). ∂[ ]IЬϵPPΔ Paludamentum concealing cuirass, no shield.

7. 12.3 31 ↙ CON Off. A ς/II 589/90 *DOC* 31a
(4670; AN 76/225).] ṬỊḄϵRPPΔ Plumed helmet.

8. 11.4 31 ↗ CON Off. Δ ς/II 589/90 *DOC* 31d
(4657; AN 76/212). ∂NMΔVRI TIЬϵRPPΔVC Plumed helmet.

9. 12.1 30 ↗ CON Off. Δ ς/II 589/90 *DOC* 31d
(4656; AN 76/209). ∂NMΔV[ ]PPΔ Plumed helmet.

10. 12.2 31 ↗ CON Off. B ςI/II 590/1
(4675; AN 76/230). ∂NMΔVRIC TIЬϵRPPΔV Plumed helmet.

Officina B not listed in *DOC* 32, but see Bates 1537, and *MIB* 67D, p. 113.

11. 11.8 30 ↗ CON Off. Γ ςI/II 590/1
(4654; AN 76/211). ∂NMΔVRC TIЬϵRPPΔ̣ Plumed helmet.

Officina Γ with this form of regnal year is not listed in *DOC* 32 or Seaby, but cf. Waage 2186, *MIB* 67 D, p. 113, and Ismirlier, pp. 318–22.

12. 13.3 32 ↗ CON Off. A X/I 592/3 Bates 1548
(4665; AN 76/220). δNMΔV[ ]PΔV Paludamentum type.

13. 11.4 29 ↙ CON Off. B X/II/I 594/5 *DOC* 36b
(4676; AN 76/231). δNMΔVR TIbERIᴘPPΔ Plumed helmet.

14. 10.5 32 ↓ CON Off. B X/II/II 595/6 Metcalf, 47
(4677; AN 76/232).]ΔVRIC TIbERPPΔV Plumed helmet.

15. 11.4 34 ↗ CON Off. Γ X/ϛ 596/7 *DOC* 39a
(4679; AN 76/234).] TIbERPPΔVC Plumed helmet.

K Above, cross

Armored bust facing, holding shield and plumed helmet

*16. 5.2 21 ↓ No mint Off. A ϛ III 590/1
(4647; AN 76/202).]ṆMΔṚC TIbERPPΔV

Probably Constantinople mint (*DOC*, p. 311, footnote). Obverse legend resembles that of no. 11 (Constantinople mint) which belongs to the same regnal year.

THESSALONICA

K Above, cross

Armored bust facing, wearing cloak and crown

17. 5.8 24 ↓ TEC ϛ 586/7 *DOC* 77
(4681; AN 76/236). δNMΔURC TIB[

NICOMEDIA

M Above, cross

Armored bust facing, crown with cross?

*18. 13.1 32 ↓ NIKO Off. B II 583/4 *DOC* 92b?
(4680; AN 76/235). Legend unclear.

19. 12.8 30 ↙ NIKO′ Off. A II/II 585/6 *DOC* 94
(4651; AN 76/206).] NIPPAC

Armored bust, helmet with plume instead of crown

20. 11.8 34 ↙ NIK° Off. A ɢ I 588/9 *DOC* 97a
(4658; AN 76/213).]TIbERP

Armored bust, crown

21. 15.2 32 ↙ NIKO Off. A X 591/2 *DOC* 100a
(4668; AN 76/223).]NM AVTIB

CYZICUS

M Above, cross

Armored bust facing, helmet with plume?

*22. 10.8 33 ↙ KYZ Off. B Ꞔ II 589/90
(4652; AN 76/207).]ИΜΔURI [ ]ΔV

Off. B not listed in *DOC* 124 with this form of regnal year, but it does appear in *BMCByz* 152 and Tolstoi, 143.

K Above, cross

23. 5.2 23 No mint Off. obscure Ч 587/8
(4682; AN 76/237).

Obverse remains uncleaned, since the corrosion bears clear traces of the fabric of the cloth wrapping that had contained the hoard; details obscure.

Mint is uncertain, but the shape of the obverse head suggests Cyzicus (*DOC*, 311, footnote).

ANTIOCH

m Above, cross

Consular bust facing, crown with trefoil ornament

24. 12.1 29 ↓ ꝾHЄUP′ Ч/II 588/9 *DOC* 158c
(4655; AN 76/210).]IΛU

M Above, cross

Consular bust facing, crown with trefoil ornament

25.	13.2	31	↓	ƧHЄUP′	Off. Γ	ɥ/III	590/1	*DOC* 161
	(4663 ; AN 76/218). ꝺNMAUΓI CNP̄AЧΓ							
26.	11.9	30	↙	ƧHЄUP′	Off. Γ	X	591/2	*DOC* 162c
	(4669 ; AN 76/224).]CNP̄AUΓ							
27.	11.2	30	↓	ƧHЄUP′	Off. Γ	X	591/2	*DOC* 162c
	(4671; AN 76/226). ꝺ̄N̄MAUΓI CNP̄AUT							
28.	10.0	28	↓	ƧHЄUP′	Off. Γ	[X]/III	594/5	*DOC* 165b
	(4662; AN 76/217). ꝺ̄N̄MAUΓ CNP̄AUT This coin is sharply bent.							
29.	11.4	29	↓	ƧHEUP′	Off. Γ	X/IIII	595/6	*DOC* 166b
	(4673; AN 76/228). ꝺ̄N̄MAUΓI CNP̄AUT							
*30.	11.4	29	↖	ƧHЄUP′	Off. Δ	X/Ч	596/7	*DOC* 167
	(4650; AN 76/205).]AUT							

Officina Δ not listed in *DOC* but see Hahn *MIB*, p. 121, 96c.

31. 11.0 28 ↓ ƨ HЄUP′ Off. Γ X/ЧI 597/8 *DOC* 168b
(4659; AN 76/214).]CNP̄AUT

32. 11.3 31 ↓ ƨ HЄUP′ Off. Γ X/ЧIII 599/600 *DOC* 170b.1
(4674; AN 76/299).]CNP̄AU[

33. 12.2 31 ↓ ƨ HЄUP′ Off. Γ X/ЧIII 599/600 *DOC* 170b.1
(4664; AN 76/219). ǫИmAẎ PẠUT Inscription somewhat blundered.

*34. 10.2 30 ↑ ƨ HЄUP′ Off. illegible. X/ЧIII 599/600 *DOC* 170
(4653; AN 76/208). ǫNmAUΓṢ]APT

35. 9.8 27 ↓ ƨ HЄUP′ Off. Γ X/X 601/2 *DOC* 172b
(4672; AN 76/227).]P̄AUT

36. 11.2 29 ↓ ƨ HЄUP′ Off. Γ X/X 601/2 *DOC* 172b
(4666; AN 76/221). ǫNmAUΓ CNP̄

37. 10.1 29 ↓ ƨ HЄUP′ Off. Ƨ X/X 601/2 *DOC* 172d
(4649; AN 76/204). ǫNmAUΓI CNP̄AUT

Table 1. Comparative Distribution of Mints for Years 578-602 in Syrian Hoards of Copper Issues

	Tell Bisa	%	*Coele-syria*	%	*Myers*	%	*Cyrrhes-tica*	%	*Ane-murium*	%
Constantinople	124	38.27	45	42.06	9	52.95	74	42.05	15	40.55
Thessalonica	5	1.54					3	1.70	1	2.70
Nicomedia	50	15.43	18	16.82	1	5.88	18	10.23	5	13.50
Cyzicus	16	4.94	10	9.35			15	8.52	2	5.40
Antioch	129	39.82	34	31.77	6	35.29	66	37.50	14	37.85
Cherson					1	5.88				
Total	324	100.00	107	100.00	17	100.00	176	100.00	37	100.00

The hoard came to light in the service area at the rear of a small bathing establishment (III 15) located in the northern part of the city fronting the west side of the major street that traverses the site from north to south.[2] The find spot lies close to a small service passage situated in the middle of the west wall of the tepidarium, the central room in a row of three chambers serving the three stages of the bathing process. The coins were not found on the floor of the service area but lay in earth fill at a height of 0.26 m. above the floor. When discovered most of the coins were stuck together in small groups, with a few remaining loose. Evidence for the cloth bag in which they had been wrapped appeared in the impression of the fabric visible on the corrosion of one of the coins. The hoard comprises a total of 37 copper coins, 34 folles and three half folles ranging in date from 578 to 601/2, all but one belonging to the reign of Maurice Tiberius. The mints of Constantinople and Antioch are represented almost equally, with fifteen and fourteen coins each respectively, Nicomedia with five, Cyzicus with two and Thessalonica with one. This distribution of mints corresponds quite closely to the

[2] For the location of this and other buildings in the city plan see Rosenbaum (above, n. 1), plan 1; Russell, (above, n. 1), "Kleinstadt," abb. 4. For description and plan of the baths themselves, see J. Russell, "Excavations at Anemurium (Eski Anamur)," *Turk Arkeoloji Dergisi* 22:2 (1975), pp. 125–26, fig. 13; 25:1 (1980), pp. 266–67, figs. 6–7, 27–28; *Proceedings of Xth International Congress of Classical Archaeology* (Ankara, 1978), pp. 921–22. For a brief report of the hoard and its context, see J. Russell in "Recent Archaeological Research in Turkey," *Anatolian Studies* 27 (1977), pp. 26, 28; *Classical News and Views* 21:1 (1977), pp. 6, 9, fig. 2.

mints of the coins issued in the period 578–602 in three large Syrian hoards previously published, viz. Tell Bisa,[3] Coelesyria[4] and Cyrrhestica[5] (Table 1). The similarity in distribution between the very large hoard of Tell Bisa and that of Anemurium is particularly striking, with almost equal representation of coins of the Constantinople and Antioch mints, Nicomedia fairly well represented and with very limited appearance of the Cyzicus and Thessalonica mints. Coelesyria and Cyrrhestica display the same general pattern with some variation.[6] On this evidence at least it would seem that the coastal regions of Isauria shared with Syria the same pattern in the circulation of copper currency in the last quarter of the sixth century.[7]

[3] E. Leuthold, "Monete bizantine rinvenute in Siria," *RIN* (1952–3), pp. 31–49.

[4] G. E. Bates, "A Byzantine Hoard from Coelesyria," *ANSMN* 14 (1968), pp. 67–109.

[5] E. Leuthold, "Monete bizantine rinvenute in Cirrestica," *RIN* 73 (1971), pp. 9–24.

[6] A fourth large Syrian hoard now in the Museum of the American Numismatic Society is not included in the comparative table since only 17 coins from that hoard fall within the time span represented by the Anemurium hoard. The distribution in this case is Constantinople 9 (53%), Nicomedia 1 (6%), Antioch 6 (35%), and Cherson 1 (6%). Although the pattern is not gravely inconsistent with the others, the numbers involved are perhaps too few to be statistically meaningful. W. E. Metcalf, "A Heraclian Hoard from Syria," *ANSMN* 20 (1975), pp. 109–37, see in particular Table 1 for a comparative table of distribution by mints of all the coins of this hoard and those of Tell Bisa and Coelesyria.

An additional hoard, discovered at Paphos on Cyprus, is also of some relevance to the discussion. The hoard comprised a total of 117 coins ranging in date from 579/80–616/7. Twenty of these fall within the period covered by the Anemurium hoard, with a mint distribution pattern as follows: Constantinople 6 (30%), Nicomedia 2 (10%), and Antioch 12 (60%). See P. J. Donald and P. D. Whitting, "A VIIth Century Hoard from Cyprus," *NCirc* 75:6 (1967), pp. 162–65.

[7] In the absence of published hoards of the period from other parts of Anatolia, the degree to which circulation patterns represented by this Syrian-Isaurian group differed from patterns in other parts of Asia Minor remains a matter for speculation. The conspectus of coins found in the excavations at Sardis from 1958–68, however, suggests a substantially different mint distribution for the reigns of Tiberius II and Maurice. The cumulative totals for the two reigns by mint are Constantinople 86 (57.33%), Thessalonica 20 (13.33%), Nicomedia 23 (15.33%), Cyzicus 13 (8.66%), Antioch 7 (4.66%), Rome 1 (0.66%). The predominance of Constantinople here is in sharp contrast to the scanty representation of the Antioch mint. See G. E. Bates, *Byzantine Coins*, Archaeological Exploration of Sardis, monograph 1 (Cambridge, Mass., 1971), Table 2, p. 5.

The latest coins (nos. 33–35) provide a clear terminus post quem of 601/2 for the deposit of the hoard. There is no lack of events in the following decade or so to account for the hoard's burial. The unsettled conditions surrounding the death of Phocas (608) and the imminent threat of Persian invasion, especially after the capture of Antioch (611), might well have provided the occasion for the owner's action. On the other hand, the absence of any coins of Phocas perhaps indicates a date for the deposit of the hoard earlier in that reign. The possibility that troubles of a local nature not otherwise recorded afflicted the coast of Isauria early in Phocas's reign gains strength from a small hoard of seven gold coins discovered at Selinus (modern Gazipaşa), a coastal city, 91 kilometers west of Anemurium. Consisting of one solidus and one tremissis of Justin II and five solidi of Maurice Tiberius it spans a period comparable to the Anemurium hoard (565–602).[8] Though not dated precisely, the condition of the coins reported as "somewhat worn" might suggest that they continued in circulation as late as the early seventh century. Troubled conditions in this region around this date may also account for the enormous lamp hoard discovered at Anemurium in 1968. Found stacked in the abandoned hypocaust system of one of the baths it consists of some 650 whole terracotta lamps apparently never used. No datable material was found with the lamps, but it was assumed at the time of their discovery that they represented a merchant's stock hidden away sometime after 650 when the Isaurian coast was exposed to Arab raids from Cyprus.[9] The possibility that the lamps were concealed fifty years before in connection with the circumstances that prompted the coin hoards, however, should not be overlooked.

The Anemurium coin hoard has also provided welcome confirmation for the rapid decline of the city's material prosperity in the last quarter of the sixth century. The burial of the coins in loose earth mixed with much broken pottery overlying the floor of the service area of the baths clearly suggests that the baths had ceased to fulfill their original function

[8] S. M. Mosser, *A Bibliography of Byzantine Coin Hoards* (New York, 1935), p. 78.

[9] H. Williams and P. Taylor, "A Byzantine Lamp Hoard from Anamur (Cilicia)," *Anatolian Studies* 25 (1975), pp. 77–84.

some considerable time before 602, the terminus post quem for the deposit of the hoard. There is in fact good evidence that a destructive earthquake struck the city toward the end of Justin II's reign in 578. This caused the collapse of at least one of the city's churches (III 10 C) which was never repaired and probably accounts for widespread damage in two others.[10] The small baths, III 15, survived the earthquake more or less intact, but the burial of the hoard in the now derelict service area at the rear provides incontrovertible evidence that the building had been turned to other uses at some interval before. It is virtually certain that the city's aqueduct system suffered irreparable damage in the earthquake. This forced the inhabitants to seek an alternative water supply in the form of wells, of which one example, securely dated to the first half of the seventh century, has been excavated in the reused palaestra area of the large Roman baths (E III 2 B).[11] With the destruction of the aqueduct we may assume also the closing of the city's baths. In the case of the baths that produced the hoard, the well constructed heated chambers continued in active use for a further three generations, housing various forms of retail activity, to judge from the finds. The service area at the rear, however, probably rendered useless by the collapse of its flimsy tile roof in the earthquake, quickly became a rubbish dump. By the beginning of the seventh century enough earth had accumulated to afford a suitable hiding place for a small cloth bag of copper coins, representing some poor man's modest savings.[12]

[10] For a brief report of the evidence for this occurrence, consisting primarily of a worn follis of Justin II dated 569/70 (AN 78/61) sealed beneath the debris of the collapsed roof, see J. Russell, "Recent Archaeological Research in Turkey," *Anatolian Studies* 29 (1979), p. 185, and *Classical News & Views* 23:1 (1979), p. 6.

[11] For details see C. Williams, "A Byzantine Well-Deposit from Anemurium (Rough Cilicia)," *Anatolian Studies* 27 (1977), pp. 175–90.

[12] The total value of the hoard amounting to 35 folles approximates to one sixth of a solidus, or a half-tremissis. I owe this interesting observation to Prof. Philip Grierson to whom I am also indebted for much general advice in the preparation of this report. Besides Professor Grierson, I am deeply obliged to Mustafa Gürdal, Director of the Alanya Museum, and his staff for assistance in preparing this report, and to my colleague, Professor Hector Williams, for supplying photographs of the obverse and reverse of no. 18 and the obverse of no. 16.

ANSMN 28 (1983)

A GOLD DINAR OF THE SASANIAN QUEEN BURAN

Roger Kuntz and William B. Warden, Jr.

By the courtesy of the Museum of Fine Arts, Boston, Massachusetts, and through the kindness of Mr. Timothy Kendall, we are permitted to publish a heretofore undocumented issue in gold of the Sasanian Queen Buran[1] who ruled the Persian Empire in A.D. 630–31. Very little is known of this queen other than the fact that she was the daughter of Khusro II, and sister of Kavad II and Ardaser III. She succeeded Ardaser III to the throne and appears to have concluded a treaty of peace with the Byzantine Emperor Heraclius.

[1] F. D. J. Paruck, *Sasanian Coins* (Bombay, 1924), p. 117, mentions a gold coin of Buran, but it is actually a silver drachm. The references he gives are obscure, and there seem to be problems with the dates of the publications he cites.

Buran, AV dinar regnal year 2 = A.D. 630, with no mint name.[2]

Obv. Full face portrait of queen, with crown surmounted by spreading wings enclosing globe with smaller globe on top;[3] crown adorned with three rosettes and two dotted borders; star to either side; queen's hair plaited in tresses at either side of face flowing down in front of bust; pendant of pearls for breast ornament, crescent and star on either shoulder; to l. of bust,  = *'pzwn*; to r. 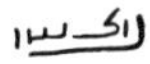 = *bwl'nw* = Buran.[4]

Rev. Queen, standing, robed, wearing same crown as on obv.; crescent and star to either side of face; flowing ribbons to either side of body; to l. of body 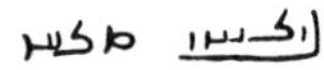 = *bwl'nw TLYYN* (for *TLYN*)[5] = Buran, two; to r. 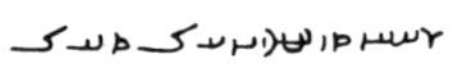 = . . . *ntw GDH nyw bwll'l.*

Museum of Fine Arts Collection, 35–272,[6] 26 mm and 4.390 g.[7]

This is the first example of a coin struck in gold by any of the successors of Khusro II.[8] It is remarkable in that it features our only

[2] According to F. D. J. Paruck, "The Drachm of the Sassanian Queen Bōrān," *JASB* 13 (1917), *Num. Suppl.* 28, p. 43–45, the so called "regnal years" appearing on the coins were reckoned according to the calendar and not from the date of succession. Thus, a monarch who began his reign two months prior to the end of the calendar year would enter his second regnal year at the end of the second month. According to many historians, Buran probably reigned for only 16–17 months.

[3] We expect Prof. Robert Göbl, Director of the Institut für Numismatik of the University of Vienna, to publish a more detailed crown synopsis in the near future.

[4] The inscription reads *'pzwn bwl'nw*, literally "increase, Buran," but the two are not connected since the first word on the left is a pious wish to be bountiful or to increase, while the second word to the right is her name.

[5] *TLYN* in Middle Persian is the ideogram *dō* = "two."

[6] The coin was acquired by the Museum of Fine Arts in 1935 as part of a lot of five Sasanian gold coins donated anonymously to honor the memory of Zoe Wilbour.

[7] The coin has been worn as jewelry and has been mounted with a loop, thus it is hard to estimate the actual weight, but we think ca. 4.2 g, as in coins of her predecessors. See Robert Göbl, *Sasanian Numismatics* (Braunschweig, 1971), pp. 27–29.

[8] Göbl, p. 54.

known frontal portrait of this queen and her crown. In this respect, it is similar to the earlier gold issues of her father's regnal years 33 and 34.[9] The queen is wearing a totally new crown not found on any examples of her rare silver coinage.[10]

The reverse inscription to the right side of the standing figure is a bit enigmatic. Especially the first word, which is either an adjective or possibly a word ending in *ntw*, meaning "attested, or declared"? Then follows *GDH nyw bwlt'l* (= "farn nēv Burdār") which can be translated as "good bearer of glory,"[11] probably copied from the coins of her father which have "maker of the world without fear."

We look forward to seeing contributions by other experts in this field as to the inscription and the iconography of this queen's rather enigmatic gold issue.

9 Göbl, p. 80 and pl. 14, coins 220 and 221, type combination V/6 and VI/7.

10 We wish to thank Prof. Robert Göbl for confirming that this is a new variety of crown for this queen, and for help in our initial research for this article.

11 We also would like to thank Prof. Richard Frye of Harvard University for his generous assistance in deciphering the Middle Persian inscription on this coin. In a letter he says, "It is also possible to assume that one letter fell away in the last line and one could read *GDH (-i) nyk bwlt'l* (*nyk* for the older *nywk*) and interpret this as "bearer of good fortune," although I feel this is a modern interpretation read back to Sasanian times as "good fortune."

ANSMN 28 (1983)

THE STRUGGLE FOR SYRIA AND MESOPOTAMIA (330-58/941-69) AS REFLECTED ON ḤAMDĀNID AND IKHSHĪDID COINS

Ramzi Jibran Bikhazi

Medieval historians, as a rule, give scant attention to provincial areas, particularly when the events concerned are of a transitional nature. In the first half of the fourth/tenth century, a transitional period, Syria and Mesopotamia were "provincial," and the literary sources treat them in a gloss. The numismatic evidence is fortunately a supportive source of information which on close examination yields many useful clues.

During the middle decades of the fourth/tenth century, Syria and Mesopotamia were the theater of a complicated struggle in which local and regional policies did not follow a neat pattern. This inconstancy was due to three important facts. First, the breakdown of the ʿAbbāsid empire caused ideological disorientation as well as political disarray, hence realistic policy sometimes lost out to outdated dogma. Second, the Fāṭimids, the Buwayhids, and the Byzantines, all of whom had interests in the region, did not consistently push their claims, as they were sometimes hindered by domestic problems. And third (partially a result of the first two), the balance of power made several dramatic shifts, the most unforseen of which was the decline of Ikhshīdid Egypt after 336/947 from a regional power to a dependency of the Fāṭimids.

THE ḤAMDĀNIDS, THE IKHSHĪDIDS, AND THE ʿABBĀSID CALIPHATE, 324–33/936–44

Despite al-Muqtadir's disastrous reign (295–320/908–32) and the attendant breakdown of the ʿAbbāsid government, the ʿAbbāsid caliphate enjoyed a residual political influence which survived for almost two decades. The struggle of al-Muqtadir's immediate successors to save the caliphate was the central issue around which revolved the foreign policies of Mosul, Egypt, and, of course, Iraq.

Nāṣir al-Dawla, the Ḥamdānid emir of Mosul, regarded the caliphate with mixed feelings rooted in the history of his family. The Ḥamdānid emirate of Mosul was a tribal chiefdom with no regular army and little ability to defend itself against a powerful neighbor. Its independence had become an accomplished fact in the early 320s/930s as a result of the ʿAbbāsid government's inability to hold on to Mesopotamia. Since economic chaos and agricultural deterioration were among the root causes of Iraq's weakness, it was moreover to be expected that the reforming caliphs would be anxious to regain control of Mesopotamia's rich agricultural resources.

Nāṣir al-Dawla fought twice to defend the Ḥamdānid emirate against the Caliph al-Rāḍi (in 323/935 and again in 327/938). But what he feared most was the alien military class of Iraq and, beyond that, the unfathomable and still more alien Buwayhids of Persia. Against these two forces Nāṣir al-Dawla was helpless. He could not overthrow the military class of Iraq any more than he could stop the Buwayhids in their tracks. But he could hope that the one would keep the other in check. With Ḥamdānid interests dependent on the balancing of these two potential enemies, Nāṣir al-Dawla hoped that the caliphate would remain strong enough to temper the militarism of Iraq and rally the anti-Buwayhid forces, but not grow so strong as to pose a threat to Mesopotamia's independence.

Nāṣir al-Dawla's interest in the political survival of the caliphate was one of two determining factors in his policy in another area of vital interest, northern Syria. The continued stability of the emirate of Mosul necessitated a policy of expansion in northern Syria both to circumscribe the unruly migratory tribes of the Euphrates region, which threatened the tribal balance in Mesopotamia,[1] and to acquire a military outpost against the Byzantine empire. Nāṣir al-Dawla's younger brother, Sayf al-Dawla, advocated this policy of expansion in the expectation that Syria would be his prize. Legally, however, the Ḥamdānids possessed no claim to Syria that the ʿAbbāsid caliphs recognized. Nāṣir al-Dawla, therefore, could not both uphold the authority of the ʿAbbāsid caliphate and authorize his brother to annex northern Syria. The other important factor concerning northern Syria was that the powerful Ikhshīdids of Egypt were currently interested in extending their influence over the country and would undoubtedly parry any attempt by the Ḥamdānids to lay claim to it.

Egypt was a relatively stable country with little cause for worry about current events in Iraq. But Egypt's autonomous governor al-Ikhshīd, inspired by the deterioration of political and public order in Iraq, was taken by the notion of becoming the protector of the ʿAbbāsid caliph. For almost a decade (from ca. 324/935 until 333/944) Egypt's foreign policy was determined by al-Ikhshīd's hope to induce the ʿAbbāsid caliph to abandon Baghdad and take up a new capital in Syria under Ikhshīdid protection.

During this decade, the idea of moving the caliphate away from Iraq gained some adherents at the ʿAbbāsid capital. As early as 324/936, the caliphal guard was driven to near mutiny by rumors that the Caliph al-Rāḍī intended to leave for Mosul.[2] The sources do not connect al-Ikhshīd with these events, but a letter sent to al-Ikhshīd by the Fāṭimid caliph al-Qā'im shortly after the abortive Fāṭimid attack on Egypt in 324/936 very strongly suggests that this was indeed the case.

[1] Abū al-Qāsim ibn Ḥawqal, *Kitāb Ṣurat al-Arḍ*, ed. J. H. Kramers, 2nd ed., 2 vols., Bibliotheca Geographorum Arabicorum (Leiden: Brill, 1938–39), 1, pp. 226, 228; Ibrāhīm b. Muḥammad al-Iṣṭakhrī, *Al-Masālik wa al-Mamālik*, ed. M. J. A. al-Ḥusaynī and Sh. Ghurbāl (Cairo: Al-Idāra al-ʿĀmma lil-Thaqāfa, 1961), p. 54; cf. M. Canard, *Histoire de la dynastie des H'amdanides de Jazîra et de Syrie* (Algiers: Publications de la Faculté des lettres d'Alger, 1951), pp. 575–76.

[2] Muḥammad b. Yaḥyā al-Ṣūlī, *Akhbār al-Rāḍī billāh wa al-Muttaqī lillāh*, ed. J. Heyworth-Dunne (Cairo: Maṭbaʿat al-Ṣāwī, 1935), p. 53. This incident should be compared with al-Ṣūlī's account of al-Rāḍī's expedition of 327/938 against Mosul, pp. 108ff., especially pp. 108–15. Many persons opposed the expedition because they suspected that al-Rāḍī intended to abandon Baghdad.

In this letter, which Ibn Saʿīd preserves verbatim,[3] al-Qā'im reminded al-Ikhshīd how the ʿAbbāsids had failed to heed his advice, trust his promises, or even reward him for his faithfulness. We know of nothing in contemporary ʿAbbāsid-Ikhshīdid relations which warrants this statement. Al-Rāḍī, to be sure, was to appoint Ibn Rā'iq in Ṣafar 327/ December 938, as governor of Diyār Muḍar and northern Syria, and Ibn Rā'iq's subsequent activities were to give al-Ikhshīd cause for umbrage. But al-Qā'im's statement could hardly refer to Ibn Rā'iq's appointment, for Ibn Saʿīd is clear that this letter arrived some two years earlier, when Ibn Rā'iq still held the office of *amīr al-umarā'* in Baghdad.

The most plausible explanation of al-Qā'im's statement is that al-Ikhshīd had offered to house the ʿAbbāsid caliphate and had been repulsed by al-Rāḍī, who then created the office of *amīr al-umarā'* and raised Ibn Rā'iq to power in a radical move to bring stability to Iraq. Al-Ikhshīd's offer would not have only evoked al-Qā'im's derisive words but would have also been cause enough to make him try a countermove. Indeed, the primary object of the Fāṭimid caliph's letter was to invite al-Ikhshīd to recognize Fāṭimid suzerainty. Al-Qā'im, the letter said, would not press al-Ikhshīd to embrace the Fāṭimid creed; he would be satisfied if al-Ikhshīd were to recognize his primacy as though he, al-Qā'im, were a senior member of al-Ikhshīd's family.

Ibn Rā'iq arrived in Syria in 327/939. He had been toppled by Bajkam, the commander of Baghdad's elite army corps, and had subsequently been appointed by al-Rāḍī as governor of Aleppo and Diyār Muḍar. Ibn Rā'iq marched into Ramla, overstepping his terms of appointment, and al-Ikhshīd, after waiting in vain for an explanation from Baghdad, decided in a fit of anger to accept al-Qā'im's offer.[4]

[3] ʿAlī b. Mūsā ibn Saʿīd al-Andalusī, *Al-Sifr al-Rābiʿ min Kitāb al-Mughrib fī Ḥulā al-Maghrib*, ed. K. L. Tallquist (Leiden: Brill, 1899), pp. 25–26.

[4] Ibn Saʿīd, pp. 26–28; Muḥammad b. Yūsūf al-Kindī, *Kitāb al-Wulāt wa Kitāb al-Quḍāt*, ed. R. Guest, E. J. W. Gibb Memorial Series 19 (Beirut: Maṭbaʿat al-Ābā' al-Yāsuʿiyyīn, 1908), pp. 288–89. For the terms of Ibn Rā'iq's appointment see Aḥmad b. Muḥammad Miskawayh, *Kitāb Tajārib al-Umam*, in *The Eclipse of the ʿAbbāsid Caliphate: Original Chronicles of the Fourth Islamic Century*, ed. and tr. H. F. Amedroz and D. S. Margoliouth, 7 vols. (Oxford: B. Blackwell, 1920–21), 2, pp. 408–9; *Kitāb al-ʿUyūn wa al-Ḥadā'iq fī Akhbār al-Ḥaqā'iq*, ed. O. Saïdi (Damascus: Institut français de Damas, 1972–73), vol. 4, pt. 1, p. 329.

The Ikhshīdid army had meanwhile engaged Ibn Rā'iq in an intermittent war in which it achieved various indecisive victories until it was stalled at al-Lajjūn in Palestine. An agreement was finally reached at the end of 328/late 940, by the terms of which al-Ikhshīd relinquished Damascus and northern Syria to Ibn Rā'iq, and retained Palestine against the payment of an annual sum of money.[5] Mollified by this agreement, al-Ikhshīd retracted his decision to recognize the Fāṭimid caliph.

The sources do not give us the slightest hint that this agreement was anything but a quid pro quo in Syria. One year later, however, when Ibn Rā'iq returned to the office of *amīr al-umarā'* in Baghdad, al-Ikhshīd appears to have assumed that his chances of convincing the ʿAbbāsid caliph to move to Syria had improved. An Ikhshīdid embassy of undisclosed intent left for Iraq soon after Ibn Rā'iq had regained power in the ʿAbbāsid capital.[6] By the time it arrived, however, the caliph (now al-Muttaqī) and Ibn Ra'iq were in flight, driven forth by Iraq's war lords, and Ibn Rā'iq was determined to take the caliph to Syria. This circumstance suggests that the agreement of 328 included at least a tentative understanding between al-Ikhshīd and Ibn Rā'iq to transfer the ʿAbbāsid capital to Syria.

We know in retrospect that neither al-Rāḍī nor his successor al-Muttaqī gave serious thought to al-Ikhshīd's aspirations; but contemporaries who lived day by day through the difficult events of 329–32/940–44, could not rule out the possibility that al-Muttaqī might resign himself to the Ikhshīdid option. Al-Ikhshīd's policy was specially opposed by the Ḥamdānids. To the Ḥamdānids, the caliphate was of little use unless it remained in Iraq. Relocated to Syria, it might indeed prove inimical to their interests by impelling al-Ikshhīd to extend his authority into the sensitive Euphrates region, where the establishment of strong rule would inevitably accelerate the eastward migration of nomadic tribes. Al-Ikhshīd's policy therefore forced Nāṣir

[5] Kindī (above, n. 4), pp. 289–90; Ibn Saʿīd (above, n. 3), pp. 28–29; Jamāl al-Dīn ibn Taghribirdī, *Al-Nujūm al-Zāhira fī Mulūk Miṣr wa al-Qāhira*, 16 vols. (Cairo: Maṭbaʿat Dār al-Kutub al-Miṣriyya, 1929–72), 3, pp. 252–53.

[6] Ṣūlī (above n. 2), p. 225; *K. al-ʿUyūn* (above, n. 4), vol. 4, pt. 2, p. 375.

al-Dawla to become much more involved in the affairs of the caliphate than he would have otherwise desired.

The earliest extant Ikhshīdid coins were struck in 329/940, the very year that the Amīr al-Umarā' Bajkam had introduced his name on the coinage of Iraq.[7] Al-Ikhshīd, who did not recognize the overlordship of the *amīr al-umarā'*, seems to have intended this step as a reminder that he held office under the caliph's sole authority.

For the Ḥamdānids, it was not politic to take a principled stand on the coinage. A necessity of Nāṣir al-Dawla's policy until 330/942 was to avoid legal disputes with the regimes of Iraq. A rejoinder to Bajkam in the manner adopted by al-Ikhshīd would have been incompatible with this low profile.

It was therefore more than a year later, and only when circumstances had forced him to accept the office of *amīr al-umarā'* (Shaʿbān 330/April 942), that Nāṣir al-Dawla assumed the right of adding his name to the coinage. The early Ḥamdānid coins were evidently not intended as dynastic issues but as ʿAbbāsid ones, with Nāṣir al-Dawla's state title included, as Bajkam's had been, in recognition of his rank in the central government of the caliphate. One might further note in support of this contention that Sayf al-Dawla was not cited on the coinage until, four months later, he had likewise received a state title and been promoted in rank.[8]

This point has to be emphasized because it has been all too easy to ascribe the wrong motives to Nāṣir al-Dawla's policy in 330, particularly in the territories seized by the Ḥamdānids three years later. Nāṣir al-Dawla had not coveted the office of *amīr al-umarā'*, nor did he subsequently manipulate his power of office to expand Ḥamdānid possessions. Late in the previous year he had actually connived in Ibn Rā'iq's return to Baghdad and had furnished him with some financial assistance in the hope that he would be able to put an end to the disorders which raked Iraq after Bajkam's death in Rajab 329/April 941.[9] What shook

[7] J. Bacharach, "Al-Ikhshīd, the Ḥamdānids and the Caliphate: The Numismatic Evidence," *JAOS* 94 (1974), p. 362.

[8] R. J. Bikhazi, "Ḥamdānid Coins of Madīnat al-Salām, A. H. 330–331," in D. K. Kouymjian, ed., *Near Eastern Numismatics, Iconography, Epigraphy and History: Studies in Honor of George C. Miles* (Beirut, 1974), pp. 258, 269.

[9] Bikhazi, p. 257.

Nāṣir al-Dawla's determination to stay on the sidelines was Ibn Rā'iq's flight to Mosul with the Caliph al-Muttaqī in tow only six months after returning to office. Ibn Rā'iq intended (against the caliph's desire) to proceed with al-Muttaqī to Syria, and put the caliphate under Ikhshīdid protection there.[10]

This plan forced Nāṣir al-Dawla to liquidate Ibn Rā'iq and accept the office of *amīr al-umarā'*;[11] it is the backdrop against which the Ḥamdānid coins of Syria as well as Nāṣir al-Dawla's Syrian policy in 330–31/942–43 must be seen. The task which faced Nāṣir al-Dawla on assuming office was not simply to return the caliph to Baghdad, but more urgently to curb al-Ikhshīd who, on hearing of Ibn Rā'iq's death, occupied Damascus and seemed ready to implement his plan by force. Nāṣir al-Dawla's first priority, even while he prepared to march on Iraq, was to bring Diyār Muḍar and northern Syria under direct rule and thereby block all practicable routes between Syria and Iraq. Once occupied, the mints of these territories were made to cite the Ḥamdānids on the coinage, but this was only in the spirit that impelled Nāṣir al-Dawla to assume the right of coinage in Iraq. During the next year Nāṣir al-Dawla made no attempt to incorporate Diyār Muḍar and northern Syria into the Ḥamdānid domain any more than he did so with Iraq. His administration outside the Ḥamdānid domain was staffed by ʿAbbāsid functionaries, not Ḥamdānid ones.[12]

The guiding principles of Ḥamdānid policy towards the caliphate underwent only a slight change after Nāṣir al-Dawla had given up the office of *amīr al-umarā'* in Shaʿbān 331/April 943. Iraq's many problems made him lose faith in the caliphate's political future, but he did not abandon the view that the caliph should remain in Baghdad. The Ḥamdānid policy of keeping the caliph in Baghdad had not been dictated solely by Nāṣir al-Dawla's concern about the caliphate's survival; it had equally been determined by his fear of what might ensue from setting up the caliphate in Syria. Back in Mosul, Nāṣir al-Dawla was

[10] See the conversation between Ibn Rā'iq and al-Muttaqī in *K. al-ʿUyūn* (above, n. 4), vol. 4, pt. 2, p. 368 (after Dhukā the chamberlain, an eyewitness).

[11] Nāṣir al-Dawla did not order the killing of Ibn Rā'iq until he had failed to dissuade him from his plan. *K. al-ʿUyūn*, vol. 4, pt. 2, pp. 371-72 (after Dhukā); Miskawayh (above, n. 4), 2, pp. 27–28.

[12] Canard (above, n. 1), pp. 428–40, 490-92.

still careful not to fly unnecessarily in the face of caliphal authority. He laid no claim to northern Syria or any other territory to which he had no title. Nevertheless, having lost faith in the caliphate's power to hold back the Buwayhids, he no longer felt the need to maintain a deferential attitude towards the caliphate's military mentors. On the contrary the prospect of a Buwayhid takeover of Iraq impelled him to assert his dynastic rights by making a clear distinction between his loyalty to the caliph and his attitude to the government of Baghdad. Accordingly, he retained the right to cite himself and his brother on the coins issued in the Ḥamdānid principality.

Al-Muttaqī's second flight from Baghdad, in Ṣafar 332/October 943, proved more embarrassing to the Ḥamdānids than the first. The caliph left Baghdad under the illusion that the Ḥamdānids would send forces to overthrow Tūzūn, the new *amīr al-umarā'*, and was greatly surprised to discover that Nāṣir al-Dawla had no such intention.[13] Disappointed with the Ḥamdānids, al-Muttaqī seemed to fall under the influence of the pro-Ikhshīdid party at court. He appealed to al-Ikhshīd for help and presently invited him to a meeting at Rakka. In this awkward situation, Nāṣir al-Dawla was determined to restore al-Muttaqī to Baghdad without either taking an active part in the matter or subjecting the caliph to unnecessary humiliation.[14] But Tūzūn, who smarted at Nāṣir al-Dawla's refusal to recognize his overlordship and desperately wanted the caliph back, was more inclined to fight the Ḥamdānids than to settle amicably. Hence, while Nāṣir al-Dawla bore the blunt of Tūzūn's backlash and sought ways to settle the issue with him, he had to undertake military action in Syria to delay contact between the caliphal party and al-Ikhshīd.

The army which Nāṣir al-Dawla sent into Syria was not meant to annex the country (an impossible task under the circumstances) but simply to delay al-Ikhshīd's advance to Rakka and give Nāṣir al-Dawla enough time to negotiate a settlement with Tūzūn. Nāṣir al-Dawla

[13] Ṣūlī (above, n. 2), pp. 246–48; Muḥammad b. ʿAbd al-Malik al-Hamadhānī, *Takmilat Ta'rīkh al-Ṭabarī*, ed. A. Kanʿān, 2nd ed. (Beirut: Impr. Catholique, 1961), p. 136; ʿIzz al-Dīn ibn al-Athīr, *Al-Kāmil fī al-Ta'rīkh*, 13 vols. (Beirut: Dār Ṣādir, 1965–66), 8, p. 407.

[14] Ṣūlī, pp. 256, 258; Miskawayh (above, n. 4), 2, pp. 49–50; Hamadhānī, p. 138.

entrusted the expedition to his cousin al-Ḥusayn b. Saʿīd, who had little political ambition, rather than to his more ambitious brother Sayf al-Dawla. I do not believe that al-Ḥusayn b. Saʿīd assumed administrative functions in Syria, and disagree with Bacharach's suggestion that he might have been responsible for two ʿAbbāsid dirhams of uncertain date struck in Emessa and Tiberias in the name of al-Muttaqī.[15] The purport of Bacharach's argument is that al-Ḥusayn b. Saʿīd issued these ʿAbbāsid dirhams (rather than Ḥamdānid ones) to demonstrate that he wished to honor Nāṣir al-Dawla's treaty of 1 Shawwāl 332/27 May 944 with Tūzūn, which had defined the limits of the Ḥamdānid territories. Al-Ḥusayn, in fact, set out for Syria on 1 Rajab 332/28 February 944.[16] The Ḥamdānid war against Tūzūn was at its height and the treaty still three months in the future.[17] Al-Ḥusayn did not advance as far as Tiberias; he reached Emessa briefly and turned back to Aleppo almost certainly before Nāṣir al-Dawla and Tūzūn had concluded the treaty.[18] He could have hardly controlled much of the country outside the army camp. Many Ikhshīdid supporters, however, decamped as he approached;[19] and the two ʿAbbāsid coins in question (like a few others to be discussed) probably represent the unsupervised minting activities of local authorities in Emessa and Tiberias, reflecting their preference for ʿAbbāsid rule.

While al-Ḥusayn b. Saʿīd campaigned in Syria, Sayf al-Dawla kept a close watch on the caliph, who awaited al-Ikhshīd at Rakka. Al-Ikhshīd approached Rakka at the end of 332/944, heralded by al-Ḥusayn b. Saʿīd's retreating army, and Sayf al-Dawla retired to Haran, 80 kilometers due north, where he was presently joined by his cousin. Sayf al-Dawla's sojourn in Rakka and Haran is marked by Ḥamdānid coins for 332 from both towns.[20]

[15] Bacharach (above, n. 7), nos. 42, 44, and discussion p. 364.

[16] Ṣūlī (above, n. 2), p. 256.

[17] For the date of this treaty (1 Shawwāl 332/27 May 944) see Ṣūlī, p. 258.

[18] *K. al-ʿUyūn* (above, n. 4), vol. 4, pt. 2, pp. 397–98. The exact date of al-Ḥusayn's return to Aleppo, however, is not given.

[19] *K. al-ʿUyūn*, vol. 4, pt. 2, pp. 397-98; cf. Ibn Saʿīd (above, n. 3), p. 32.

[20] U. S. Linder-Welin, "Sayf al-Dawlah's Reign in Syria and Diyarbekr in the Light of the Numismatic Evidence," *Commentationes de nummis saeculorum, IX-XI, in Suecia repertis* (1961), 1, nos. 2, 3, and discussion p. 41. See also Canard (above, n. 1), pp. 498–99.

COIN TYPES

Except for citing al-Ikhshīd, the early Ikhshīdid issues adhered to the established ʿAbbāsid format. It was only in 336/947, that al-Ikhshīd's successors departed from this practice by adding the ʿAlid legend *Ṣallā Allāhu ʿalayhi wa ʿalā ālihi* after the *kalima* on the reverse. Even then they continued to follow the ʿAbbāsid format in other respects.

Nāṣir al-Dawla's coins adhered likewise to the conventional ʿAbbāsid type. The place of honor beneath the caliph's name on the reverse was reserved for Nāṣir al-Dawla, while Sayf al-Dawla was cited on the obverse. The coins of the Mosul emirate, issued mainly in Mosul city and Niṣībīn, retained this format until Sayf al-Dawla's death in 356/967.

During the lifetime of Nāṣir al-Dawla and Sayf al-Dawla, when the Ḥamdānids observed the appearances of family solidarity, the coinage of Sayf al-Dawla's mints in northern Syria, Diyār Bakr, and Diyār Muḍar, followed roughly the format laid down by Nāṣir al-Dawla in 330. Nevertheless significant divergences occurred from time to time. The ʿAlid legend *Ṣallā Allāhu ʿalayhi wa ʿalā ālihi* appears on a large number of Sayf al-Dawla's coins after the *kalima* on the reverse. A few coins contain one or more of three uncommon Qur'ānic legends, namely, *Qur'ān* 30:3 mixed with 30:11 or 13, *Qur'ān* 9:34 mixed with 28:68 or 23:93, and *Qur'an* 9:34, sometimes in addition to the usual *Qu'ān* 9:33 and 30:3–4 (for the wording and translation of these legends see pp. 171-72). In layout, Sayf al-Dawla's most important departure from Nāṣir al-Dawla's format was an extra-marginal legend citing Nāṣir al-Dawla and Sayf al-Dawla; but only a few coins bear this extra-marginal inscription.[21]

In his earliest issues (1–5) Nāṣir al-Dawla published his full proper name "al-Ḥasan b. ʿAbd Allāh" beneath his state title; but this was replaced in all subsequent issues by the *kunya* "Abū Muḥammad." Sayf al-Dawla's state title, when it appeared on the coinage a few

[21] See Linder-Welin, p. 63.

months later, included the *kunya* "Abū al-Ḥasan." The son whom Nāṣir al-Dawla actually prepared for the succession was not Muḥammad, however, but Abū Taghlib Faḍl Allāh al-Ghaḍanfar, born ca. 318/930.[22] It therefore seems fairly obvious that Nāṣir al-Dawla's object of crowding the *kunya*s on the coinage was to make a display of religious creed rather than lay down the order of successsion. Nāṣir al-Dawla and Sayf al-Dawla were, by their proper names, the namesakes in inverse order of the first two Shīʿite imāms, ʿAlī and al-Ḥasan, who likewise bore the *kunya*s Abū al-Ḥasan and Abū Muḥammad.

Whether the *kunya*s in question also represent the names of Nāṣir al-Dawla's and Sayf al-Dawla's first male issue cannot be established conclusively, but I am inclined to believe they do. Al-Fāriqī, who provides us with the only complete list of Nāṣir al-Dawla's male issue, puts Abū al-Qāsim first and Muḥammad and Abū Taghlib in second and third place respectively, but does not state whether his list is arranged in order of age.[23] Ibn Ẓāfir's list of Sayf al-Dawla's sons, which is arranged by age,[24] is not helpful either, because Sayf al-Dawla's eldest son (who pre-deceased Sayf al-Dawla by two years) is known to us only by his cognomen, Abū al-Barakāt. Freytag, relying on a source which he does not acknowledge, and followed in turn by Canard, maintains—without explaining the numismatic evidence—that Abū Taghlib was Nāṣir al-Dawla's eldest son. Muḥammad he places among Nāṣir al-Dawla's younger sons without suggesting his age.[25]

Very little is known about Muḥammad b. Nāṣir al-Dawla, but of his age one thing seems certain: in 338/949, when Abū Taghlib was twenty, Muḥammad was likewise a grown man, for he deputized for Sayf al-Dawla in Aleppo while the latter made a lengthy trip in Mesopo-

[22] See Aḥmad b. Yūsūf ibn al-Azraq al-Fāriqī, *Ta'rīkh Mayyāfāriqīn* (British Museum MS. Or. 5803), fol. 111*a*.

[23] *Ta'rīkh Mayyāfāriqīn*, fol. 114*b*.

[24] Jamāl al-Dīn ibn Ẓāfir, *Kitāb Akhbār al-Zamān fī Ta'rīkh Banī al-ʿAbbās* (*Al-Duwal al-Munqaṭiʿa*) (British Museum MS. Or. 3685), fol. 11*b*.

[25] G. W. Freytag, "Geschichte der Dynastien der Hamdaniden in Mosul und Aleppo," *Zeitschrift der Deutschen Morgenländischen Gesellschaft* 10–11 (1856–57), 10, pp. 441, 485, and table p. 440; Canard (above, n. 1), pp. 541–42.

tamia.[26] After that we hear no more of Muḥammad until Sayf al-Dawla gives him a commanding position in the army of Aleppo in 348/959.[27] What prompted Sayf al-Dawla to rescue Muḥammad from obscurity after a lapse of nine years is, again, left unstated, but the reason appears to bear more than a coincidental relationship to the family quarrel which pitted the two Ḥamdānid courts against each other earlier that year. This family quarrel gave Sayf al-Dawla good reason to feel uneasy about Abū Taghlib's growing influence in Mosul. His sudden promotion of Muḥammad was probably intended as a challenge to Abū Taghlib's right of succession.

None of this proves that Muḥammad and al-Ḥasan were Nāṣir al-Dawla's and Sayf al-Dawla's eldest sons. It nevertheless appears hardly reasonable that Sayf al-Dawla would use Muḥammad to contest Abū Taghlib's right of succession if the man did not have the right of premogeniture: he would have more likely fallen back on his own tribal right of seniority. It is to be expected, at any rate, that the religious considerations which impelled the brothers to publish these *kunya*s on the coinage had likewise determined their choice of names for their first male issue. Whatever the case, the format which Nāṣir al-Dawla devised for Ḥamdānid coins managed to convey a Shīʿite persuasion without actually flouting the Sunnī caliph's claim of being the only legitimate head of the community.

THE BUWAYHID OCCUPATION OF BAGHDAD

On 21 Jumādā II 334/28 January 946, barely a week after occupying Baghdad, Muʿizz al-Dawla overthrew the Caliph al-Mustakfī and raised al-Muṭīʿ. This event was greatly deplored in the lands of the ʿAbbāsid caliphate for it seemed to confirm a widespread belief that the Buway-

[26] Yaḥya b. Saʿīd al-Anṭākī, *Ta'rīkh*, ed. I. Kratchkovsky and A. Vasiliev, 2 vols. (Paris: Patrologia Orientalis 18 and 23, 1932), 18, p. 767; Kamāl al-Dīn ibn al-ʿAdīm, *Zubdat al-Ḥalab min Ta'rīkh Ḥalab*, ed. S. Dahhan, 3 vols. (Damascus: Institut français de Damas, 1951–68), 1, pp. 120–21.

[27] Hamadhānī (above, n. 13), p. 178; Muḥammad b. Aḥmad al-Dhahabī, *Kitāb Ta'rīkh al-Islām al-Kabīr* (Bibliothèque Nationale MS. Ar. 1581), fol. 193*b*.

hid occupation of Baghdad would entail a fundamental change in the constitutional position of the caliphate. Several autonomous rulers refused to recognize the legality of this act and continued for varying lengths of time to strike coinage in the name of the deposed caliph.

The Ḥamdānids were more vulnerable to the change of regime in Baghdad than most of their contemporaries. Nāṣir al-Dawla instantly put his forces on a wartime footing and, in Ramaḍān 334/April 946 invaded Iraq, entered Baghdad, and engaged the Buwayhids in battle until the end of the year. During the three-month battle of Baghdad Nāṣir al-Dawla was in control of part of the capital and is reported to have operated the mint, using old dies from the period when he had occupied the office of *amīr al-umarā'* under the Caliph al-Muttaqī.[28] He took this measure in Baghdad undoubtedly because in the midst of battle it was difficult to make a die of his choosing. But in Mesopotamia, where there were no impediments, he struck coins in the name of al-Mustakfī (26, a Ḥamdānid coin of Mosul, 335 H. bearing the name of al-Mustakfī). This coin must have been struck during, or not much later than the end of, Muḥarram 335/August 946. At the end of Muḥarram, Nāṣir al-Dawla concluded a peace treaty with the Buwayhids and henceforth struck his coins in the name of al-Muṭīʿ.

In contrast to 26, there are two earlier Ḥamdānid issues which bear the name of the new caliph al-Muṭīʿ rather than the fallen al-Mustakfī (25, 55). These two coins were struck in 334 by the two mints under Nāṣir al-Dawla's direct control, Mosul and Niṣībīn. Since Nāṣir al-Dawla in the latter part of that year rescinded the obligation of citing al-Muṭīʿ on Ḥamdānid coins, these two coins must have been struck during the three months between the accession of al-Muṭīʿ in Jumādā II and the outbreak of the Ḥamdānid-Buwayhid war in Ramaḍān. They suggest that Nāṣir al-Dawla was initially willing to recognize the change of caliph effected by Muʿizz al-Dawla. Nāṣir al-Dawla's reaction to the Buwayhid occupation must therefore be reconsidered in the light of these coins.

In the course of the 320s, the obvious weakness of most of the Daylamite chiefdoms dispelled much of the irrational fear earlier inspired by these people. In 334/945, the prospect of a Buwayhid takeover

[28] Bikhazi, pp. 260–61, 270–71.

of Iraq was less unpalatable to Nāṣir al-Dawla than years before. Twice before 334/945, Nāṣir al-Dawla had demonstrated his changing attitude toward the Buwayhids. In the fall of 331/942, while holding office in Baghdad, he had negotiated with Muʿizz al-Dawla a two-pronged attack against their common enemy, the Barīdīs of southern Iraq[29] (who, incidently, were another bulwark against Buwayhid expansion); and in 333/944, when Tūzūn's deteriorating health made the Buwayhid occupation of Iraq a possibility, Nāṣir al-Dawla sent an embassy to Muʿizz al-Dawla in Fārs, bearing money and gifts.[30]

By 334/945, Nāṣir al-Dawla was willing to acquiesce in a Buwayhid occupation of Baghdad, though not to the point of recognizing Buwayhid overlordship. When the Buwayhids entered Baghdad, Nāṣir al-Dawla struck the coins in the name of Muʿizz al-Dawla's protégé, the Caliph al-Muṭīʿ, as a sign of good will, though leaving out Muʿizz al-Dawla's name, as he was always to do. Simultaneously, as a back-up measure, he made a well-publicized military build-up in Mosul. Muʿizz al-Dawla, as Nāṣir al-Dawla had feared, would not respond to friendly overtures without testing his other options: he was only too aware of Mesopotamia's economic importance to Iraq. Unlike the former Caliph al-Rāḍī, however, Muʿizz al-Dawla had little chance of winning grass roots tribal sympathy in Mesopotamia, and was fairly realistic about it. When the Ḥamdānids put up a determined fight in Baghdad, he eventually consented to an agreement which gave the Ḥamdānids their independence from the Buwayhid state but secured for Iraq its basic economic interest.[31]

THE BEGINNINGS OF THE ḤAMDĀNID EMIRATE OF ALEPPO

We must now go back two years in time to pick up the threads of Mosul's policy in northern Syria. Al-Muttaqī's return to Baghdad from

[29] Ṣūlī (above, n. 2), p. 233; Miskawayh (above, n. 4), 2, p. 37; Hamadhānī (above, n. 13), p. 130. The attack was not carried out, however.

[30] Fāriqī (above, n. 22), fol. 112*a*.

[31] For the terms of this agreement, concluded in Muḥarram 335/August 946, see Miskawayh (above, n. 4), 2, p. 108.

the Rakka conference, his ignominious deposition by Tūzūn in Ṣafar 333/October 944, and the accession of the more tractable al-Mustakfī, inaugurated a new period in the history of the Ḥamdānid emirate. The political authority of the caliphate had received a severe blow from which it never really recovered; the possibility of removing the caliphate to Damascus was eliminated; al-Ikhshīd's interest in northern Syria instantly diminished; and the moral and political considerations which had prevented the Ḥamdānids from occupying northern Syria were gone. During the lull which preceded the Buwayhid takeover of Iraq, Nāṣir al-Dawla provided Sayf al-Dawla with financial and military assistance and set him on the road for Aleppo.

In 333/944 and for four years thereafter, the coins of Syria provide invaluable evidence about Sayf al-Dawla's policy objectives. They substantiate what the literary sources indicate by default, namely, that in 333 Sayf al-Dawla made no attempt to subjugate northern Syria, but considered Aleppo a stepping stone for the occupation of Damascus, which he intended to have as his capital.

Of particular interest are the *amīr al-umarā'* coins of Antioch, al-Maṣṣīṣa, and Emessa (105, 127, 140) and the ʿAbbāsid coin of Tarsus (125) all issued in 333. These must have been struck after Sayf al-Dawla's occupation of Aleppo since the country had earlier been ruled by representatives of al-Ikhshīd. With regard to the *amīr al-umarā'* coins, Bacharach suggests that they were struck by Sayf al-Dawla as a sign of compliance with the agreement which his brother and Tūzūn had concluded a few months earlier.[32] This theory does not account for the above mentioned ʿAbbāsid coin of Tarsus; nor does it resolve Sayf al-Dawla's change of mind and shift to the Ḥamdānid type, which—in this same year—he struck in Aleppo and Emessa (80, 139); and, finally, it does not explain why another ʿAbbāsid coin should be issued in Antioch in 337 (108) fully four years after Aleppo had begun to strike Ḥamdānid coins.

The non-Ḥamdānid coins under study reflect the changing political map of northern Syria. Sayf al-Dawla entered Aleppo on 9 Rabīʿ I 333/30 October 944, and rode within two weeks to fight the Byzantines. He crossed the border at al-Maṣṣīṣa, but made no attempt to enforce

[32] Bacharach (above, n. 7), p. 365.

his authority on Cilicia. Returning to Aleppo, he passed the winter of 333 doing nothing which the sources consider worth mentioning. Left to their own devices, the local mints opted for the ʿAbbāsids with or without recognizing Tūzūn's ascendancy. The coins they issued suggest that northern Syria preferred the remote authority of the ʿAbbāsids to the direct rule threatened alternately by the Ikhshīdids and the Ḥamdānids.

In the second half of the year, Sayf al-Dawla embarked on an ambitious plan of conquest which took him to the borders of Palestine. He defeated the Ikhshīdids near Emessa and marched into Damascus in Ramaḍān 333/April 945. Emessa began to issue Ḥamdānid coins (139) and it has been suggested that Filastīn did too.

Linder-Welin attributes a coin in the Bibliothèque Nationale to the mint of Filasṭīn, 333.[33] The coin, however, is anomalous in that it bears the name of the caliph al-Muttaqī even though Sayf al-Dawla had recognized his successor al-Mustakfī before setting foot in central Syria. Further, it is epigraphically different from other Filasṭīn coins, being quite similar to the contemporary issues of Rakka and Haran. This coin needs further study before inclusion in the corpus of Ḥamdānid coins from Filasṭīn.[34]

Within a month of entering Damascus, Sayf al-Dawla was evicted by the Ikhshīdids and forced to withdraw to Rakka. Before the end of the year, he reached an agreement with al-Ikhshīd; under its terms he obtained the districts of Aleppo and Emessa in return for giving up his claims to the central and southern parts of Syria.

During 334/945, northern Syria belonged legally to Sayf al-Dawla, but how much of it came under effective rule is difficult to say. The literary sources are vague on this point and the numismatic evidence speaks only for Aleppo, Emessa, and Haran, all of which issued Ḥamdānid coins (81–84, 141, 148). The frontier districts appear to have

[33] Linder-Welin (above, no. 20), pp. 44, 6.

[34] Some time ago, Steve Album saw the coin and suggested to Michael L. Bates of the ANS that the mint is Wasit. Arlette Negre has provided a photograph of the coin, and Dr. Bates has compared it with a similar coin in the ANS collection. This coin had originally been attributed to Filasṭīn but was reattributed to Wasit by Album. Dr. Bates has concluded that the mint is correctly Wasit, based on the style of the epigraphy and the layout, and that the date is 331.

remained outside Sayf al-Dawla's authority. Tarsus, at any rate, did not recognize him until 335/946.[35] Antioch came under his authority in the early months of 335/946,[36] probably at the same time as Tarsus.

The death of al-Ikhshīd at the end of 334/mid 946, induced Sayf al-Dawla to make another attempt on Ikhshīdid Syria. He was routed near Damascus in the spring of 335/947, and retreated to Rakka. The Ikhshīdids entered Aleppo in Dhū al-Ḥijja 335/July 947, and for three months northern Syria declared for them. The Ikhshīdid coin of Emessa, 336 H. (142) must have been struck during this interval.

In Rabīʿ II 336/October 947, Sayf al-Dawla recaptured Aleppo and presently reached a new agreement with the Ikhshīdids which established him definitively in northern Syria. As in 334, the country did not instantly accept his authority. The literary sources offer a fairly clear idea of the opposition he encountered in the regions of Emessa and the Ḥadath-Marash-Raʿbān triangle. The numismatic evidence provides a piece of information which the literary sources overlook, namely, that Antioch did not return to him until a year later. In the meantime, it declared for the ʿAbbāsids only. Antioch's return to the Ḥamdānids in 337/948, is marked by the occurence of two coin types:

35 ʿAlī b. al-Ḥusayn al-Masʿūdī, *Kitāb al-Tanbīh wa al-Ishrāf*, ed. M. J. de Goeje, Bibliotheca Geographorum Arabicorum 8 (Leiden: Brill, 1894), pp. 194–95; Dhahabī (above, n. 27), fols. 160a, 162a; Taghribirdi (above, n. 5), 3, pp. 293–94. Al-Masʿūdī, in particular, gives the impression that recognition was granted when Sayf al-Dawla supervized the exchange of prisoners of Rabīʿ I 335/October 946. Cf. Athīr (above, n. 13), 8, p. 468; Canard (above, n. 1), pp. 758–60; Linder-Welin (above, n. 20), pp. 48–49; A. Toynbee, *Constantine Porphyrogenitus and His World* (London, 1973), pp. 499, 503–4.

36 The date of Sayf al-Dawla's acquisition of Antioch can be roughly fixed in reference to the invitation which the poet al-Mutanabbī received from Abū al-ʿAshāʾir, Sayf al-Dawla's governor for Antioch. See the historical introductions to the relevant poems by al-Mutanabbī in Abū al-Ṭayyib al-Mutanabbī, *Dīwān Abī al-Tayyib al-Mutanabbī, wa fī Athnāʾ Matnihi Sharḥ al-Imām al-ʿAllāma al-Wāḥidī*, ed. F. Dietrici (Berlin, 1861), pp. 206, 316; *Dīwān Abī al-Ṭayyib al-Mutanabbī*, ed. ʿA. W. ʿAzzām (Cairo: Maṭbaʿat Lijnat al-Taʾlīf wa al-Tarjamah wa al-Nashr, 1944), pp. 123 and n., 195, 228 and n.; *Dīwān abī al-Ṭayyib al-Mutanabbī* (Bibliothèque Nationale MS. Ar 3091), fols. 86*a–b*. See also R. Blachère, *Un poète arabe du IVe siècle de l'Hégire: Abou ṭ-Ṭayyib al-Montanabbī; Essai d'histoire littéraire* (Paris: Librairie d'Amérique et d'Orient, 1935), pp. 95ff.; ʿAdīm (above, n. 26), 1, p. 118.

one ʿAbbāsid and the other Ḥamdānid, both issued in Antioch in that year (108, 109).

One year after these events, Sayf al-Dawla augmented his domain still further by inducing Nāṣir al-Dawla to recognize his authority over Diyār Bakr and parts of Diyār Bakr and parts of Diyār Muḍar.

RELATIONS BETWEEN THE TWO BRANCHES OF THE ḤAMDĀNID DUAL PRINCIPALITY

Nāṣir al-Dawla, as head of the family, enjoyed a right of overlordship in Sayf al-Dawla's Mesopotamian territories by virtue of caliphal investiture first granted to the Ḥamdānids in 319/931. This much is faithfully reflected by the over-all format of Sayf al-Dawla's coins. But an important point which Sayf al-Dawla's coins do not reflect is that northern Syria belonged, legally, to the Ikhshīdids. It was granted to al-Ikhshīd and his progeny for a period of thirty years by al-Muttaqī at the Rakka conference of 14 Muḥarram 333/6 September 944, and the investiture was confirmed at intervals by al-Muttaqī's two successors, al-Mustakfī and al-Muṭīʿ.[37] Sayf al-Dawla's position in Syria was legitimatized, in effect, by his treaties with the Ikhshīdids rather than by a caliphal patent. Nāṣir al-Dawla's title to northern Syria was even more dubious since it depended on Sayf al-Dawla's willingness to consider him party to these treaties.

It has been pointed out in the description of Ḥamdānid coins that Sayf al-Dawla's coins differed from his brother's in some significant respects. Most of these differences resulted from specific events beyond Sayf al-Dawla's power or from minting practices peculiar to the territories of the Aleppo emirate; but other differences, of which the ʿAlid legend is the most striking, cannot be put down to incidental causes.

While the *kunyah*s of Nāṣir al-Dawla and Sayf al-Dawla convey a simple statement of faith, the ʿAlid legend is too flagrantly significant to be anything but an ouright political statement. There are two things

[37] Yaḥyā (above, n. 26), 18, p. 735; ʿAdīm (above, n. 26), 1, p. 107; Kindī (above, n. 4), pp. 290–91, 294; Taghribirdi (above, n. 5), 3, pp. 255–56; *K. al-ʿUyūn* (above, n. 4), 2, pp. 460–61.

which make this legend difficult to explain. Although the Ḥamdānids were often ready to manipulate religion for political ends, their rule was less Shīʿite in character than that of their fellow Twelvers, the Buwayhids (who, incidentally, did not adopt the ʿAlid legend). Secondly, the legend does not appear consistently on Sayf al-Dawla's coinage. There are some issues without it from every mint in the Aleppo emirate.

At one point I was inclined to connect these coins with the Ikhshīdid issues which likewise juxtapose the ʿAlid legend with the name of the ʿAbbāsid caliph; it seemed likely that Sayf al-Dawla found it politic on occasion to follow the Egyptian practice in recognition of the Ikhshīdid right of overlordship in northern Syria. This explanation would have been valid had the ʿAlid legend appeared simultaneously on both Ḥamdānid and Ikhshīdid coins. But whereas it appeared on Sayf al-Dawla's coins as early as 333/944, I have encountered no Ikhshīdid coin of the same type predating 336/947—and that disposes of this explanation.

For a while, I also considered the possibility that the legend was meant to please the Qarmaṭian tribes of Syria and their coreligionists who inhabited and ruled Bahrain. The Ḥamdānids were eager to cultivate the friendship of the Qarmaṭians; but the absence of doctrinal agreement between the Twelver Shīʿites and the Qarmaṭians would have made a religious manifestation on the coins superfluous unless the Ḥamdānids were willing to recognize the overlordship of Bahrain, which they certainly were not. Moreover, the Ḥamdānids of Mosul were equally involved with the Qarmaṭians, yet they did not strike the ʿAlid legend on their coins until well after the fall of Nāṣir al-Dawla in 356/967.

It is even less likely that these coins constitute evidence of a political understanding with the Fāṭimids. Relations between the Fāṭimids and Sayf al-Dawla, while hardly discussed by the sources, appear to have been far from amicable.[38] In a study of the Ḥamdānid dynasty which I am currently preparing for publication, I shall suggest that the Caliph al-Muʿizz made an attempt around 346/957 to secure for him-

[38] See the statement attributed to the Fāṭimid caliph al-Muʿizz in ca. 358/969, in Aḥmad b. ʿAlī al-Maqrīzī, *Al-Khiṭaṭ al-Maqrīziyyah al-Musammāt bil-Mawāʿiẓ wa al-Iʿtibār bi-Dhikr al-Khiṭaṭ wa al-Āthār*, 4 vols. (Cairo: Al-Malījī, 1906–8), 2, p. 165. Cf. Canard (above, n. 1), p. 677.

self recognition in northern Syria, but in vain, and that this episode—perhaps along with others—made him feel that the Ḥamdānids were unreliable fellow travellers.

To return to the ʿAlid legend, I finally reached the conclusion that it was adopted by Sayf al-Dawla simply to distinguish his coins from his brother's. It was, in other words, an occasional assertion of independence within the family, intended to fall short of outright secession.

That Sayf al-Dawla's assertion of independence should take this circuitous form is not surprising, for the factors involved defied a clear-cut arrangement. Sayf al-Dawla needed no reminder that the dynasty was more securely entrenched in Mosul than in the territories he himself held. This alone gave him a real interest in family solidarity and was sufficient to make him accept Nāṣir al-Dawla's primacy. Nevertheless, Sayf al-Dawla's function in the over-all Ḥamdānid political scheme (defending the border against Byzantium and policing the turbulent Euphrates region) set the Aleppo emirate on an independent course. Aleppo's military-political establishment did not merge well with Mosul's familial-tribal system. There was no administrative unity between the two emirates and little agreement on priorities. Sayf al-Dawla was torn between his interest in his family connections and the requirements of his position in Aleppo.

While the textual sources are largely silent on the subject, the numismatic evidence suggests that the political relations between Aleppo and Mosul sometimes verged on rupture. Sayf al-Dawla would sometimes remove Nāṣir al-Dawla's name from the coinage by either partially or completely leaving it off flan (90, 120–23, 126, 137).

In this numismatic war, Nāṣir al-Dawla was helpless. He could not retaliate in kind because Sayf al-Dawla's subsidiary place on the coins was a symbolic expression of Nāṣir al-Dawla's theoretical overlordship. The quarrels between the brothers expressed themselves only on Sayf al-Dawla's coins, with one exception: 89, struck in Aleppo in the name of al-Muṭīʿ and Nāṣir al-Dawla without citing Sayf al-Dawla. The date is uncertain, but I believe it was issued at the turn of 347–48/early 969, when Nāṣir al-Dawla was in temporary control of Aleppo.[39]

[39] Linder-Welin (above, n. 20), p. 70, reads the year as possibly 340, but attributes the coin to 347 on historical grounds.

The events which led up to this had been set in motion by a change of policy in Baghdad. For more than a decade, Muʿizz al-Dawla had based his relations with the Ḥamdānids on a bilateral agreement solely with Nāṣir al-Dawla, who was more vulnerable than his brother to pressure from Baghdad. Nāṣir al-Dawla sometimes withheld the tribute from Baghdad, and Ḥamdānid-Buwayhid relations floundered each time this happened. Yet until 347/958, Muʿizz al-Dawla does not seem to have entertained the idea of regulating his relations with the Ḥamdānids except through Mosul. His official view was that the unity of the Ḥamdānid family bound Sayf al-Dawla to the terms contracted by Nāṣir al-Dawla.

In 347/958, Muʿizz al-Dawla suddenly abandoned this attitude. He occupied Mosul and Diyār Rabīʿa on the pretext that Nāṣir al-Dawla had again defaulted on the tribute, and refused to settle with the Ḥamdānids except by agreement with Sayf al-Dawla. The Buwayhid emir, according to the sources, did not aim to dislodge Nāṣir al-Dawla; he had simply lost confidence in him and intended henceforth to deal solely with Sayf al-Dawla, whom he held in high regard.[40] In effect, Muʿizz al-Dawla intended to bring Aleppo into direct relationship with Baghdad.

Nāṣir al-Dawla had in fact withheld the tribute as was his habit whenever he thought he could. But there is reason to believe that Muʿizz al-Dawla's change of policy was precipitated by suspicions that Sayf al-Dawla was planing a deal with the Fāṭimid government. Sayf al-Dawla was presumably to recognize Fāṭimid suzerainty and the Fāṭimid caliph was to reciprocate by arranging for a much needed peace between Aleppo and Byzantium.[41] As the protector of the ʿAbbāsid

[40] For the Ḥamdānid-Buwayhid conflict of 347–48/958–59, see Miskawayh (above, n. 4), 2, pp. 170–72, 174–75; Athīr (above, n. 13), 8, pp. 522–24; Abū Firās al-Ḥārith b. Saʿīd al-Ḥamdānī, *Dīwān Abī Firās*, ed. S. Dahhan, 3 vols. (Beirut: Impr. Catholique, 1944), 2, pp. 151–52 (comment on verse 212); Yaḥyā (above, n. 26), 18, p. 777; Fāriqī (above, n. 22), fol. 114*b*.

[41] The evidence in question is contained in an account of a Byzantine embassy to the Fātimid court, by al-Qāḍī al-Nuʿmān b. Muḥammad, *Al-Majālis wa al-Musāyarāt wa al-Mawāqif wa al-Tawqīʿāt*, published, translated and discussed by S. M. Stern, "An Embassy of the Byzantine Emperor to the Fātimid Caliph al-Muʿizz," *Byzantion* 20 (1950), pp. 239–58. Supportive evidence is provided by Mis-

caliphate, Muʿizz al-Dawla was obliged to abort this agreement. He could not hope to coerce Sayf al-Dawla, but he could hold Mosul in ransom until Sayf al-Dawla came to terms.

Whatever Muʿizz al-Dawla's motives, the crucial point for the Ḥamdānids was that his terms carried the adjunct that Sayf al-Dawla rather than Nāṣir al-Dawla would henceforth be regarded by Baghdad as head of the family. Nāṣir al-Dawla hung around in the unoccupied part of Mesopotamia for five months, willing to settle with the Buwayhids on all their terms except this. Towards the end of the year he repaired in person to Aleppo to dissuade Sayf al-Dawla from negotiating with Muʿizz al-Dawla.

In Aleppo, Nāṣir al-Dawla and his party seized every opportunity to flaunt their ascendency in the face of Sayf al-Dawla and his court, and a series of unpleasant scenes occurred. Abū Taghlib's irritating inclination to dictate policy to his elders added fuel to the fire. The historical sources, however, miss the whole point of Nāṣir al-Dawla's ostentatious behavior. Nearly all of them maintain that he travelled to Aleppo to seek military assistance against the Buwayhids. (This actually was Abū Taghlib's idea, not Nāṣir al-Dawla's.)[42] The continuous squabbling between members of the two courts is put down to arrogance on the part of the one and over-sensitivity on the part of the other. The one literary source that alludes to the question of primacy is the *Dīwān* of Abū Firās, prince of Manbij and cousin of the reigning emirs, who took Sayf al-Dawla's side in every family quarrel. In commenting on Nāṣir al-Dawla's haughtiness, Abū Firās submits that primacy should belong to the abler brother, Sayf al-Dawla.[43] But he does not go as far as to suggest that Nāṣir al-Dawla behaved haughtily because his primacy had been called in question to begin with; nor does he connect this behavior with the peace agreement which Sayf al-Dawla was even then negotiating with Muʿizz al-Dawla. The coin under discussion,

kawayh (above, n. 4), 2, p. 172, in his account of an embassy from Muʿizz al-Dawla the Buwayhid to the Ikhshīdid court.

42 See two poems in al-Sariy al-Raffā', *Dīwān al-Sariy al-Raffā'* (Cairo: Maktabat al-Qudsi, 1355 A.H.), pp. 111–14. This poet was then in the employ of the Mosul Ḥamdānids, and was particularly attached to Abū Taghlib.

43 Abū Firās (above, n. 40), 3, pp. 366–68 (no. 293), 416–17 n. (no. 336).

89, confirms that Nāṣir al-Dawla was not being pointlessly unpleasant or undecorous, but was simply eager to assert his primacy.

At the end of the year, with Nāṣir al-Dawla still in Aleppo, Sayf al-Dawla made a foray into Byzantium.[44] The raid was unimpressive as military operations go, and was probably intended only to assure Muʿizz al-Dawla that Sayf al-Dawla had no desire to suspend Holy War, and therefore had no reason to make a deal with the Fāṭimids. Nevertheless, considering that Aleppo's regular forces had suffered severe human losses earlier in the year,[45] the raid must have occupied a large proportion of what troops were still available. Sayf al-Dawla could not have left a big garrison in Aleppo, and it must have been possible for Nāṣir al-Dawla to seize the mint and issue the coins represented by 89.

NORTHERN SYRIA, BYZANTIUM, AND THE ḤAMDĀNIDS: THE LEGEND *QUR'ĀN* 9:34

Among the Ḥamdānid specimens that have come to my attention, the Qur'ānic legend 9:34, with its dire warning to those who hoard gold and silver instead of spending them in the service of God, occurs for the first time on issue 138 from the year 350/961, bearing the mint name *Thaghr al-Shāmiyya* (Syria's frontier city). Mrs. Linder-Welin has established on epigraphic grounds that this coin was issued in al-Maṣṣīṣa, in the autonomous frontier district Cilicia.[46] Following its appearance on this unique coin, the legend in question appears on all subsequent Ḥamdānid coins from al-Maṣṣīṣa (128–36). It also appears on coins from the mints of Aleppo and Emessa, both of which were usually under Sayf al-Dawla's direct authority. The Aleppo coin bears an uncertain date which could be read as 351 or 353, while the Emessa coins were undoubtedly struck in 363 (91, 145–47).

[44] Fāriqī (above, n. 22), fol. 114*b*.

[45] Sayf al-Dawla's losses were incurred during two battles against a Byzantine invading force led by John Tsimisces. Yaḥyā (above, n. 26), 18, p. 775; ʿAdīm (above, n. 26), 1, pp. 127–28; Dhahabī (above, n. 27), fol. 193*a*; Hamadhānī (above, n. 13), p. 172.

[46] Linder-Welin (above, n. 20), pp. 78–80.

Cilicia had overcome its initial reluctance to recognize the Ḥamdānids not because Sayf al-Dawla intimidated it by force, but because the Byzantine military threat dictated a policy of close relationship with whoever governed northern Syria. The failure of the Ḥamdānids to provide the country with adequate protection subsequently led to a resurgence of opposition. Following the paralyzing military débacle which shattered Aleppo's forces in 349/960, Sayf al-Dawla drew fire from Tarsus's governor Ibn al-Zayyāt for negotiating for peace at the very moment Byzantium was preparing to reduce Anazarba and the network of fortresses which served as Cilicia's first line of defense. Unable to induce Aleppo to participate in Anazarba's defense, Ibn al-Zayyāt severed ties with Sayf al-Dawla, whom he accused of dealing with the enemy at Cilicia's expense, and rode out for the border at the head of Tarsus's army.[47]

Outside Tarsus, the preponderant feeling in Cilicia was that while Sayf al-Dawla was incapable of standing up to Byzantium, there was nothing to be gained by breaking away from the Ḥamdānid emirate. Al-Maṣṣīṣa had lost heavily during the previous year's fighting and its governor, loyal to Sayf al-Dawla, was able to keep the populace under control. But when Ibn al-Zayyāt revealed the extent of the danger which threatened Anazarba, the citizens of al-Maṣṣīṣa likewise revoked their allegiance to Sayf al-Dawla and sent their enfeebled force to serve under Ibn al-Zayyāt in the defense of the border.

After the rout of the Cilician forces near Anazarba, al-Maṣṣīṣa repented but did not abandon its belligerent mood. Its populace proclaimed once more for Sayf al-Dawla, and asked its governor (who had remained loyal to him throughout) for arms to carry on with the war that was still raging along the border. The governor, however, confessed that he did not have the means; and the citizens, infuriated, sent a delegation to Tarsus, whither Ibn al-Zayyāt had returned, to renew their allegiance

[47] Our most detailed source on this episode is the *K. al-ʿUyūn* (above, n. 4), vol. 4, pt. 2, pp. 501–8. See also Yaḥyā (above, n. 26), 18, pp. 783–84; Miskawayh (above, n. 4) 2, pp. 190–91; Athīr (above, n. 13), 8, pp. 538–39; Gregory Abū al-Faraj Bar Hebraeus, *The Chronography*, ed and tr. E. A. W. Budge, 2 vols. (London, 1932), 1, pp. 167–68.

to him.[48] There can be little doubt that the occurrence of *Qur'ān* 9:34 owes itself to the failure of Sayf al-Dawla's governor of al-Maṣṣīṣa to assume the cost of defense. The mint name *Thaghr al-Shāmiyya* was obviously adopted to emphasize that following the fall of Anazarba, al-Maṣṣīṣa had become the most forward bulwark on Syria's approaches from the direction of the Cilician border.

The delegation of al-Maṣṣīṣa arrived in Tarsus to find that Ibn al-Zayyāt had in the meantime committed suicide, having first turned the city over to the pro-Ḥamdānid party. What happened next is unknown, for our source, the *Kitāb al-ʿUyūn*, ends abruptly at this point. It is hardly likely that disaffection with Ḥamdānid rule abated. In al-Maṣṣīṣa, Sayf al-Dawla's representative does not seem to have regained much authority, as we may infer from the survival of the Qur'ānic injunction on subsequent coins. But the pro-Ḥamdānid party in Tarsus seems to have remained firmly in charge, and was able to prevent the feelings of discontent from taking official form.

The appearance of *Qur'ān* 9:34 on coins from Aleppo and Emessa was undoubtedly inspired by its presence on the coins of al-Maṣṣīṣa; but here it conveys a different message. On purely epigraphic grounds, it is not clear whether the Aleppo coin bears the date 351 or 353. It was at first inclined to connect this coin with the looting of Sayf al-Dawla's palace in 351/962. In Dhū al-Qaʿda/December of that year, a Byzantine army sacked Aleppo and took off with, among other things, Sayf al-Dawla's treasure and store of arms. From that moment Sayf al-Dawla was in financial difficulties, and it seemed likely that he could have adopted the anti-hoarding legend because he was raising funds to replenish his treasurey. But Sayf al-Dawla hardly had the time to institute this change in 351. He had left the city just before the Byzantines forced an entry and did not return until practically the end of the year.[49] In addition, the other mints under his control did not pick up this legend as they would have logically done had he adopted it to serve his fund raising purposes. Everything considered, it seems probable that the Aleppo coin 91 was struck in 353 along with the Emessa

48 *K. al-ʿUyūn* (above, n. 4), vol. 4, pt. 2, p. 507.

49 Yaḥyā (above, n. 26), 18, p. 785; Ẓāfir (above, n. 24), fol. 10*b*; ʿAdīm (above, n. 26), 1, p. 145.

coins, and expresses, as they do, the doubts and apprehension aroused by Sayf al-Dawla's absence from Syria between 353 and 355/964 and 966.

Sayf al-Dawla's departure for Mayyāfāriqīn in Shawwāl 353/October 964, left his officials and allies in Syria with uneasy feelings, exacerbated by the knowledge that the emir was seriously stricken by paralysis and might not recover. There was a widespread unwillingness to submit to Sayf al-Dawla's *ghulām*, Qarghawayh the chamberlain, who had been left in charge of government in Aleppo. The first to revolt was Marwān al-ʿUqaylī, governor of the litoral province and one of the few Arab tribal leaders still holding a ranking position in northern Syria. Marwān took Emessa, then occupied Aleppo after defeating Qarghawayh in battle. He remained in control of Aleppo until his death from battle wounds shortly afterward.[50] As for this sedition's date, the literary evidence narrows it down to within a year of Sayf al-Dawla's departure from Aleppo. However, if the coins under study were struck by Marwān as I believe, we can then date this affair to the last two months of 353/964.

During this affair, Marwān was quick to assure Sayf al-Dawla of his loyalty, and the latter reciprocated by confirming him in authority over northern Syria. The numismatic evidence, however, indicates that Marwān took Sayf al-Dawla publicly to task for staying in Mayyāfāriqīn while the Greeks overran northern Syria.

Sayf al-Dawla had withdrawn to his eastern possessions for two reasons: to stay away from the main theater of war pending the conclusion of peace with Byzantium, and to restore his authority in Diyār Bakr, recently grown shaky.

The negotiations with Byzantium had started earlier in the year but were not making easy progress. Sayf al-Dawla pressed for a general peace while Byzantium was interested only in an exchange of prisoners. Arab prisoners far outnumbered Byzantine ones, and the balance had to be freed by outright purchase. Sayf al-Dawla shrank from an agreement limited to prisoners because, in addition to being prohibitively costly, it would have scarcely improved his desperate political and military position. Sayf al-Dawla's tribal allies in northern Syria, grow-

[50] Athīr (above, n. 13), 8, p. 566; ʿAdīm, 1, p. 148.

ing impatient for the prince to return, do not seem to have grasped the full difficulty of his position. The appearance of the anti-hoarding legend on Marwān's coins reveals that they suspected him of being unwilling to spend his personal fortune on the sacrosanct duty of buying the freedom of Moslem prisoners of war.

Two years later *Qurān* 9:34 was worked (in Rajab 355-June 966) into an official Ḥamdānid document which proclaimed the recent exchange of prisoners effected by Sayf al-Dawla with Byzantium.[51] Drafted by the poet Abū al-Faraj al-Babbaghā', the document in question dwells on the large sum of money which the prince expended on this religious duty. Sayf al-Dawla's munificence was a favorite theme for poets, but his generosity was usually panegyrized as a sign of power and greatness rather than in the religious sense expressed in this document. On Marwān al-ʿUqaylī's coins *Qurān* 9:34 reflected the prevailing doubts over Sayf al-Dawla's negotiations with Byzantium, while on Sayf al-Dawla's official proclamation it was used as a retort to these doubts.

THE IKHSHĪDIDS AND THE FĀṬIMIDS

On the coins of the Ikhshīdids, a Sunnī dynasty, the ʿAlid legend "*. . . wa ʿalā ālihi*" concedes to Fāṭimah's descendants an exclusive political right which Sunnīs did not recognize despite the special status they accorded the House of the Prophet. The same legend on Sayf al-Dawla's coins does not constitute a similar departure from political principle because the Ḥamdānids, as Twelver Shīʿites, conceded these rights as a matter of faith, though they were prevented from putting them in practice by the concealment of the Twelfth Imām.

Egygt's special relation with the Fāṭimids, which is epitomized by the ʿAlid legend, is rarely mentioned directly by the sources. In his biographical notice of Kāfūr, for instance, al-Dhahabī simply says that Kāfūr recognized the ʿAbbāsids and professed sympathy for the Fāṭimids,

[51] This proclamation is preserved in al-Muḥassin b. ʿAlī al-Tunūkhī, *Nishwār al-Muḥāḍara wa Akhbār al-Mudhākara*, ed. A. Shalchy, 8 vols. (Bhamdoun, 1971–73), 2, pp. 296–300.

"and used to cajole and deceive these and those."[52] Modern research into the actions of Ikhshīdid officials reveals that the relationship ran deeper than that. It was governed by an understanding which guaranteed Egypt's independence for the duration of Kāfūr's life, and allowed the Fāṭimids to have a free run for their propaganda in preparation for a peaceful takeover.[53] This arrangement complemented the truce of 325/937 with Byzantium and minimized Egypt's defense requirements.

The idea of coming to terms with the Fāṭimids in order to reduce Egypt's army budget had been contemplated by al-Ikhshīd but put off because he hoped to play host to the ʿAbbāsid caliph. Between 330 and 333/941 and 944, al-Ikhshīd came twice to the conclusion that al-Muttaqī might be induced to transfer the capital to Damascus. On the second of these occasions, he was actually invited by the caliph for a conference at Rakka. The ʿAbbāsid issue for Egypt in 333[54] was obviously struck to demonstrate al-Ikhshīd's loyalty to the caliph, and must have comprised the monetary gift which al-Ikhshīd presented to al-Muttaqī at Rakka. During the meeting, however, it transpired that the caliph wanted al-Ikhshīd to return with him to Iraq and restore order. Al-Ikhshīd turned down the invitation and al-Muttaqī returned to Baghdad by himself, where he was deposed in favor of al-Mustakfī. And there ended all prospect of removing the caliphate from Iraq.

Meanwhile, the Fāṭimids had been crippled by the revolution of Ibn Kaydād, so al-Ikhshīd did not have a pressing reason to revive his old plan. It was only during the reign of al-Ikhshīd's son Anūjūr that the Fāṭimids restored order to northern Africa and again posed a threat to Egypt. By then, the man in control of Egypt was the eunuch Kāfūr who, unlike al-Ikhshīd, did not have dynastic interests to protect. Kāfūr could afford to take his arrangements with the Fāṭimids much further than al-Ikhshīd had planned.

[52] Dhahabī (above, n. 27), fol. 277*a*.

[53] S. I. Kāshif, *Miṣr fī ʿAṣr al-Ikhshīdiyyīn*, 2nd ed. (Cairo: Dār al-Nahḍa al-ʿArabiyya, 1970), pp. 380–84. Cf. F. Dachraoui, "La Crète dans le conflit entre Byzance et al-Muʿizz," *Les cahiers de Tunisie* 7 (1959), p. 316.

[54] *BMCOR* 1, 473.

The Fāṭimid caliph al-Manṣūr put an end to the last remnants of Ibn Kaydād's revolution by Ramaḍān 336/March 948. But it had been apparent since the end of the previous year that the Fāṭimid caliphate would survive. Kāfūr appears to have made his arrangements early in 336/mid 947, for I have found no coins from Egypt of the old type for that year. The lone Ikhshīdid coin from Emessa for 336 (142), which must have been struck fairly early in the year, likewise bears the ʿAlid legend.

Byzantium's strident policy in the eastern Mediterranean, which in the late 340s/early 960s threatened to cut Egypt off from major sources of timber for its two maritime fleets, underlined the incompatibility of Egypt's and north Africa's respective interests and appears to have generated some friction between the two governments. In 349/960, Kāfūr attempted to interest the Fāṭimid caliph al-Muʿizz in a joint venture to defend Crete against Byzantium.[55] Al-Muʿizz dodged the issue, but apparently at so much loss of countenance that al-Nuʿmān b. Muḥammad, chief propagandist and highest ranking qādī of the Fāṭimid empire, was later at pains to belittle Egypt's attempt to aid the beleaguered island.[56] In the years which followed, Egypt made feeble attempts to aid Cyprus (in 352/963) and Tarsus (in 354/965) against Byzantium,[57] while the Fāṭimids made none.

The most likely places for Kāfūr's Fāṭimid policy to run into opposition were Damascus and Palestine, the Ikhshīdid family's original sinecures, where effective power remained in the hands of members of the family. The ʿAlid legend on the Ikhshīdid coins of Syria for 336/947 (142, 166–67, 183) must have been struck on the direct orders of Kāfūr, who was in Syria fighting the Ḥamdānids during the first part of the year. One may also conjecture that Kāfūr's sojourn in Syria was spent mainly in Damascus as one coin from that city (167) bears his

[55] Al-Nuʿmān b. Muḥammad, *al-Majālis wa al-Musāyarāt wa al-Mawāqif wa al-Tawqīʿāt* (American University of Beirut MS. photocopy, MS. 297.8:N17mA), pp. 323–29; F. Dachraoui (above, n. 53), pp. 307–8.

[56] Al-Nuʿmān, p. 324.

[57] Yaḥyā (above, n. 26), 18, pp. 794–97; Muḥammad b. Aḥmad al-Dhahabī, *Kitāb Ta'rīkh al-Islām al-Kabīr*, excerpts in M. Canard, ed., *Sayf al-Dawla: Recueil des textes relatifs à l'émir Sayf al-Dawla le Hamdanide avec annotations* (Algiers: Edition Jules Carbonel, 1934), pp. 185–86; ʿAdīm (above, n. 26), 1, pp. 142–43.

initial *kāf* —the earliest such specimen to my knowledge. Tiberias, the one Ikhshīdid Syrian mint which does not seem to have adopted the ʿAlid legend in 336,[58] remained outside the scope of Ikhshīdid military activities.

In Ramla (mint name, Filasṭīn) where the governor was al-Ikhshīd's nephew al-Ḥasan b. ʿUbayd Allāh, the ʿAlid legend disappeared from the coinage in 337/948, the year after Kāfūr returned to Egypt (185–94). It was, however, retained on the sole Damascus specimen of the next year (168). The governor of Damascus in that year was al-Ikhshīd's surviving brother al-Ḥasan b. Ṭughj,[59] so it does not appear that al-Ikhshīd's family were of one mind on Kāfūr's Fāṭimid policy. After 338/949, there are no extant Ikhshīdid coins for Damascus, so we cannot ascertain al-Ḥasan b. Ṭughj's opinion of the policy of his nephew and namesake al-Ḥasan b. ʿUbayd Allāh. Anyway, Ibn Ṭughj died three years later, in 341/952.[60]

The little we know of al-Ḥasan b. ʿUbayd Allāh's activities after the Fāṭimid occupation of Egypt suggests that he headed the anti-Fāṭimid party and attempted to organize military resistance in Syria.[61] There is, however, a curious account of al-Ḥassan's last years which does not tally with this. He allegedly embraced the Fāṭimid call and, being at odds with Kāfūr and the military establishment of Egypt, was then induced by a Fāṭimid agent to seek Fāṭimid backing against the Ikhshīdid government. The Fāṭimid occupation of Egypt is then said to have occurred in the immediate wake of al-Ḥasan's appeal for Fāṭimid help.[62]

[58] P. Balog, "Tables des références des monnaies ikhchidites," *RBN* 102 (1956), p. 130 (2 specimens). To these must be added two uncatalogued specimens in the collections of the American Numismatic Society and the Bibliothèque Nationale. All these coins were struck in Tiberias in 336, without the ʿAlid legend.

[59] Taghribirdī (above, n. 5), 3, p. 297.

[60] Taghribirdī, 3, p. 310.

[61] Aḥmad b. ʿAlī al-Maqrīzī, *Ittiʿāẓ al-Ḥunafā' bi-Akhbār al-A'immah al-Faṭimiyyīn al-Khulafā'*, ed. J. D. Shayyāl, 3 vols. (Cairo: A-Majlis al-Aʿlā lil-Shu'ūn al-Islāmiyya, 1967–73), 1, pp. 120, 122; Taghribirdī, 4, p. 26; Athīr (above, n. 13), 8, p. 591.

[62] Taghribirdī, 4, pp. 72–74, citing a contemporary account by the Qadi ʿAbd al-Jabbār al-Baṣrī, who seems to have been hostile to the Fāṭimids.

One is inclined to treat this account as apocryphal because, aside from overlooking Kāfūr's dealings with the Fāṭimids, it fails to account for al-Ḥasan's belated anti-Fāṭimid stand and contains what appears to be a fanciful account of the last months of al-Ḥasan's life, spent in captivity at al-Manṣūriyya. The numismatic evidence indicates, however, that the reported estrangement between al-Ḥasan and Kāfūr and al-Ḥasan's subsequent contact with the Fātimids contain a substratum of truth, though both incidents must have occurred at an earlier date and in the opposite causal relationship.

While reluctant to condone Kāfūr's Fāṭimid policy, al-Ḥasan b. ʿUbayd Allāh does not seem to have initially challenged Kāfūr himself. He introduced Kāfūr's *kāf* on the coinage of Filasṭīn in 337/948 (185–93), the very year he dropped the ʿAlid legend, and at least a decade before Kāfūr ventured to publish his initial on Egypt's coins.[63] Once he began to recognize the futility of resisting Fāṭimid influence, however, al-Ḥasan must have realized that his family's chance of political survival might be forfeited should Kāfūr remain the conduit between the Ikhshīdid government and the Fāṭimids. Al-Ḥasan therefore did not merely acquiesce in Kāfūr's Fāṭimid policy, but tried to cut him out and cast himself as the foremost ally of the Fāṭimids. In 341/952 Kāfūr's initial was removed from Filasṭīn's coins, and did not reappear until five years later (196–208). The prolonged absence of the *kāf* from Filastin's coins roughly coincides with the reappearance of the ʿAlid legend. It is moreover to be noted that Anūjūr b. al-Ikhshīd's attempt in 343/954 to free himself from Kāfūr's tutelage (in the course of which he bethought of seeking refuge with his cousin in Ramla)[64] occurred midway during the interval when the *kāf* did not appear on any of the extant coins from Filasṭīn.

[63] There is a gap in the numismatic evidence for Egypt for the four years preceding the appearance of the *kāf*. One may reasonably conjecture, however, that Kāfūr introduced his initial on the Egyptian coins immediately after the death of Anūjūr and accession of ʿAlī b. al-Ikhshīd toward the end of 349/960, at which point Kāfūr tightened his control over the Egyptian government. The first extant Egyptian coins to carry Kāfūr's initial were issued in 350/961. Balog (above, n. 58), p. 125 (2 specimens).

[64] Taghribirdī (above, n. 5), 3, pp. 292–93.

Unable to outbid Kāfūr, al-Ḥasan was left with the one real option of preparing to resist the Fāṭimids. But since he restored the *kāf* to Filasṭīn's coinage in 346/957, and thereafter retained it along with the ʿAlid legend during a whole decade (209–48), he appears to have chosen to get on Kāfūr's bandwagon instead. The futility of this policy must have become apparent by 355/966, which was the first year of Kāfūr's personal reign as well as the year in which the Fāṭimids started to prepare in earnest for the occupation of Egypt.[65] All but one specimen from Filasṭīn for this year bear the ʿAlid legend and the *kāf* as before (244–48, but without the name of an Ikhshīdid prince since none was associated in power). The one exception of the same year carried the ʿAlid legend without the *kāf* (249, listed here as ʿAbbāsid). What the coins for 355 imply is that al-Ḥasan initially acquiesced in Kāfūr's accession, but changed heart some time during the year, and attempted once again to guarantee his personal future by a separate agreement with the Fāṭimids.

In 357/968, Kāfūr died. The establishment in Egypt raised the son of the last Ikhshīdid prince to nominal rule and formally associated him in power with al-Ḥasan b. ʿUbayd Allāh. Real power in Egypt was exercised for a while by the minister Abū al-Faḍl Jaʿfar b. al-Furāt, a determined anti-Fāṭimid who immediately took steps to curb the Fāṭimid party. Al-Ḥasan b. ʿUbayd Allāh arrived in al-Fusṭāṭ around the turn of 357–58/968 and removed the anti-Fāṭimid minister from power, treating him horribly.[66] This behavior, left unexplained by the sources, is best understood in light of al-Ḥasan's confidence that he could come to terms with the Fāṭimids. The specimen from Filasṭīn for 357 and two of the five specimens for 358 (250–51) are Ikhshīdid issues bearing the ʿAlid legend. They indicate that in 357/968, al-Ḥasan pursued his contacts with the Fāṭimids and overthrew Ibn al-Furāt in an attempt to suppress the anti-Fāṭimid party in Egypt and thereby appease the Fāṭimids. But after returning to Ramla in Rabīʿ II 358/February 969, al-Ḥasan appears to have recognized the failure of his policy of appeasement, for the ʿAlid legend was again dropped from the coinage of Filasṭīn (252–54). His decision to take up arms

[65] Maqrīzī, *Ittiʿāẓ* (above, n. 61), 1, p. 96.

[66] Taghribirdī, 4, pp. 21–23.

against the Fāṭimids must have been made only after he had given up trying to reach a favorable agreement with them.

While the Egyptian establishment did not wholeheartedly support Kāfūr's passive foreign policy, it is also obvious that those who wished to undo Kāfūr's arrangement with the Fāṭimids would have had to challenge Kāfūr's authority, throw Egypt's politics in disarray, and perhaps hasten the Fāṭimid takeover. Fāṭimid propaganda did not go entirely unopposed,[67] but the sources do not record that the opposition faced the root of the problem by attempting to constrain Kāfūr to rebuild Egypt's armed forces and suppress Fāṭimid agents. The crux of the matter for most members of the Ikhshīdid establishment was personal survival rather than Egypt's political future. Hence Kāfūr adhered to his policy until the end of his life; the Egyptian armed forces went to seed and were neither able to maintain Egypt's status in the eastern Mediterranean nor act as a lever against the Fāṭimids.

CATALOGUE

The catalogue which follows consists of three sections: a list of abbreviations, translations of religious formulae found on the coins, and the actual catalogue. The headings in the catalogue reflect issues raised in the article rather than constituting a complete description of the coin types.

ABBREVIATIONS

ANS	The American Numismatic Society, New York.
Ash	The Ashmolean Museum, Oxford.
AUB	The American University of Beirut.
Bach	J. L. Bacharach, "Al-Ikhshīd, the Ḥamdānids and the Caliphate: The Numismatic Evidence," *JOAS* 94 (1974), pp. 360–70.

[67] Taghribirdī, 3, p. 326.

Balog	P. Balog, "Tables des références des monnaies ikhchidites," *RBN* 102 (1956), pp. 107–34.
BM	The British Museum, London.
BMC	*BMCOR*.
Cons	Müzé humâyûn, *Mäskûkât qadîme islâmiye qatâlôghî*, by Edhem Isma'il Ghalib et al. (Constantinople: Matba'at seh, 1312–34 A.H.).
Dama	The National Museum, Damascus.
"Déc"	C. J. Tornberg, "Découvertes récentes de monnaies koufique en Suède," *Revue de la numismatique belge*, 5th ser., 2 (1870), pp. 221–45.
"FasA"	S. Lane-Poole, "Fasti Arabici, 6. Arabian and Other Rare Coins from the Collections of Colonel Gosset, Major Trotter, and J. Avent, Esq.," *NC*, 3rd ser., 7 (1887), pp. 324–39.
Herm	The State Hermitage Collection, Leningrad.
Lavoix	H. Lavoix, *Catalogue des monnaies musulmanes de la Bibliothèque National*, 3 vols. (Paris: Impr. Nationale, 1887–96).
L-W	U. S. Linder-Welin, "Sayf al-Dawlah's Reign in Syria and Diyarbekr in the Light of the Numismatic Evidence," *Commentationes de nummis saeculorum, IX-XI, in Suecia repertis* (1961), 1, pp. 17–104.
Naq	N. Naqshabandī, "Al-Dīnār al-Islāmī li-Mulūk al-Ṭawā'if, *Sumer* 3, 2 (1947), pp. 270–311.
NumC	C. J. Tornberg, *Numi Cufici Regii numophylacii Holmiensis quos omnes in terra Sueciae repertos digessit et interpretatus est* (Upsala: Excudebant Leffler et Sebell, 1848).
Paris	Bibliothèque Nationale, Paris.
RIC	G. C. Miles, *Rare Islamic Coins*, ANSNNM 118 (1950).
Stoc	The Central Office and Museum of National Antiquities and the Royal Coin Cabinet, Stockholm.
"Sym"	C. J. Tornberg, "Symbolae ad rem numariam Muhammedanorum ex Museo regio Holmiensi," 4 pts., *Nova acta Regiae Societatis Scientiarum Upsaliensis* 13 (1846); 3rd ser., 1 (1855); 2 (1858); 4 (1863).
YKB	Yapi ve Kredi Bankasi, Istanbul.

RELIGIOUS FORMULAE

ʿAlid legend

صلى الله عليه وعلى آله.

May God bless him (the Prophet) *and his family.*

Kalimah

The profession of faith at the beginning of the area inscriptions.

Qur'ān 9:33

محمد رسول الله ارسله بالهدى ودين الحق ليظهر الدين كله ولو كره المشركون.

Muḥammed is the Apostle of God, He has sent him with guidance and the true religion that it may prevail over all other religions, even if the disbelievers are averse.

Qur'ān 9:33 mixed with 28:68 or 23:93

هو الذي ارسل رسوله بالهدى ودين الحق ليظهره سبحان الله وتعالى عمّا يصفون.

He it is who has sent his Apostle with the guidance and the true religion that it may prevail; exalted be God, He is high over what they affirm of Him.

Qur'ān 9:34

والذين يكنزون الذهب و الفضة ولا ينفقونها في سبيل الله فبشّرهم بعذاب اليم.

Those who store up gold and silver and expend it not in God's way, unto them bring the glad tidings of a painful punishment.

Qur'ān 30:3–4

لله الامر من قبل ومن بعد ويومئذ يفرح المؤمنون بنصر الله.

To God belongs the order before and after and in that day the believers shall rejoice in help from God.

Qur'ān 30:3 mixed with 30:11 or 13

لله الامر من قبل ومن بعد ويومئذ الساعة يفرح المؤمنون بنصر الله.

To God belongs the power before and after and on that day, when the (last) hour comes, the believers shall rejoice in help from God.

Qur'ān 30:3 mixed with 30:11, 13, and 54

لله الامر من قبل ومن بعد ويومئذ ويوم يقوم الساعة نصر الله.

To God belongs the power before and after, and on that day, and (it is) that day when the (last) hour comes, help from God.

CATALOGUE

No.	*Year*	*Metal*	*g*	*mm*	*Reference*

Al-Mawṣil (Mosul)

Ḥamdānid al-Muttaqī
Obv. below field, Nāṣir al-Dawla cited as Nāṣir al-Dawla al-Ḥasan b. ʿAbd Allāh
Sayf al-Dawla not cited

No.	Year	Metal	g	mm	Reference
1	330	Æ	3.77	28	Paris
2	330	Æ	3.92	26.5	Paris
3	330	Æ	1.69	25.5	Herm 2989:6745
4	330	Æ	2.43	25.5	Herm 3184:4662
5	330	Æ	3.48	27	Herm 3184:4664

Ḥamdānid al-Muttaqī

No.	Year	Metal	g	mm	Reference
6	330	Æ	1.84	26	*BMC* 3, 3
7	330	Æ	3.23	26	Paris
8	330	Æ	2.41	24.5	Herm 2989:6760
9	330	Æ	–	–	Cons 2, 828
10	332	Æ	2.64	26	Paris
11	332	Æ	3.04	28.5	Stoc 3547:220

No.	*Year*	*Metal*	*g*	*mm*	*Reference*
12	332	Æ	4.95	26	YKB
13	332	Æ	4.75	28	Herm 2989:6762
14	332	Æ	3.48	25	Herm 2989:6763
15	332	Æ	3.62	–	ANS 1975.73.25
16	333	Æ	3.46	25	Paris
Ḥamdānid al-Mustakfī, Imām al-Ḥaqq					
17	334	Æ	5.60	27	*BMC* 3, 7
18	334	Æ	3.52	26	Paris
19	334	Æ	3.92	28	Paris
20	334	Æ	4.40	26	AUB C.8893
21	334	Æ	4.42	26	AUB C.8894
22	334	Æ	2.86	26	Herm 2989:6764
23	334	Æ	–	–	"Sym" 4, 135
24	334	Æ	3.37	–	ANS 1972.2.41
Ḥamdānid al-Mutīʿ					
Mint, . . . d . . . al . . . wṣil, "Madīnat al-Mawṣil?"					
25	334	Æ	3.25	28	Paris
Ḥamdānid al-Mustakfī					
26	335	Æ	3.05	28	YKB, 7
Ḥamdānid al-Muṭīʿ					
27	335	Æ	3.64	25	AUB C.8896
28	335	Æ	3.96	27	Stoc 6331
29	338	Æ	4.77	28.5	Herm 3184:3135
30	338	Æ	3.95	27	Herm 2989:6765
31	339	Æ	4.65	26	YKB, 8
32	339	Æ	3.32	27	Herm 2989:6766
33	339	Æ	3.41	27	Herm 2989:6767
34	340	Æ	3.00	28	YKB
35	341	Æ	2.44	20	ANS 1917.215.784
36	343	Æ	2.98	29	YKB, 10
37	345	Æ	2.30	28	YKB, 11
38	346	Æ	3.20	29	Stoc 12956:559

No.	*Year*	*Metal*	*g*	*mm*	*Reference*
39	347	Æ	4.30	28	YKB, 12
40	348	Æ	3.11	29	Paris
41	348	Æ	2.93	27	Paris
42	348	Æ	4.04	27	Paris
43	349	Æ	3.60	26	ANS
44	349	Æ	2.87	26.5	Paris
45	349	Æ	3.07	26.5	Paris
46	349	Æ	3.20	25	YKB
47	350	Æ	3.18	25	Herm 2989:6768
48[a]	351	Æ	3.72	28	*BMC* 3, 13
49	351	Æ	2.71	–	ANS 1917.215.785
50	354	Æ	3.13	26.5	*NumC* Cl. XV:7
51	354	Æ	–	–	*NumC* p. 260
52	356	Æ	2.53	28	Stoc

Niṣībīn

Ḥamdānid al-Mustakfī, Imām al-Ḥaqq

No.	Year	Metal	g	mm	Reference
53	334	Æ	4.34	25	Herm 3219:16047
54	334	Æ	3.66	26	Herm 2989:6774

Ḥamdānid al-Muṭīʿ

No.	Year	Metal	g	mm	Reference
55	334	Æ	–	–	Cons 3, 832
56	335	Æ	2.69	26	Stoc 6331
57	336	Æ	3.56	23	Paris
58	336	Æ	2.46	24	*BMC* 3, 8
59	336	Æ	4.80	26.5	Stoc 6331
60	337	Æ	3.72	24	Herm 2989:6776
61	338	Æ	–	–	Cons 2, 834

[a] Cf. Linder-Welin, n. 34.d, where she republishes this coin under the mint and date al-Maṣṣīṣa 351, describing it in the same terms as the coins struck in al-Massisa between 351 and 353. My own reading of this coin confirms Lane-Poole's with the only exception that the mint is possibly "Madīnat al-Mawṣil," with "Madīna" slightly contracted.

No.	*Year*	*Metal*	*g*	*mm*	*Reference*
62	339	Æ	3.23	25	Stoc
63	340	Æ	2.98	24	*BMC* 3, 9
64	340	Æ	3.17	25	Paris
65	340	Æ	3.33	25	AUB C.8901
66	344	Æ	3.02	23	Paris
67	344	Æ	4.45	25	AUB C.8903

Ḥamdānid
Rev. field illegible except for "Muḥammad"

68	346	Æ	3.19	26	Stoc

Ḥamdānid al-Muṭīʿ

69	347	Æ	3.64	26	Herm 2989:6775

Ḥamdānid
Rev. field as 68

70	349	Æ	2.15	21	*NumC* Cl.XV:6

Ḥamdānid al-Muṭīʿ

71	350	Æ	5.02	27	Herm 2989:6778
72	352	Æ	3.08	27	YKB 837.b
73	352	Æ	2.80	26	AUB, C.8904
74	352	Æ	2.94	26	Herm 3184:3695
75	354	Æ	3.09	24	*NumC* Cl.XV:5
76	354	Æ	2.96	25.5	Paris
77	355	Æ	–	–	"Déc" 84
78	355	Æ	3.33	26	*BMC* 3, 14
79	355	Æ	2.54	25.5	Paris

Ḥalab (Aleppo)

Ḥamdānid al-Mustakfī

80	333	Æ	3.80	–	ANS 1971.316.936

Ḥamdānid

81	334	Æ	3.46	–	Dama A. 1953

No.	Year	Metal	g	mm	Reference
Ḥamdānid al-Mustakfī					
ʿAlid legend					
82	334	AR	3.50	25	Paris
83	334	AR	3.56	26.5	L-W 10
84	334	AR	–	–	L-W 9
Ḥamdānid al-Muṭīʿ					
ʿAlid legend					
85	335	AR	3.45	23.5	L-W 15.a
86	335	AR	4.32	25	L-W. 15.b
87	336	AR	2.48	25	L-W 15.1
88	341	AR	3.80	26	AUB, C.8902
Ḥamdānid al-Muṭīʿ					
Sayf al-Dawla not cited					
89	347?	AR	0.52	14.5	L-W 26
Ḥamdānid al-Muṭīʿ					
Obv. and *rev.* outer margin, Sayf al-Dawla Abū al-Ḥasan					
Mint, Al-Khazna al-Shāmiyya li-Halab					
90	349	AV	3.70	27	YKB 1.2
Ḥamdānid al-Muṭīʿ					
Obv. outer margin, al-amīr ... al-Dawla					
Rev. inner margin, *Qur'ān* 9:34; outer margin, al-amīr Nāṣir al-Dawla					
ʿAlid legend					
Mint, al-Khazna al-Shāmiyya li-Ḥalab					
91	353?	AR	2.44	.25.5	L-W 35

Mayyāfāriqīn

No.	Year	Metal	g	mm	Reference
Ḥamdānid al-Muṭīʿ					
Obv. outer margin, Nāṣir al-Dawla					
Rev. outer margin, Sayf al-Dawla					
ʿAlid legend					
92	340	AR	3.00	24	BM
93	340	AR	–	23.5	L-W 21

No.	*Year*	*Metal*	*g*	*mm*	*Reference*
Ḥamdānid al-Muṭīʿ					
94	346	Æ	4.80	26.5	L-W 25
95	348	Æ	3.73	25	Paris
96	348	Æ	–	26.5	L-W 28
Ḥamdānid al-Muṭīʿ					
Mint, al-Thughūr Mayyafariqīn					
97	349	Æ	3.64	23.5	L-W 29.a
98	349	Æ	3.50	24.5	L-W 29.b
Ḥamdānid al-Muṭīʿ					
99	350	Æ	3.25	23.5	L-W 30.a
100	350	Æ	–	–	L-W 30.b
Ḥamdānid al-Muṭīʿ					
ʿAlid legend					
101	354	Æ	2.52	24.8	L-W 39
102	354	Æ	–	–	"Sym" 3:1, 40, 41
Ḥamdānid al-Muṭīʿ					
Mint, Madīnat Mayyafariqīn					
103	356	Æ	–	–	L-W 40.a
104	356	Æ	2.85	24	L-W 40.b

Anṭākiyya (*Antioch*)

No.	*Year*	*Metal*	*g*	*mm*	*Reference*
ʿAbbāsid, Tūzūn al-Muttaqī (caliph's name partly obliterated)					
105	333	Æ	4.87	25.5	Paris
ʿAbbāsid, Tūzūn al-Mustakfī, al-Khalīfa					
106	333	Æ	3.00	24	AUB, C.8857
107	333	Æ	3.57	25	L-W 8
ʿAbbāsid al-Muṭīʿ					
108	337	Æ	4.42	27	*RIC*, 118

No.	Year	Metal	g	mm	Reference
Ḥamdānid al-Muṭīʿ					
ʿAlid legend					
109	337	AR	2.20	23	L-W 20
110	337	AR	3.35	25	YKB, 1
111	337	AR	3.22	25	AUB, C.8898
Ḥamdānid al-Muṭīʿ					
112	340	AR	2.94	26	ANS 1917.215.787
113	340	AR	3.01	26	ANS 1917.215.788
114	340	AR	3.60	24	L-W 22.a
115	340	AR	5.19	26.5	L-W 22.b
116	340	AR	3.77	27	L-W 22.c
117	340	AR	3.02	27	L-W 22.d
118	340	AR	2.94	27	L-W 22.e
119	340	AR	2.95	26.5	L-W 22.f
Ḥamdānid al-Muṭīʿ					
Nāṣir al-Dawla not cited					
120	342	AR	2.72	26	L-W 23.a
121	342	AR	–	–	L-W 23.b
122	342	AR	2.41	25	L-W 23.c
Ḥamdānid al-Muṭīʿ					
Obv. and *rev.* outer margin, Sayf al-Dawla					
Mint, possibly Madīnat Anṭākiyya					
123	349	AV	4.05	29	ANS, 62.107.1

Madīnat al-ʿAwāṣim (Antioch?)[b]

No.	Year	Metal	g	mm	Reference
Ḥamdānid al-Muṭīʿ					
124	348	AR	2.85	24	L-W 27

[b] I adopt the reading of the mint name suggested with some reluctance by Mrs. Linder-Welin, who also suggests that this coin was struck in Antioch.

No.	*Year*	*Metal*	*g*	*mm*	*Reference*
			Tarsus		
ʿAbbāsid al-Mustakfī					
125	333	AR	–	–	L-W 7
Ḥamdānid al-Muṭīʿ					
Nāṣir al-Dawla not cited					
126	354	AR	3.29	25	L-W 38
			Al-Maṣṣīṣa		
ʿAbbāsid, Tuzūn al-Mustafkī, al-Khalīfa					
127	333	AR	2.54	26	*BMC* 2, 617
Ḥamdānid al-Maṭīʿ					
Rev. inner margin, *Qur'ān* 30:3 with 30:11 or 13; outer margin, *Qur'ān* 9:34					
128	351	AR	3.13	27.5	L-W 32.a
129	351	AR	2.59	25	L-W 32.b
130	351	AR	3.23	25	L-W 32.c
Ḥamdānid al-Muṭīʿ					
Obv. inner margin, *Qur'ān* 30:3 with 30:11, 13, and 54					
Rev. inner margin, *Qur'ān* 30:3 with 30:11 or 13; outer margin, *Qur'ān* 9:34[c]					
131	352	AR	4.60	27	L-W 33.a
132	352	AR	–	26	L-W 33.b
133	352	AR	2.59	25	L-W 33.c

[c] Mrs. Linder-Welin reads the third line on the rev. field of these coins *ṣallā Allāhu ʿalayhi wa ālihi* (with the proposition *ʿalā* ommitted). I have examined the first two of these coins and am of the opinion that the last word is a contraction of sallam.

No.	*Year*	*Metal*	*g*	*mm*	*Reference*
Ḥamdānid al-Muṭīʿ					
Rev. outer margin, *Qur'ān* 9:34					
ʿAlid legend					
134	353	Æ	3.74	26	L-W 34.a
135	353	Æ	3.30	27	L-W 34.b
136	353	Æ	3.53	26	L-W 34.c
Ḥamdānid al-Muṭīʿ					
Nāṣir al-Dawla not cited					
137	35x	Æ	2.28	23	Herm 2989:6789

Thaghr al-Shāmiyya

No.	*Year*	*Metal*	*g*	*mm*	*Reference*
Ḥamdānid al-Muṭīʿ					
Rev. inner margin *Qu'ān* 9:33 with 28:68 or 23:93; outer margin, *Qur'ān* 9:34					
ʿAlid legend					
138	350	Æ	2.38	28	L-W 31

Ḥimṣ (Emessa)

No.	*Year*	*Metal*	*g*	*mm*	*Reference*
Ḥamdānid al-Muttaqī					
139	333	Æ	3.11	27	AUB C.8892
ʿAbbāsid, Tūzūn al-Mustakfī					
140	333	Æ	–	–	Bach 44
Ḥamdānid al-Mustakfī					
141	334	Æ	2.12	24	L-W 12
Ikhshidid al-Muṭīʿ					
ʿAlid legend					
142	336	Æ	3.81	25	L-W 17

No.	*Year*	*Metal*	*g*	*mm*	*Reference*
Ḥamdānid al-Muṭīʿ					
ʿAlid legend					
143	342	Æ	1.64	24	*BMC* 3, 16
Ḥamdānid al-Muṭīʿ					
144	350	Æ	5.72	23.5	BM
Ḥamdānid al-Muṭīʿ					
Rev. outer margin, *Qur'ān* 9:34					
ʿAlid legend					
145	353	Æ	3.89	28.5	L-W 37.a
146	353	Æ	2.57	27	L-W 37.b
147	353	Æ	5.72	25.5	L-W 37.c

Ḥarrān (*Haran*)

No.	*Year*	*Metal*	*g*	*mm*	*Reference*
Ḥamdānid al-Mustakfī					
ʿAlid legend					
148	334	Æ	2.94	28	L-W 11
Ḥamdānid al-Muṭīʿ					
ʿAlid legend					
149	337	Æ	3.57	27	L-W 18.a

Al-Raqqa/al-Rāfiqa (*Rakka*)

No.	*Year*	*Metal*	*g*	*mm*	*Reference*
Ḥamdānid al-Muṭīʿ					
Mint, al-Raqqah					
150	338	Æ	3.10	27	AUB C.8899
Ḥamdānid al-Imām al-Muṭīʿ lillāh					
ʿAlid legend					
Mint, al-Rāfiqa					
151	356	Æ	2.82	25	*NumC* Cl.XV:8

No.	*Year*	*Metal*	*g*	*mm*	*Reference*
			Dimishq (Damascus)		
Ikhshīdid al-Muttaqī					
152	333	AR	3.05	25.5	Paris
153	333	AR	3.71	28	Lavoix 3, 49 bis
154	333	AR	4.09	26.5	L-W 5
155	333	AR	–	–	"Sym" 3:1, 42
156	333	AR	–	–	Balog p. 129 (2 spec)
Ikhshīdid al-Mustak					
157	334	AR	3.13	26	ANS 1917.215.776
158	334	AR	3.55	25	ANS 1971.316.934
159	334	AR	2.34	25	Paris
160	334	AR	4.01	26	Paris
161	334	AR	2.74	27.5	Paris
162	334	AR	3.77	26	Paris
163	334	AR	–	–	"FasA" p. 333
164	334	AR	3.40	26	AUB C.8822
165	334	AR	2.66	27	AUB C.8833
Ikhshīdid al-Muṭīʿ ʿAlid legend					
166	336	AR	4.59	27	Balog p. 130
Ikhshīdid al-Muṭīʿ ʿAlid legend *Obv.* field لك					
167	336	AR	2.87	26	Paris
Ikhshīdid al-Muṭīʿ ʿAlid legend					
168	338	AR	1.42	26	*BMC* 2, 236
			Filasṭīn (Ramla)		
Ikhshīdid al-Muttaqī					
169	333	AV	3.08	22	Lavoix 3, 49
170	333	AV	4.44	22.5	*BMC* 2, 231

No.	*Year*	*Metal*	*g*	*mm*	*Reference*
171	333	AV	3.21	22.5	*BMC* 2, 232
172	333	AV	2.92	22	ANS 1972.228.113
173	333	AV	–	–	Balog p. 121 (2 spec)
Ikhshīdid al-Mustakfī					
174	334	AR	3.41	24	Balog p. 129
175	334	AR	–	–	Bach 58
176	335	AV	–	–	Bach 59
Ikhshīdid al-Muṭīʿ					
177	335	AV	4.45	23	ANS 1957.82.2
178	335	AV	4.58	23	ANS 1972.228.114
179	335	AV	3.95	22	*BMC* 9, 232k
180	335	AV	4.58	23	Lavoix 3, 50 bis
181	335	AV	–	–	Balog p. 122 (4 spec)
182	335	AR	2.46	27	Paris
Ikhshīdid al-Muṭīʿ					
ʿAlid legend					
183	336	AR	3.12	29	ANS
Ikhshīdid al-Muṭīʿ					
Obv. field ك [d]					
184	337	AV	3.73	21	ANS
185	337	AV	3.72	22	ANS
186	337	AV	3.09	21	ANS
187	337	AV	3.37	22.5	*BMC* 2, 233
188	337	AV	3.33	22	Lavoix 3, 51
189	337	AV	3.69	21	Lavoix 3, 52
190	337	AV	–	–	Balog p. 123 (4 spec)
191	337/339	AV	3.66	21	AUB C.8825
192	337/339	AV	–	–	Balog p. 124 (3 spec)

[d] Lane-Poole and Lavoix read ṣād for kāf beneath the obv. field on 188–90.

No.	*Year*	*Metal*	*g*	*mm*	*Reference*
Ikhshīdid al-Muṭīʿ					
193	337/339	AR	3.91	23.5	Lavoix 3, 56
Ikhshīdid al-Muṭīʿ					
Obv. field ك					
194	339	AV	2.42	–	ANS
Ikhshīdid al-Muṭīʿ					
Obv. field ك					
ʿAlid legend					
195	340	AR	2.35	24	ANS
Ikhshīdid al-Muṭīʿ					
ʿAlid legend					
196	341	AV	4.34	22	ANS
197	341	AV	3.92	22	ANS
198	341	AV	3.80	24	Balog p. 124
199	341	AV	–	–	Balog p. 124 (2 spec)
200	341	AV	4.73	24	AUB C.8827
201	341	AR	2.46	24	ANS
202	342	AV	–	–	Balog p. 124
203	345	AV	2.48	23	Balog p. 124
204	345	AV	3.80	22	*BMC* 2, 235
205	345	AV	3.69	23	Lavoix 3, 53
206	345	AV	3.35	22	Lavoix 3, 54
207	345	AV	–	–	Balog p. 124
208	345	AR	–	–	Balog p. 132
Ikhshīdid al-Muṭīʿ					
Obv. field, ك [e]					
ʿAlid legend					
209	346	AV	3.11	23	ANS
210	346	AV	3.28	22	ANS

[e] Lavoix and Balog read ṣād for kāf beneath the obv. field. on 217–18.

No.	*Year*	*Metal*	*g*	*mm*	*Reference*
211	346	AV	3.54	23.5	Naq pp. 279–80
212	346	AV	4.28	22	Ash
213	346	AV	–	–	Balog p. 125 (4 spec)
214	346	AR	2.61	24	Balog p. 132
215	346	AR	–	–	Balog p. 132 (2 spec)
216	347	AV	3.42	21	Lavoix 3, 55; Balog p. 125
217	347	AV	–	–	Balog p. 125 (2 spec)
218	350	AV	4.31	22	ANS
219	350	AV	4.17	22	ANS
220	350	AV	4.84	22	ANS
221	350	AV	3.12	21.5	Lavoix 3, 57
222	350	AV	–	–	Balog p. 125
223	350	AR	–	–	Balog p. 133
224	351	AV	3.88	23	Balog p. 125
225	351	AV	3.46	22.5	Lavoix 3, 58
226	351	AV	–	–	Balog p. 125 (4 spec)
227	351	AR	3.28	26	ANS
228	351	AR	2.16	23	AUB C.8830
229	351	AR	2.56	24	L-W 36
230	352	AR	–	–	Balog p. 133
231	353	AV	3.55	23	ANS
232	353	AV	4.32	23	ANS
233	353	AV	4.08	23	Lavoix 3, 59
234	353	AV	3.07	22	Lavoix 3, 60
235	353	AV	3.88	22.5	Lavoix 3, 61
236	353	AV	2.60	24	*BMC* 2, 237
237	353	AV	4.37	23	Naq p. 280
238	353	AV	3.33	21	AUB C.8829
239	353	AV	–	–	Balog p. 125 (9 spec)
240	353	AR	3.95	25	ANS
241	353	AR	1.82	25	ANS
242	353	AR	3.42	25	ANS
243	354	AR	2.80	24	Balog p. 134
244	355	AV	2.69	21.5	ANS
245	355	AV	3.57	23	ANS

No.	*Year*	*Metal*	*g*	*mm*	*Reference*
246	355	AV	3.41	22	ANS
247	355	AV	–	–	Balog p. 125 (3 spec)
248	355	AV	1.30	21	AUB C.8761

ʿAbbāsid al-Muṭīʿ
ʿAlid legend

249	355	AV	4.94	24	*BMC* 2, 239

Ikhshīdid In the names of al-Ḥasan b. ʿUbayd Allāh and Aḥmad b. ʿAlī; al-Muṭīʿ
ʿAlid legend

250	357	AR	–	–	Balog p. 134
251	358	AV	–	–	Balog p. 125 (2 spec)

Ikhshīdid In the names of al-Ḥasan b. ʿUbayd Allāh and Aḥmad b. ʿAlī; al-Muṭīʿ

252	358	AV	3.52	22	ANS
253	358	AV	3.83	23	ANS
254	358	AV	–	–	Balog p. 125 (8 spec)

ANSMN 28 (1983)

THE WANDERING DIE OF NĪSĀBŪR: A SEQUEL

(Plate 22)

Nicholas M. Lowick

Some years ago this journal carried a note on a gold dinar of an extraordinary hybrid type, struck from an obverse die of the Sāmānid amir Nūḥ II inscribed with the mint name Nīsābūr (i.e. Nīshāpūr) and the date 375 H., and from a reverse die of the Kākwayhid Muḥammad b. Dushmanzār attributable to the mint of Iṣbahān, ca. 432 H. (Plate 22, 1).[1] It was suggested that the coin, which is plainly not a modern counterfeit, was the product of an accidental pairing of dies at the Iṣbahān mint in the period following the struggle between Muḥammad b. Dushmanzār and Masʿūd the Ghaznawid, the latter being presumed to have brought an old die with him from his headquarters in Khurasan. The recent appearance of a second, associated mule justifies a re-examination of the problem, which now presents itself in a different light. The new coin, which like its companion is now in the British Museum collection, has one side struck from the same Sāmānid obverse die; the other side is struck from a Seljuq obverse die of al-Baṣra dated 449 H. (A.D. 1057–58).[2]

[1] N. M. Lowick, "A Sāmānid/Kākwayhid Mule," in *ANSMN* 14 (1968), pp. 159–62.

[2] The coin appears in Sotheby's *Catalogue of Islamic Coins*, 29 April 1981, 321, where the problem of the two mules is first discussed.

Obverse 1 ك

لا اله الا
الله وحده
لا شريك له
الملك المنصور

Inner margin: بسم الله ضرب هذا الدينار بنيسابور سنة خمس
و سبعين و ثلثمائة

Outer margin: *Qur'ān* 33:3–4

Obverse 2 

لا الــه الا
الله وحده
لاشر يك له
القائم بامر الله

Inner margin: بسم الله ضرب هذا الدينار بالبصرة سنة تسع
و اربعين و اربعمائة

Outer margin: *Qur'ān* 30:3–4
AV 4.03 g 25 mm BM 1981.5.1.4 (Plate 22, 2)

Obverse 1, the Sāmānid side, is in some respects better preserved than the corresponding side of the Sāmānid/Kākwayhid piece. The die itself, however, was decidedly more worn when used to strike the second coin. The field shows minor flaws and raised striations, presumably caused by cracks in the die. One of these is particularly noticeable: it runs horizontally from the lower part of the isolated letter *kāf* in the upper area to the top of the *lām* in *ilāha*. There is no sign of this flaw on the first coin. It is thus clear that the new coin was struck later, when the die had already served to strike other—perhaps hundreds of other—pieces.

Obverse 2, the Seljuq side, is identical with—although not from the same die as—the obverse of a dinar of Ṭughril Beg (Plate 22, 3) in the

British Museum (*BMCOr* 3, 59). It shows, in addition to the mint name al-Baṣra and the date 449, the name of the ʿAbbāsid Caliph al-Qā'im, the Seljuq bow-and-arrow (bow-and-mace?) emblem and an isolated *jīm, khā* or *hā* above the word *ilāha*. There can be no question but that this side of the coin, like the Sāmānid side, was struck from a genuine medieval die.

It follows that the new mule must have been struck in or after 449/1057–58, that is not less than 74 Hijra years after the date of manufacture of the Sāmānid die, and 17 years after that of the reverse die used to strike the Sāmānid/Kākwayhid mule. The geographical discrepancy, also, is greater in the case of the new mule. From Nīsābūr in northeastern Iran to Baṣra in lower Iraq is a distance of some 900 miles as measured on the map, or 1,100 in terms of the distance that must have been covered by the medieval traveller. This compares with about 600 (practically speaking about 800) miles between Nīsābūr and Iṣbahān, which lie on opposite sides of the Dasht-e Kavīr or great Iranian desert. Two questions thus call for an answer. How could a medieval die survive in use for almost three-quarters of a century? And what circumstances could have brought about the linkage of three dies whose mints of origin lie so far apart?

Several lines of approach suggest themselves. The first takes as its point of departure the conclusions reached concerning the Sāmānid/Kākwayhid mule. Assuming this piece to have been struck in Iṣbahān in 432 or shortly after, the Sāmānid obverse die could be envisaged as continuing to travel west and south until it reached Baṣra, where it was again accidentally paired with a local die, this time one of the Seljuq Ṭughril Beg. The journey between Iṣbahān and Baṣra, as between Iṣbahān and Nīsābūr, was doubtless undertaken by many persons in those times, all three cities being large commercial centers. The die could be seen, too, as moving with the tide of Seljuq conquest, which began in 429 and culminated with Tughril's entry into Baghdad in 447 H. Nevertheless, any theory involving the accidental misuse of a single die by official moneyers at different mints on successive, unrelated occasions, must appear too farfetched to be tenable as an explanation. Even if a reason could be found for the die's having travelled from Jibāl province to Iraq, the chances against its being mistakenly used a second time are enormous. Had it first been employed at Iṣbahān, as suggested in my note on the Sāmānid/Kākwayhid mule, the die would certainly have been destroyed once the moneyer responsible realised his blunder. In short the discovery of the second mule, with its later Seljuq obverse, invalidates the hypothesis devised to account for the first mule, and makes it necessary to look for a different solution. Where two such exceptional hybrids are linked by an obverse die, it will obviously be desirable to explain their genesis by the same set of circumstances—to assign them, in fact, a common origin both in place and in time.

While all three dies used in the striking of the two pieces are patently genuine, it is by no means sure that the coins themselves were produced under official auspices. State interests clearly required that dies should be systematically destroyed, or re-engraved, once their legitimate period of use had expired. In the case of an obverse die, showing the date of striking, this would normally mean at the end of the year. A reverse die, showing the name of the ruler or Caliph, might remain in use for longer, but it too must normally have been destroyed at the end of the reign. Despite this, a few medieval Islamic dies have survived to the present day in usable condition[3]—evidence that dies were either put into storage (and subsequently lost or abandoned) or purloined from the mint, presumably with the object of striking counterfeit money. The chances of theft or accidental loss were of course augmented by the invasions and revolutions so frequent in Middle Eastern history.

If superannuated dies were stored away, it may well have been government policy that they should be returned to a central repository, whence they could be distributed for re-use once they had been provided with a new striking surface. That this may have been so under the ʿAbbāsid Caliphs is suggested by the existence of dirhams struck from obverse dies the mint name of which has been altered—the original mint being still partly legible beneath the new one.[4] It is doubtful if any such

[3] For a listing of extant Islamic dies see J. L. Bacharach and H. A. Awad, "The Problem of Obverse and Reverse in Islamic Numismatics," *NC* 1973, pp. 183–91. Not included in the list is the well-preserved pair of Būyid bronze dies (Majd al-Dawla, al-Muḥammadīyya 393 H.) auctioned at Bonham's *Sale of Ancient, Mediaeval and Modern Coins*, 21–22 May 1980, 794 (illus.).

[4] L. Ilisch, "Ein Dirhamfund des frühen 10. Jahrhunderts aus der Gegend von Diyarbakir," *Münstersche Numismatische Zeitung*, 9 Jahrgang (1979), Heft 1,

centralisation was practiced by the Seljuqs, under whom coins of different mints differ markedly from each other in type and style. It should be borne in mind, however, that the three mints with which we are here concerned—Nīsābūr, Iṣbahān, and al-Baṣra—all belonged to the domain of Ṭughril Beg by the time the latest of the three dies was executed. Thus if the Seljuq government *did* maintain a central repository for dies, it could well have housed the three in question. Supposing such a storehouse to have been located at Baghdad, any major disturbance such as the revolt of al-Basāsīrī in 450–51 H., could have brought about the theft or dispersal of coin dies. It is even conceivable that al-Basāsīrī himself, after profiting from Ṭughril's absence to assume control of the city, initially minted coins from dies that were not his own, although he is also known to have had coins specially struck in the name of the Fāṭimid Caliph.[5]

Alternatively, and perhaps more plausibly, all three dies may in the first instance have been stored at their mint of production. Were this the case an itinerant moneyer or other state employee with access to mint equipment may have embezzled a number of dies and either used them himself to strike dinars of less than the required fineness, or sold them to an outsider, presumably a jeweller or metalworker with access to gold bullion and the ability to convert it into planchets of an appropriate size and weight from which counterfeits could then be struck. It is established from the existence of signed dirhams that master die cutters (accomplished artists who were probably at all times in short supply) on occasion worked for more than one mint.[6] They may not have been the only mint workers to travel, carrying their equipment with them from one workshop to the next. Mints represented by the

pp. 7–14, nos. 42–46, 53, 111–15, 150. A number of other examples, of the same period or slightly later, were located among the British Museum's ʿAbbāsid coins. It is of course possible that the re-engraved dies which served to strike such coins were transferred directly from one mint to another without passing through a central holding office.

[5] *EI*², s.v. "al-Basāsīrī" (M. Canard), pp. 1073–75; and E. Zambaur, *Die Münzprägungen des Islams* (1968), pp. 231 and 234, n. 59.

[6] Carol M. Bier, "The Work of al-Ḥasan b. Muḥammad, Die Engraver at Iṣbahān and al-Muḥammadiyya," *ANSMN* 24 (1979), pp. 243–56.

signatures *ʿaskar*, *al-muʿaskar*, *urdā*, etc., were themselves evidently mobile, travelling with the army of the ruler and supplying its needs. A moneyer from, say, the mint of Nīsābūr may have been ordered to accompany the conquering army of Ṭughril Beg into the western provinces and thus have had the opportunity to equip himself with dies from mints situated many miles apart.

Adopting a more sceptical stance, it would be possible to view both mules as modern counterfeits struck from medieval dies. This might occur if a forger were to obtain, by a lucky chance, three dies of similar appearance in sufficiently good condition for him to produce what would, at a cursory glance, pass as genuine dinars. As there are so few extant medieval Islamic dies, such a forger must presumably have had access to some such store or cache as that postulated above. In that case, the same problem would remain to be answered: was there a central storehouse for dies, or how were they assembled? If the mules are modern fakes, moreover, it is surprising that not more of them have appeared on the collectors' market.

With a view to establishing whether the two pieces were struck from the same consignment of bullion, and if so whether they represent an official issue, specific gravity tests were carried out on the mules themselves and on two related coins of normal type—a Kākwayhid dinar of Muḥammad b. Dushmanzār, Iṣbahān 432 H. (*BMCOr* 9, p. 270, 42[aa]) and a Seljuq dinar of Ṭughril Beg, al-Baṣra 449 H (*BMCOr* 3, 59). The results are set out below, the estimate of gold content being valid so long as no significant amount of copper is present in the alloy.

Coin	*SG*	*Gold Content*
Sāmānid/Kākwayhid mule	15.78	ca. 73%
Sāmānid/Seljuq mule	16.58	ca. 80%
Kākwayhid dinar	17.20	ca. 85%
Seljuq dinar	18.80	ca. 96.5%

From the wide discrepancy in fineness between the two mules, it is clear that they were not struck from the same batch of gold—although they could have been struck from successive batches of a different fineness. The standard of purity of Kākwayhid and Seljuq dinars is unknown, for few have yet been analyzed. It may well be that the standard varied from mint to mint and from issue to issue at the same mint.[7] Judging simply by the fineness of the two ordinary dinars analyzed, both mules fall somewhat short of the requisite purity. This could be a reason for regarding them as counterfeits, although in that case it would be curious that their fineness were not lower still. For the time being the problem of where and how these two strange hybrids came to be made must regrettably be regarded as unsolved.

[7] Seljuq dinars of Balkh in the reigns of Berkyāruq and Muḥammad, for instance, were very much more base than contemporary dinars of the western provinces. See N. M. Lowick, "Seljuq Coins," *NC* 1970, pp. 244–46.

ANSMN 28 (1983)

A SIMPLIFIED METHOD FOR CALCULATING THE ORIGINAL NUMBER OF DIES FROM DIE LINK STATISTICS

GILES F. CARTER

Calculation of the original number of dies for issues of ancient coins is important in estimating the approximate number of coins struck, the probable lifetime of dies, number of anvils (work-stations), and the number of die combinations. Several methods have been proposed to calculate the original number of dies from die link statistics: Brown,[1] Good,[2] Guilbaud,[3] Lyon,[4] Carter and Moore,[5] Carter,[6] Mora Mas,[7] Mül-

[1] I. D. Brown, "Some Notes on the Coinage of Elizabeth I with Special Reference to Her Hammered Silver," *BNJ* 28 (1955–57), pp. 568–603; "On the Use of Statistics in Numismatics," *NCirc* 77 (1969), pp. 83–84; "Statistical Methods as a Tool in Numismatics," *Cornucopiae* 3 (1975), pp. 33–44.

[2] I. J. Good, "The Population Frequencies of Species and the Estimation of Population Parameters," *Biometrika* 40 (1953), pp. 237–64.

[3] G. T. Guilbaud, "A propos de l'estimation du nombre des coins," *BSFN* 29 (1974), pp. 625–34.

[4] C. S. S. Lyon, "The Estimation of the Number of Dies Employed in a Coinage," *NCirc* 73 (1965), pp. 180–81; "Consultation in Research," *BNJ* 35 (1966), pp. 223–33.

[5] G. F. Carter and J. W. Moore, "Calculation of the Approximate Number of Dies and Die-Combinations of Ancient Coins from Die-Link Statistics," *SCMB* 1980, pp. 172–77, 212–14, 241–46.

[6] G. F. Carter, "A Graphical Method for Calculating the Approximate Total Number of Dies from Die-Link Statistics of Ancient Coins," in *Scientific Studies in*

ler,[8] Carcassonne,[9] McGovern,[10] and Brunetti.[11] Most of these methods assume that all dies produced the same number of coins each; however, this assumption is known to be false. Three methods assume variable die lifetime[12] and are preferable because it is well known that die lifetime varied considerably.

Lyon[13] developed one of the early methods for calculating the total number of dies, and Carter extended this method to include variable die lifetime by using a computer to simulate die link statistics using random numbers. In this computer program, written by J. W. Moore,[14] random numbers are used to represent dies and coins: the *range* of random numbers represents the total number of original dies; the *number* of random numbers represents the number of coins in the study. Groups of different sizes of random numbers are established to represent variable die lifetimes. This enables one to choose any desired distribution of lifetimes of dies. Previously Carter chose an empirical die lifetime distribution that provided results in agreement with die link data obtained from Crepusius denarii.[15] These denarii, struck in 82 B.C., have each reverse die uniquely identified by a Roman numeral from 1 to

Numismatics, ed. W. A. Oddy, British Museum Occasional Paper 18 (1980), pp. 17–29, where the "Lyon-Carter" method is developed; "Die-Link Statistics for Crepusius Denarii and Calculations of the Total Number of Dies," Table Ronde Numismatique et Statistique, 17–19 Sept. 1979, Paris.

[7] F. Mora Mas, "Estimation du nombre de coins selon les répétitions dans une trouvaille de monnaies," Table Ronde Numismatique et Statistique, 17–19 Sept. 1979, Paris.

[8] J. W. Müller, "Estimation du nombre originel de coins," Table Ronde Numismatique et Statistique, 17–19 Sept. 1979, Paris.

[9] C. Carcassonne, "Tables pour l'estimation par la méthode du maximum de vraisemblance du nombre de coins de droit (ou de revers) ayant servi à frapper une émission," Table Ronde Numismatique et Statistique, 17–19 Sept. 1979, Paris.

[10] W. E. McGovern, "Missing Die Probabilities, Expected Die Production and the Index Figure," *ANSMN* 25 (1980), pp. 209–23.

[11] L. Brunetti, "Über eine Formel zur Berechnung der ungefähren Stempel-Schlagzahl," *JNG* 15 (1965), pp. 65–74.

[12] Above, nn. 5, 6, and 8.

[13] Above, n. 4.

[14] Above, n. 5.

[15] Above, n. 6, "Graphical Method."

519. Each obverse die is uniquely identified by the combination of a letter of the Roman alphabet and a group symbol. Although Buttrey[16] and Carter (unpublished) have found some mistakes by the mint officials in the numbering and lettering of Crepusius dies, it is believed that the total number of reverse dies is about 510, and the approximate number of observe dies is 479. Therefore the Crepusius issue is a good one to check methods for calculating original numbers of dies from die link statistics.

The present work involves the use of an improved, mathematically defined distribution for die lifetimes, and develops a simple equation for calculating the original number of dies. This equation should make the method easy for numismatists to use.

DISTRIBUTION OF DIE LIFETIMES

Numerous observations lead to the conclusion that ancient die lifetimes varied by a large factor within a given issue. In almost any issue of ancient coins some dies are very common, whereas a few dies are not likely to be represented even in large samples of coins. A large number of coins produced from a long-lived die usually results in a dozen or more specimens surviving to modern times. However, a die with a short lifetime would have produced relatively few coins (probably fewer than 3000 if the average die produced about 15,000 coins), and consequently zero to one, two, or at most three coins might presently exist in all the world's collections.

In calculating the original number of dies Carter at first used a die lifetime having a Gaussian distribution (bell-shaped curve).[17] However, this distribution underestimated the number of long-lived dies because of the shape of the curve. In the present study the distribution is a gamma distribution with $\alpha = 2$ and $\beta = 25$: $y = \frac{x\,e^{-x/25}}{25^2}$, where

[16] T. V. Buttrey, "The Denarii of P. Crepusius and Roman Republican Mint Organization," *ANSMN* 21 (1976), pp. 67–108.

[17] Above, n. 5.

y is the fraction of dies and x is the die lifetime in hours.[18] This distribution (Fig. 1, compare with a bell-shaped curve) describes a number of natural phenomena such as the length of life of industrial equipment and the molecular speeds of gas molecules at a given temperature. When dies failed due to cracking, their lifetimes would best be represented by a gamma distribution. The above equation gives the best fit obtained for die link statistics of Crepusius denarii. However, it probably is not applicable to all series of ancient coins.

FIG. 1

Gamma Distribution of Die Lifetimes

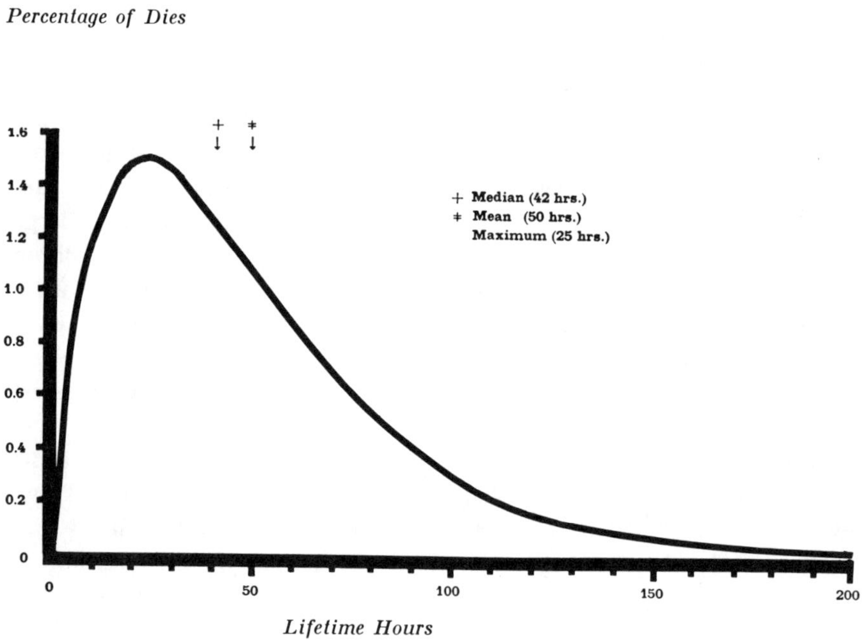

[18] P. G. Hoel, *Introduction to Mathematical Statistics*, 4th ed. (New York, 1971), pp. 86–90.

SIMPLE EQUATION FOR CALCULATING THE ORIGINAL NUMBER OF DIES

C. S. S. Lyon's equation for calculating the original number of dies assuming equal coin productivity from all dies is $\frac{d}{n} = \frac{(1 - e^{-n/D})}{\frac{n}{D}}$.[19] Lyon tabulated d/n as a function of n/D where n is the number of coins in the study, d is the number of known (different) dies in the study, and D is the calculated, approximate number of original dies. Because of the exponential nature of this equation, the curve of d/n values decreases non-linearly with increasing n/D values. In spite of several attempts, the writer was unable to derive an equation for the "Lyon-Carter" method that is based on variable lifetimes of dies.

When n/D is plotted as a function of n/d, the curve is nearly linear. In fact, it asymptotically approaches the straight line which would occur if n/D = n/d (note that for very large numbers of coins in a given issue, D = d, or all dies are known). Fig. 2 shows n/D plotted as a function of n/d using points obtained from the computer: ten computer calculations were averaged to obtain each point on the graph. Note that the curve is very nearly a straight line, particularly when n is greater than 2d. The dashed curve in Fig. 2 is a plot of the equation used by Lyon (see above) which assumes equal productivity of coins from all dies. Note that this curve reaches the asymptote much sooner than the curve assuming a gamma distribution for die lifetimes.

When the above distribution was used, it slightly changed the calculated numbers of original dies compared with Carter's previous results. In the above equation the constant, $\beta = 25$, was chosen so that the average lifetime of dies equals 50 hours, which is believed to be close to the average lifetime of Crepusius obverse dies. Using the gamma distribution, Table 1 indicates the projected distribution of die life-

[19] Above, n. 4.

times by percent. For instance 6.2% of the dies would usually have failed within the first 10 hours of use, assuming an average lifetime of 50 hours per die. Also 0.3% of the dies should have had a lifetime greater than 200 hours.

Table 1. Distribution of Die Lifetimes by Percent

Lifetime Range, Hrs.	*Percentage of Dies*	*Cumulative % of Dies*[a]	*Lifetime Range, Hrs.*	*Percentage of Dies*	*Cumulative % of Dies*
0–5	1.8	1.8	105–10	1.2	93.4
5–10	4.4	6.2	110–15	1.0	94.4
10–15	6.0	12.2	115–20	0.9	95.2
15–20	6.9	19.1	120–25	0.7	96.0
20–25	7.3	26.4	125–30	0.6	96.6
25–30	7.3	33.7	130–35	0.5	97.1
30–35	7.1	40.8	135–40	0.4	97.6
35–40	6.7	47.5	140–45	0.4	97.9
40–45	6.2	53.7	145–50	0.3	98.3
45–50	5.7	59.4	150–55	0.3	98.5
50–55	5.1	64.5	155–60	0.2	98.8
55–60	4.6	69.2	160–65	0.2	99.0
60–65	4.1	73.3	165–70	0.2	99.1
65–70	3.6	76.9	170–75	0.1	99.3
70–75	3.2	80.1	175–80	0.1	99.4
75–80	2.8	82.9	180–85	0.1	99.5
80–85	2.4	85.3	185–90	0.08	99.6
85–90	2.1	87.4	190–95	0.07	99.6
90–95	1.8	89.3	195–200	0.06	99.7
95–100	1.6	90.8	200–2000	0.30	100.0
100–105	1.4	92.2			

[a] "Cumulative percentage of dies" means that 1.8% of all dies had a lifetime of 5 hours or less, 6.2% of all dies had a lifetime of 10 hours or less, etc. All numbers in the above table were calculated and then rounded off; slight discrepancies are due to rounding. The percentages were calculated by determining the appropriate area underneath the curve in Fig. 1 by using calculus.

Average, or mean, lifetime = 50.0 hours; median lifetime = 42.0 hours (half of the dies lasted less than 42.0 hours); maximum number of dies occur at a lifetime of 25 hours.

FIG. 2

n/D Plotted as a Function of n/d Obtained from Computer Simulation[a]

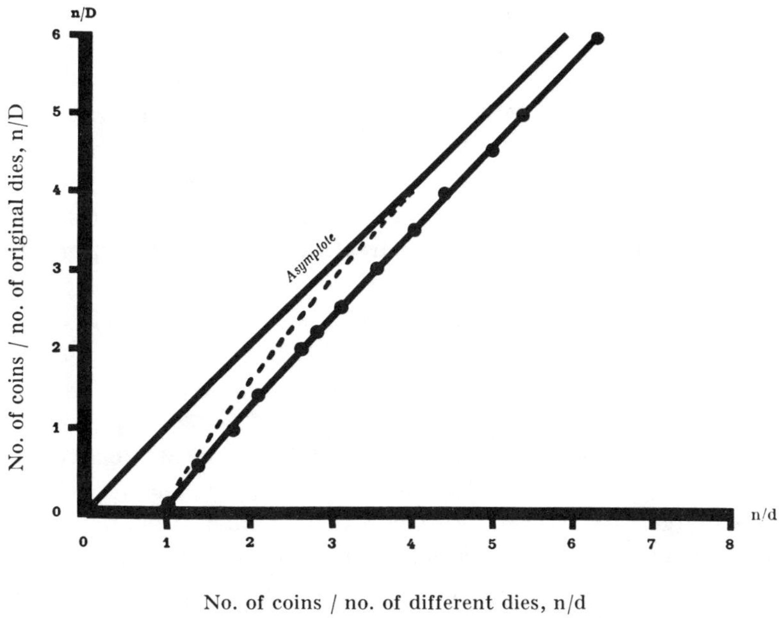

[a] The dashed curve is a plot of the equation used by Lyon which assumes equal coin productivity from all dies. The lower curve is the plot obtained from the computer simulation.

Because the line of n/D versus n/d obtained from computer simulation is only slightly curved, it can be closely approximated by three straight lines. Although the equation for the curve is not known[20] the equations for the three straight lines may be easily determined from linear regression ("least squares"). The three equations for calculating D, the original number of dies, are as follows.

[20] This equation is relatively unimportant because it would be much more difficult to use than one of the three following equations.

$$(1)\quad D = \frac{n \cdot d}{1.214n - 1.197d} \qquad \text{used in the range } n < 2d;$$

$$(2)\quad D = \frac{n \cdot d}{1.124n - 1.016d} \qquad \text{used in the range } n = 2 \text{ to } 3d;$$

$$(3)\quad D = \frac{n \cdot d}{1.069n - 0.843d} \qquad \text{used in the range } n > 3d;$$

where d = number of known (different) dies, n = number of coins in the study.

Previously when one used the Lyon or Lyon-Carter method it was necessary to use a table of d/n values listed as a function of n/D values. Interpolation was necessary plus a final calculation, dividing n by n/D to obtain D. It is much simpler to use one of the above equations. If several or many calculations for D need to be made, it is convenient to use a programmable calculator.

Tables 2 and 3 illustrate the use of the above equations to calculate D using data obtained for Crepusius denarii. Excellent agreement was obtained with estimates made by Buttrey:[21] 479 obverse dies (Buttrey) versus 475 ± 10 calculated from equations 1, 2, and 3. There are approximately 519 reverse dies (the exact number is unknown due to errors of omission and duplication of die numbers), whereas the calculated number of obverse dies is 494 ± 10. Also listed in the tables are standard deviations for the calculated number of dies using Carter's empirical equation, $s = \frac{D\sqrt{D}}{n-1}$, where s is the standard deviation, D is the calculated total number of dies, and n is the number of coins in the study.[22] In all cases there is at most a very small difference between the number of dies calculated using the equation and the number found from a table of d/n versus n/D values. The standard deviation is always at least ten times this difference meaning that the equations give results that are almost identical to the table values, and these results are just as good as the ones obtained from the table.

[21] Above, n. 16.

[22] Unpublished, mentioned in "Graphical Method" (above, n. 6), p. 20.

Table 2. Calculation of Numbers of Obverse of Crepusius Denarii[a]

Group Number	*Symbol*	*No. of Coins, n*	*No. of Known Dies, d*	*Calculated No. of Dies, D ± S*[b]	*Probable No. of Dies*
1	None	62	20	24.9 ± 2.0	22
2	Thunderbolt	61	20	25.0 ± 2.1	22
3	Feather	40	14	17.9 ± 1.9	21
4	Wheat	53	17	21.1 ± 1.9	22
5	Grasshopper	51	16	19.7 ± 1.8	21
6	Grapes	48	19	25.7 ± 2.8	21
7	Ivy Leaf	61	19	23.4 ± 1.9	21
8	Flower	49	16	20.0 ± 1.9	21
9	Thyrsus	25	5	5.5 ± 0.5	7
10	Bird	63	17	20.0 ± 1.4	21
11	Poppy	61	20	25.0 ± 2.1	24
12	Lizard	53	20	26.4 ± 2.6	21
13	Crescent	50	17	21.5 ± 2.0	21
14	Bidens	24	12	18.6 ± 3.5	21
15	Ear	59	17	20.4 ± 1.6	21
16	Star	49	17	21.6 ± 2.1	21
17	Branch	33	14	19.6 ± 2.7	21
18	Hooked Staff	31	11	14.1 ± 1.8	15
19	Cornucopiae	50	20	27.2 ± 2.9	21
20	Altar	16	5	6.2 ± 1.0	7
21	Turtle	32	14	20.0 ± 2.9	21
22	Wing	40	16	21.7 ± 2.6	22
23	Shell	25	13	20.8 ± 4.0	21
24	Palm Branch	39	14	18.1 ± 2.0	17
				484	473[c]
Total		1075	373	475 ± 10	

[a] Using the equations presented in this paper.

[b] S is the standard deviation calculated from $S = \frac{D\sqrt{D}}{n-1}$.

[c] T. V. Buttrey gave 479 as the probable number of obverse dies.

Table 3. Calculation of Numbers of Reverse Dies of Crepusius Denarii[a]

Reverse Die Numbers[b]	*Number of Coins,* n	*Number of Known Dies,* d	*Calculated No. of Dies,* D ± S[c]	*Probable No. of Dies*
1–25	79	22	26.1 ± 1.7	26
26–50	54	18	22.6 ± 2.0	25
51–75	59	19	23.6 ± 2.0	25
76–100	70	22	27.1 ± 2.0	25
101–125	79	18	20.3 ± 1.2	< 25
126–150	42	18	25.4 ± 3.1	25
151–175	71	20	23.8 ± 1.7	25
176–200	68	19	22.6 ± 1.6	25
201–225	58	19	23.8 ± 2.0	27
226–250	60	19	23.5 ± 1.9	26
251–275	34	15	21.5 ± 3.0	25
276–300	41	16	21.5 ± 2.5	25
301–325	50	20	27.2 ± 2.9	27
326–350	44	19	26.9 ± 3.2	25
351–375	40	17	23.8 ± 3.0	25
376–400	48	20	27.7 ± 3.1	28
401–425	39	19	29.0 ± 4.1	25
426–450	45	18	24.4 ± 2.7	25
451–475	44	19	26.9 ± 3.2	25
476–500	35	15	21.1 ± 2.9	25
501–519	22	12	20.0 ± 4.2	19
			509	< 519
Total	1082	384	494 ± 10	

[a] Using the equations presented in this paper.

[b] The dies were arbitrarily separated into groups of 25 to enable multiple checks of the calculations.

[c] S is the standard deviation calculated from $S = \frac{D\sqrt{D}}{n-1}$.

CONCLUSION

A simple equation (or equations) now enables rapid calculation of the total number of dies for issues of ancient coins made from at least several dies. A gamma distribution was used as the model for the distribution of die lifetimes. The results obtained from using the equations are in excellent agreement with die link data for over 1000 Crepusius denarii. However, it is not known yet whether the calculations give reasonable results for other series of ancient coins. Obviously it is important to test these equations using die link statistics for other series. It is entirely possible that early Greek minting procedures were so different from Roman ones that other equations will apply to Greek series of coins.

A NOTE ON CALCULATOR PROGRAMMING[23]

It is possible to linearize the curve of Fig. 2 so that the original number of dies, D, can be calculated from a single expression, regardless of the range of number of coins, n, to the number of observed dies, d, with results equivalent to those obtained from the three linear regression equations. Thus, the need to decide which of the three equations to use is obviated and the calculator has to be programmed only once for all groups of coins studied.

One such single equation is
(4) D = n/1.3584 (n/d) 0.9087–1.2801, which is easily solved on a hand calculator for values from D of known figures for n and d. An inexpensive hand calculator such as the Texas Instruments TI-55 makes short work of the arithmetic. For this calculator the program is:

[23] Dr. Dexter C. Seymour was one of the ANS's reviewers of Dr. Carter's article. In his enthusiasm for things mathematical, and with Dr. Carter's permission, he developed this note. The two equations below, (4) and (5), were developed generally from the methods of D. S. Davis, *Nomography and Empirical Equations*, 2nd ed. (New York, 1962).

Memory 1: reserved
Memory 2: value of "d"
Memory 3: 0.9087
Memory 4: 1.3584
Memory 5: 1.2801

Program: Sto 1, ÷ , Rcl 2, =, y^x, Rcl 3, X, Rcl 4, -, Rcl 5, =, 1/x, X, Rcl 1, =, 2nd R/S, 2nd Rst.

Another equation which can be used with equally good results is (5) D = n/22.52 tanh (0.05522 n/d + 0.1477)-4.421. The TI-55 program for equation (5) is

Memory 1: reserved
Memory 2: value of "d"
Memory 3: 0.05522
Memory 4: 0.1477
Memory 5: 22.52
Memory 6: 4.421

Program: Sto 1, ÷ , Rcl 2, X, Rcl 3, +, Rcl 4, =, 2nd tanh, X, Rcl 5, -, Rcl 6, = , ÷ , Rcl 1, =, 1/x, 2nd R/S, 2nd Rst.

PLATES

Plate 1

1 2 3 4 5 6 7 8 9 10 11 12 13 14

Facing Head Coinage of Larissa

Plate 2

A

1

2

3

4

Theon Adelphon Octadrachm (A) and Group 1 Decadrachms (1-4)

Plate 3

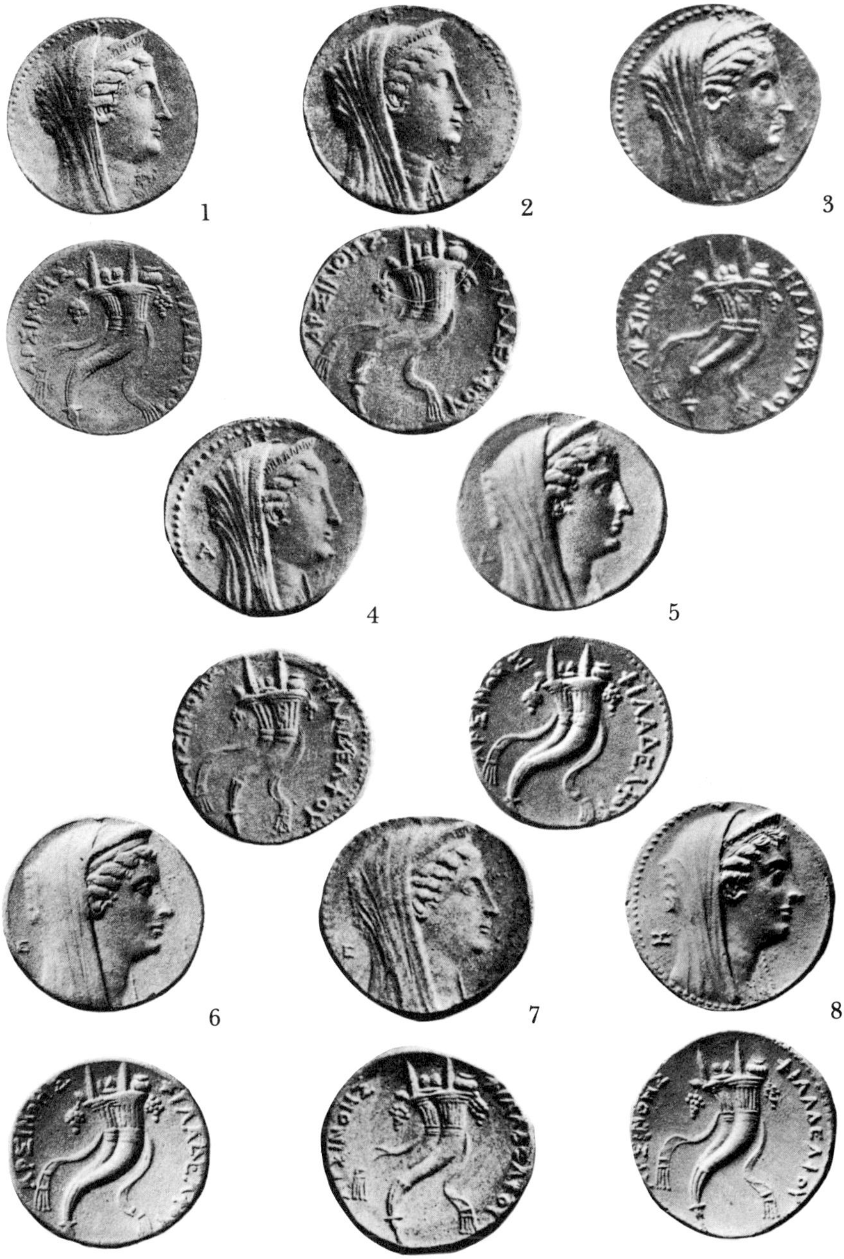

Group 2 Octadrachms

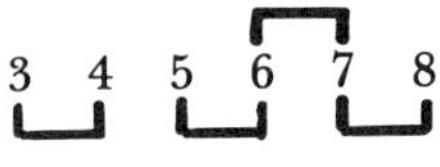

Plate 4

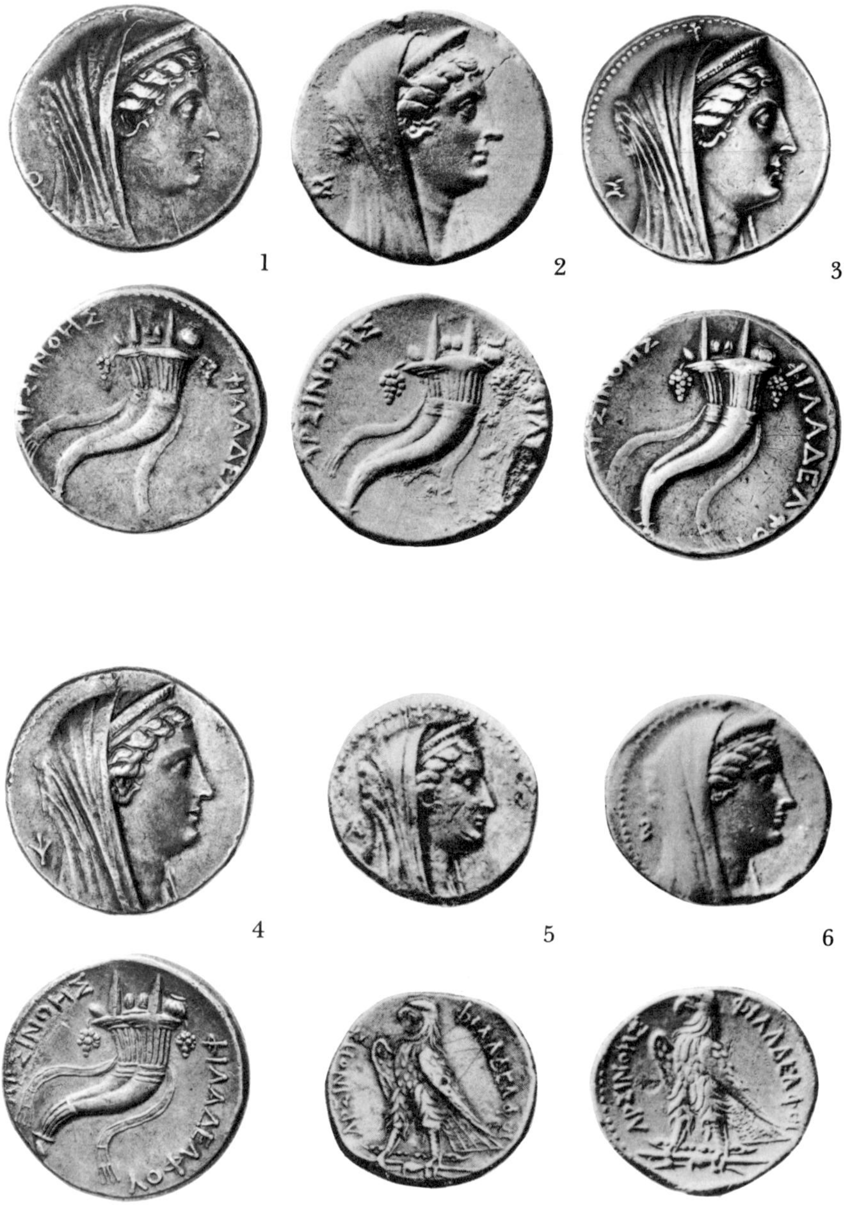

Group 2 Decadrachms (1-4) and Tetradrachms (5-6)

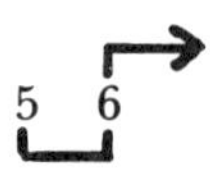

Plate 5

Group 2 Tetradrachms

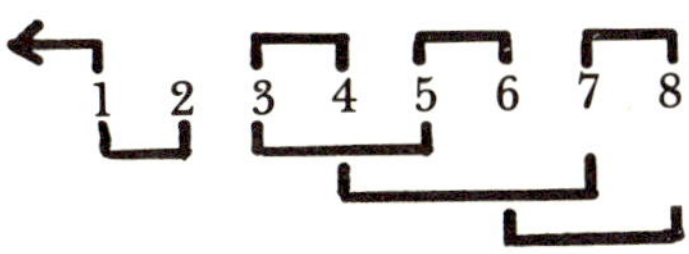

Plate 6

Transitional Octadrachms (1-3) and Decadrachms (4-6)

Plate 7

Group 3 Octadrachms (1-4) and Decadrachms (5-7)

1 2 3

Plate 8

Group 4 Octadrachms (1-4) and Decadrachms (5-7)

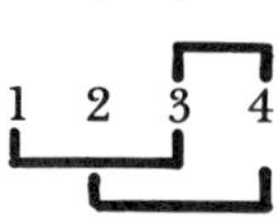

Plate 9

A, 261/0 B, 253/2 C, 253/2

D, 251/0 E, 251/0

F, 246/5 G, 244/3 H, 242/1

Phoenician and Palestinian Octadrachms

Plate 10

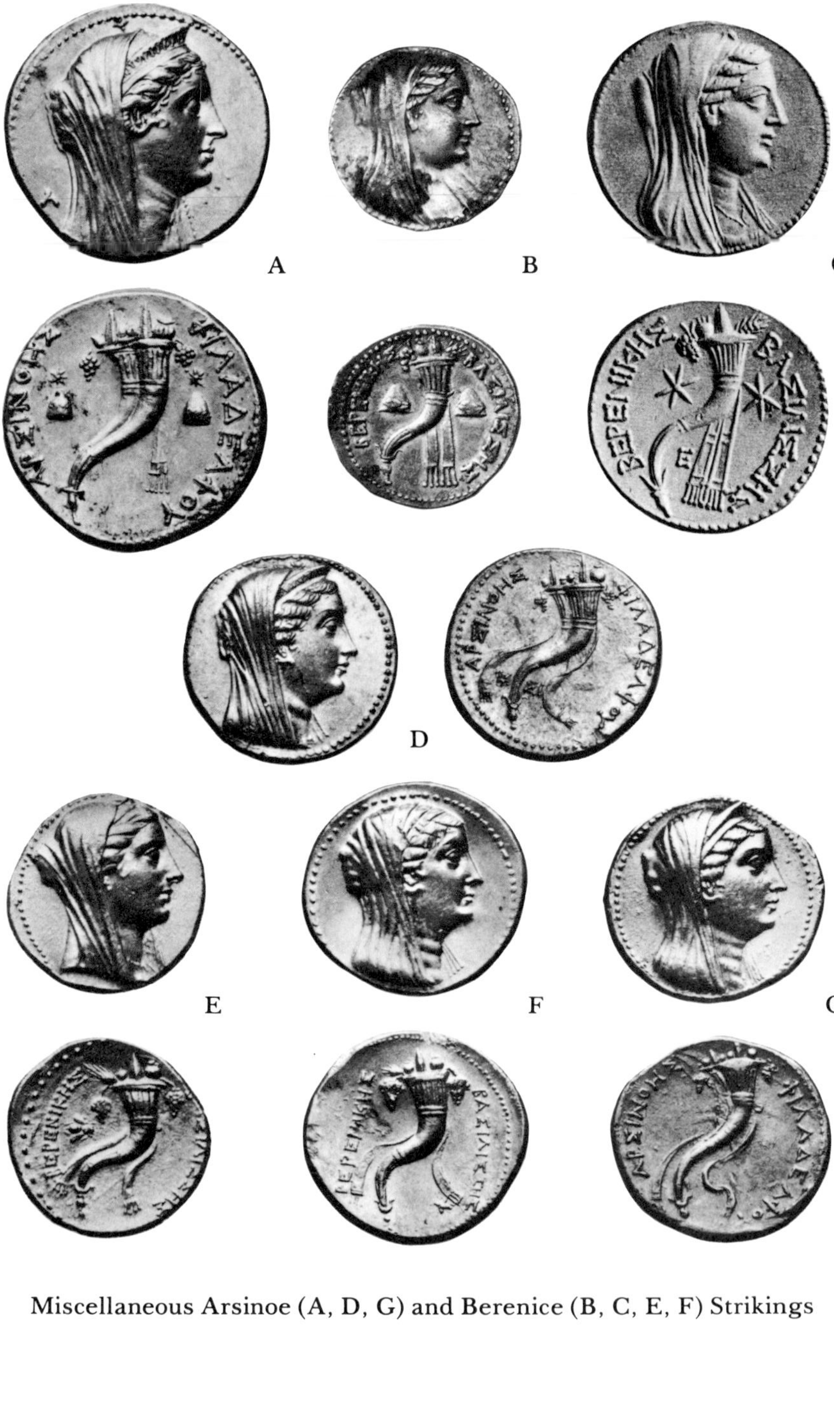

Miscellaneous Arsinoe (A, D, G) and Berenice (B, C, E, F) Strikings

Plate 11

Armenian Kingdoms of Sophene and Commagene

Plate 12

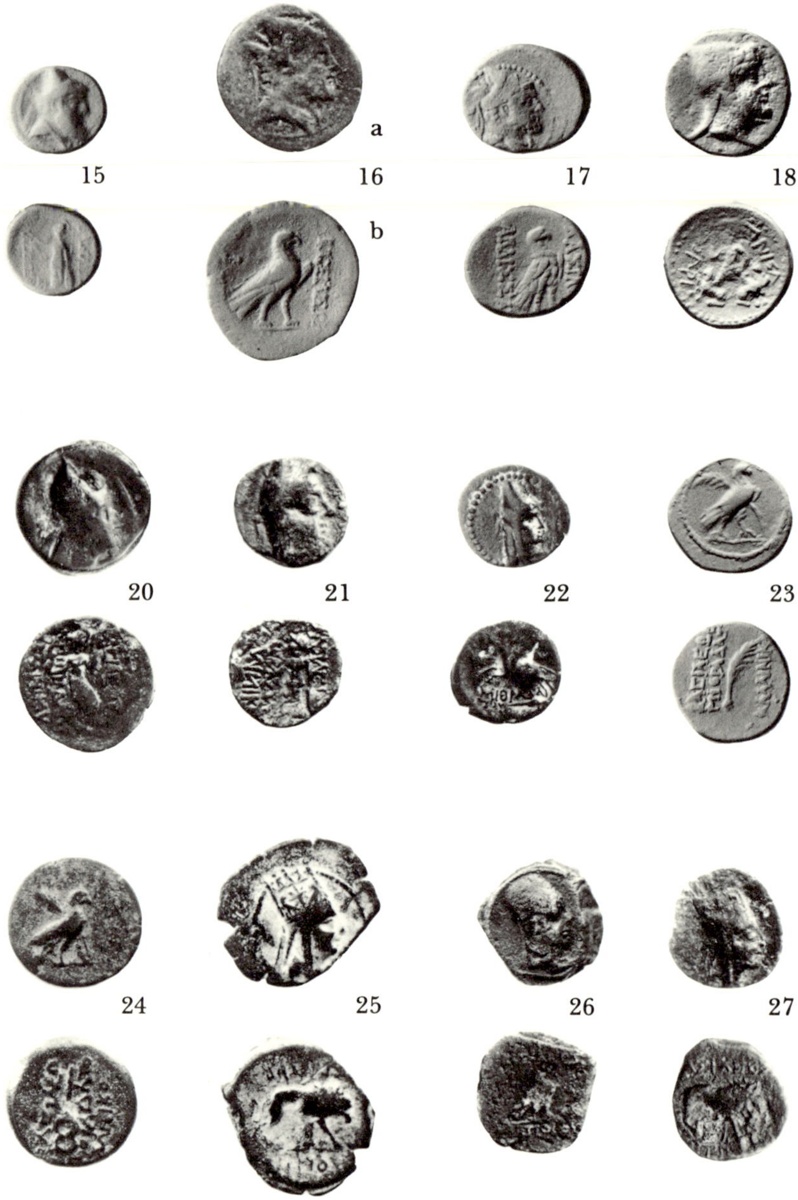

Armenian Kingdoms of Sophene and Commagene

Plate 13

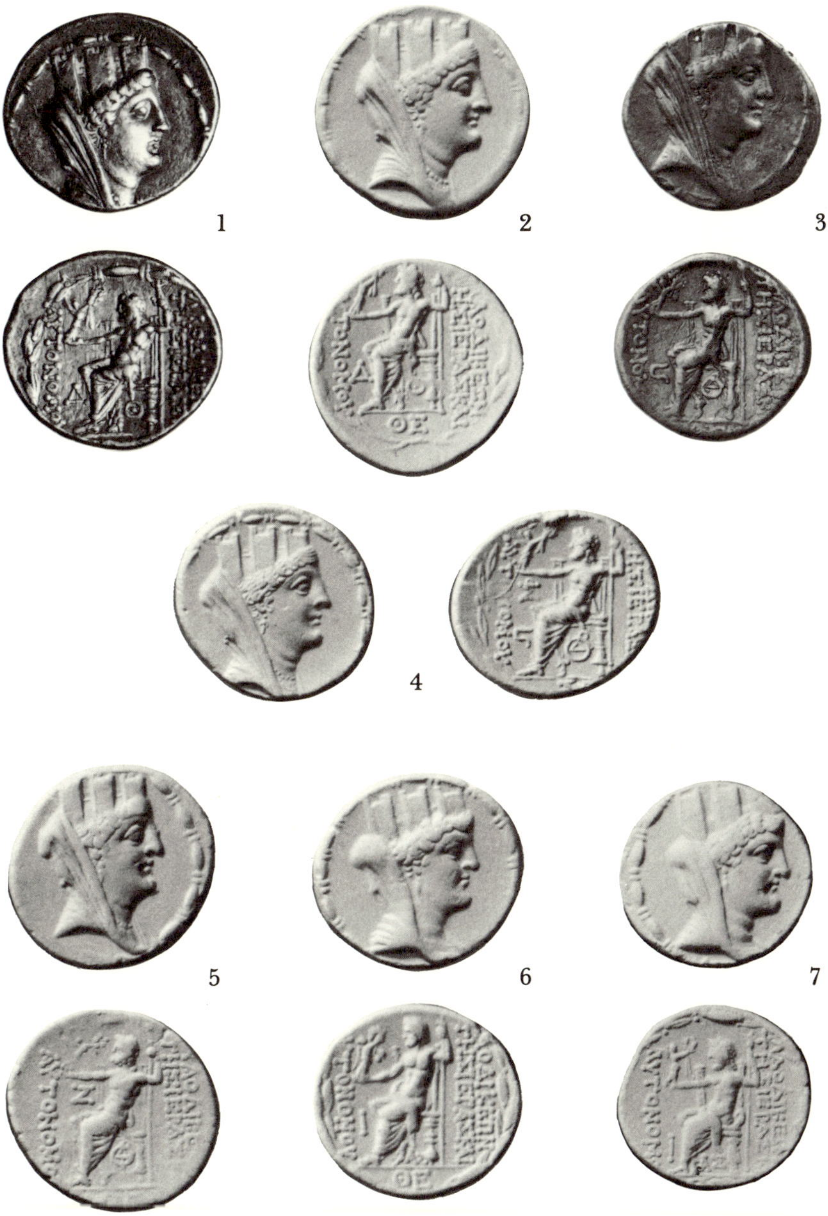

Autonomous Tetradrachms of Laodicea ad Mare

Plate 14

Autonomous Tetradrachms of Laodicea ad Mare

Plate 15

15 16 17

18

19 20 21

Autonomous Tetradrachms of Laodicea ad Mare

Plate 16

22 23 24

25

26 27 28

Autonomous Tetradrachms of Laodicea ad Mare

Plate 17

29 30 31

32

33 34 35

Autonomous Tetradrachms of Laodicea ad Mare

Plate 18

Autonomous Tetradrachms of Laodicea ad Mare

Plate 19

43 44 45

46

47 48 49

Autonomous Tetradrachms of Laodicea ad Mare

Plate 20

Egyptian Tetradrachms under Severus Alexander

Plate 21

3 16 18

22 30 34

Hoard from Anemurium

Plate 22

1 (2x)

2 (2x)

3 (2x)

Wandering Die of Nīsābūr: Sequel